NEVADA'S KEY PITTMAN

Nevada's Key Pittman

by
FRED L. ISRAEL

UNIVERSITY OF NEBRASKA PRESS · LINCOLN

Publishers on the Plains

UNP

To my *Mother* and *Father*

Preface

Key Pittman's name was scarcely known abroad when he became chairman of the United States Senate Foreign Relations Committee in 1933. A member of the Senate since 1912, he had rarely spoken about foreign affairs. But, because of the unwritten rule of seniority, the Senator served as head of this important committee during one of the most crucial periods of American history. Pittman proudly described himself as "a frontier statesman." And this he was. But his frontier stopped at the Nevada borders and his statesmanship was too often limited to the economic welfare of his constituents whose views he championed throughout his twenty-eight years in the Senate. Pittman represented the least populated state of the union in the National Legislature. As the protector of his state, he defended it against all adversaries, even the general welfare of the United States. As a product of Nevada, Pittman successfully stamped this imprint on federal legislation.

It is my hope that my interpretation of the Senator will cause readers to reflect about the structure of our political system which enabled him to obtain high office.

In the researching, organizing, and writing of my biography, I have naturally incurred many agreeable debts of gratitude. My first obligation is to Professor Richard Hofstadter, my sponsor and critic throughout my graduate studies at Columbia University. I wish to express my deep appreciation to Professor William E. Leuchtenburg for his careful and critical reading of my work. His advice and sharp editorial comments have been of vital importance. During the research stage of my work, the staff of the Manuscript Room of the Library of Congress gave me invaluable assistance. Mr. Herman Kahn, formerly director of the Franklin D. Roosevelt Library, and his associate Mr. Robert Jacoby helped me considerably. The excellent librarians who serve at the Information Desk of Butler Library, Columbia University patiently answered my many and varied questions. Mrs. Shirley Lerman skillfully typed the several drafts of this manuscript and I am grateful for her assistance. My friend and former colleague Dr. Robert Dallek of Columbia University listened to my ideas and offered countless suggestions and criticisms of which I am appreciative. Professor Joseph C. Vance of the Mary Washington College, University of Virginia suggested this topic to me.

FRED L. ISRAEL

The City College of New York
January 1963

Table of Contents

A Section of Photographs Follows Page 86

Introduction

Of whom and of what indeed can I say: "I know that!" This heart within me I can feel, and I judge that it exists. There ends all my knowledge, and the rest is construction. For if I try to seize this self of which I feel sure, if I try to define and to summarize it, it is nothing but water slipping through my fingers. I can sketch one by one all the aspects it is able to assume, all those likewise that have been attributed to it, this upbringing, this origin, this ardor or these silences, this nobility or this vileness. But aspects cannot be added up. This very heart which is mine will forever remain indefinable to me. Between the certainty I have of my existence and the content I try to give to that assurance, the gap will never be filled.

ALBERT CAMUS, *The Myth of Sisyphus*

Leadership in politics is one of the most interesting and, at the same time, one of the most involved questions in political science. In the feudal and monarchical periods leadership was based on birth, and political figures inherited their position as they did property. In the modern democracies leaders are elected. Their power, theoretically at least, depends on the will of the people.

In a series of speeches delivered at the University of Chicago in 1939, Eduard Beneš incisively defended democracy, especially its guiding heads, whom he described as people who have a deep sense of national responsibility and who carefully weigh and constantly consider public opinion. "They are generally people inclined to close analysis and to profound reasoning," he continued. In a government by the people, a leader "should be extremely well educated and informed as to general conditions in his country, and . . . must be of wide erudition. . . . He must be a sort of hero of industry, of honesty, of self-sacrifice and patience." [1]

Key Pittman probably never read Beneš' speech. If he did, he undoubtedly snickered at the intellectual's views on politics. Pittman was not elected and re-elected because of his "wide erudition" or his "self-sacrifice and patience." He was elected and re-elected because of his stand on local issues and his success in satisfying the narrow demands of his constituents. Silver, reclamation, and irrigation interested Nevadans—and Pittman. A small fluctuation in local opinion would have cost the Senator his seat. Pittman realized this and therefore he devoted his energies to the needs and interests of his state. Too often the Senator confused Nevada interests with public policy. In a national legislature, Pittman did not represent the American people but was, instead, the spokesman of his state, safeguarding the interests of 110,000 people from the rest of the 130 million.

Pittman's chief aim was re-election. The people of Nevada, therefore, were his principal concern—their petty problems, their attitudes, their votes. To satisfy the home interests, the Senator became a master of manipulating amendments, riders, and conference committee compromises. Controversial speeches were carefully avoided as he deliberately straddled issues in order not to antagonize his colleagues and supporters. Pittman confined his world to Nevada, and the folks back home shaped his ideas. "There are Congressmen elected year after year," Walter Lippmann has written, "who never think of dissipating their energy on public affairs. They prefer to do a little service for a lot of people on a lot of little subjects rather than to engage in trying to do a big service out there in the void." [2] Pittman fit this description.

Pittman's defense of silver was not only a result of the pressures on him, but also a result of strong personal feeling. The Senator believed that silver should be used as a metallic base for currencies and for actual money itself. Silver, he thought, constituted an important part of the United States monetary structure as well as of international trade. From time immemorial, he argued, mankind, almost instinctively, selected gold and silver for monetary purposes. Their beauty, their malleability for coins, their durability, and their relative scarcity made these metals ideal for use as money. Unlike inconvertible paper, quantity could not be increased at the mere behest of governments. No war or revolution, no sudden government decision or change of policy could increase the physical amount of gold and silver beyond that mined from the earth.

Many very learned people frequently wrote to Pittman, spoke to him, and argued with him in an attempt to convince him that the use of gold and silver for money was an idea just as dead as the dodo bird. Pittman responded that gold and silver would still remain acceptable when no other medium of exchange purchased an iota of bread. All the wisdom of economists, all the laws, regulations, and penalties would not stop people from trying to obtain them. When paper currencies shrank to the value of waste paper, these metals still would purchase something to eat.

Pittman was a political realist. Knowing the strength of the opposition to free-coinage bills, he concentrated on obtaining a higher price for the white metal through silver purchase programs. The ultimate aim of these laws would be free coinage. The immediate goal, however, was a higher price for domestic silver. By welding the representatives of the seven Rocky Mountain states into the unwavering core of an economic and sectional group and through the skillful political use of this bloc, the Senator obtained concessions for silver. Critics labeled these purchasing schemes as selfish subsidies to a powerful minority, but the Senator ignored their arguments. He knew what was essential for the prosperity of his state and adroitly obtained the necessary legislation.

Although Pittman sought election to the Foreign Relations Committee in 1916, he was not really interested in foreign affairs. Appointment to a "national committee," he thought, would increase his prestige back home. For seventeen years he attended committee meetings, rarely speaking unless, of course, international monetary agreements were discussed. The defeat, death, and retirement of Democratic members caused Pittman's leather chair to be shifted closer to the head of the long green-baize–covered table. With the Democratic landslide in 1933, Pittman was elected chairman because of the unwritten rule of seniority of service—the chairmanship going to that member of the majority party who has the longest unbroken service on the committee.

Seniority, however, too often implies wisdom. Key Pittman, whose seven and one-half–year tenure as chairman of the Foreign Relations Committee ranks fifth in length in the history of the committee, was not well versed in foreign affairs. Never before, with the possible exception of the post–Civil War decade, had foreign relations taken such an important twist. Never had a chairman such an opportunity to emerge as a statesman because of the issues of the day. Pittman was not made for this role. He was a politician and not a philosopher-statesman. Unlike Sumner, Lodge, and Borah, he failed to grasp the fine points of American foreign relations. Pittman was not forceful in guiding the committee for fear of offending supporters of domestic issues which interested him, and his years as chairman were marked by vacillating and equivocal actions.

In the course of formulating a neutrality program, President Roosevelt had to accept the Senator's empty promises, his erroneous observations, and his emotional outbursts. The administration had to work with Pittman because of his senatorial position. An attempt to by-pass him through an appeal to the more sympathetic members of the Foreign Relations Committee would have automatically doomed any proposal. The administration, therefore, tried to maintain Pittman's support in foreign relations by adopting a somewhat obsequious attitude toward him.

A few months after the Senator's death, his wife attempted to summarize his career—the carefree days in Alaska, settling in Tonopah, the Senate, the Democratic conventions, silver, the London conference, the Foreign Relations Committee. After many erasures and much crossing out, she simply wrote: "Key loved our State and its people."

CHAPTER I

"I Will Succeed"

I

The Mississippi River coils like a muddy snake as it outlines the western border of the State of Mississippi. On the highest of a line of bluffs overlooking the great river, just south of its junction with the Yazoo, stands Vicksburg, a city of precipitous streets, terraces, and wooded ravines, rich in historic associations and natural beauty. In the antebellum years Vicksburg was proud to be known as the center of social activities for the state's aristocracy, but in the 1870's the main concern of its citizens was repairing the damages left by the Civil War. Reconstruction leaders had hoped to make the city into the inland port of the New South, but the erratic Mississippi changed its course, leaving Vicksburg high and dry, and in any case the depression of 1873, followed by an era of railroad expansion, signaled the end of active river trade.

Outwardly almost untouched by these events were the fine antebellum homes built by Vicksburg's founding fathers, stately mansions set in well-kept grounds crowning the city's bluffs. Into such surroundings Key Pittman was born on September 19, 1872.

Pittman's parents died when he was a child—his mother in 1883, his father in 1884—and he knew little of his family history. In his adult years he searched the country for records of his forebears, and as he advanced in his senatorial career, especially after he became chairman of the Foreign Relations Committee, Keys and Pittmans from all over the world sent him long, detailed genealogical charts. One chart showed among his ancestors Richard III of England, James IV of Scotland, and Hugh Du Puy, a crusader who had accompanied Conrad III in 1147. Replying to the newly found cousin who had sent it, Pittman wrote: "The family tree is very interesting. It appears that

5

I have more and better ancestors than I have descendants." When his correspondents could not agree as to whether the Pittmans had originated in England or in Denmark, moving to England with William the Conqueror, the Senator commented dryly that some of his relatives in the back country of Virginia were Baptist preachers, which at least showed evolution on his part.[1] On the whole his researches pleased him. "I have never seen a Pittman I wasn't willing to claim kin with," he wrote later on.[2]

The Senator was convinced that his mother, Catherine Key, traced her ancestry to William Rufus King and Francis Scott Key. "My grandmother Key was a descendant of W. R. King," he wrote in a 1934 letter. "He left her property in Louisiana in his will. My great-grandfather was Dr. Richard King. He died shortly after the Mexican War. Grandmother Key died when I was young. All of the members of the family have passed away except for some of my cousins."[3]

His father's family, the Senator knew, came from Virginia. From there "my grandfather, whose name I think was William Pittman, went into Kentucky and married one of the Bukner family. The family, shortly before the Civil War, moved to St. Joseph, Missouri. When the war broke out my father and his brothers joined the Confederate Army while his cousins joined the Federal Army."[4] The Senator described his father as a dashing Civil War captain who had distinguished himself on the battlefield, and took pride in quoting General Martin E. Green's citation written during the Battle of Corinth. It commended him for "promptness in conveying an order through the field when the very atmosphere seemed filled with shot, grape, and cannister." Again, during the siege of Vicksburg, Captain Pittman's superior officer recorded that he had discharged his duties with "coolness and pre-eminent gallantry, untiring energy and perseverance."[5]

After the war William Pittman, Jr., moved his family to Vicksburg, where he earned a brilliant reputation as an attorney.[6] During the trying reconstruction years he opposed the carpetbag municipal authorities and took part in the Vicksburg "riots" of 1874 which, as he wrote, ousted the "ignorant and corrupt officials."[7] He practiced extensively before the State Supreme Court and on one occasion successfully represented Jefferson Davis in litigation to maintain control of his Brierfield estate.[8]

On their father's death in 1884, twelve-year-old Key and his three younger brothers were sent to live with his maternal grandmother on her cotton plantation in East Carroll Parish, Louisiana. Despite the beauty of the setting—the plantation fronted on the banks of the Mississippi, and was thick with cypress and magnolia trees—it probably was an unhappy home for young Pittman. His official biographical sketches omit mention of this period and the Senator himself dismissed inquiries about it, saying that his grandmother and an aunt pampered him and he became "somewhat spoiled." His youngest brother Vail recalls that a governess gave Key daily instruction and that he passed a university entrance examination before his fifteenth birthday.[9]

His relatives belonged to the Presbyterian church, and Key matriculated at the synod university, Southwestern Presbyterian, which was in Clarksville, Tennessee, about forty miles north of Nashville. Several southern synods had taken over the institution in 1875, establishing "one grand University for the whole church South." The university's aim, as expounded by the Board of Directors, was "to furnish to the church and to the World an intellectual training of the highest standard and moral training on a scriptural basis"; its boast was that it furnished "one-fifth of the ministers of the Southern Presbyterian church and more than one-third of the ministers of that Church in the Southwestern section." Students were allowed "a large liberty of choice of classes" except for Bible courses, which were required *"each year."* "Those who object," the Chancellor bluntly announced, "must go elsewhere." Pittman and twenty-five other freshmen registered for the 1887 fall semester.[10]

As he demonstrated proficiency in Latin, Pittman was placed in the intermediate course (Caesar and Cicero), in a program of study concentrated on the classics, mathematics, history, literatures, and the Bible. His marks at Southwestern, however, were never outstanding; he never received a grade above 90 per cent except in English literature. During his second year he failed elementary French, and although he continued with his class, he had to drop the intermediate course during the middle of the following semester.[11]

Every faculty member, by the terms of the college charter, had to be "interested in the moral and spiritual training of his students as well as in their intellectual progress," and was required to be "a Christian gentleman with a love for the Christian Church and possessing the Christian graces that would make his influence felt among the students entrusted to his care." Pittman's Bible instructor was Dr. Joseph Wilson, father of the future President, but Bible instruction, Pittman recalled, bored him, and he proved only moderately competent in Wilson's course.[12] It would be difficult to show that any of his instructors exerted an influence on young Pittman: he never corresponded with them after he left Southwestern and, in fact, could not recall their names.

The student body, as described in Southwestern's catalogue, was "substantial and conservative, rather than frivolous and extravagant and there is an entire absence of that semi-infidel class whose influence is so pernicious to young men." [13] Student social life during the eighties and nineties centered upon the two literary organizations and the national fraternities, five of which had campus chapters by 1887. Soccer and baseball comprised the athletic program. The university newspaper reported on October 1, 1888, that "football made its appearance on the campus last week, at first in the hands of only a few boys but before the afternoon was over about twenty-five enthusiastic fellows were pursuing the ball and good health." [14] College records do not indicate that Pittman held any major society office or took an extensive part in athletic activities.

Despite the adjuration of the *Alma Mater* to

> Keep lighted in our hearts the flame
> Once kindled there of thee,

Pittman rarely mentioned his college days at Southwestern. An attack of typhoid fever forced him to withdraw in his third year, by which time he had completed the "School of History, English Literature and Rhetoric." This was insufficient for the baccalaureate and he received no degree, but nonetheless in years to come biographical releases from the Senator's office carried the information that he had graduated from Southwestern with high honors. Although he was awarded an honorary doctorate in 1919, he never earned a degree.

While recuperating from the fever at an aunt's home in Tuscaloosa, Pittman decided—on impulse, as he recalled—to cast his lot with the rapidly developing new states of the Far West. Business in the South was bad, money scarce, and cotton, the measuring rod of commodity prices, was selling at four cents a pound. To Pittman, a restless eighteen-year-old, eager for adventure, money, and fame, it seemed that the West offered the best opportunities. Within a few days of making up his mind, he was on his way. He carried a single letter of recommendation, given to him by a friend of his late father. The friend remembered that a town dandy called Dude Lewis, whom he had known in his younger days back in Georgia, had gone West to practice law. When Pittman arrived in Seattle in the spring of 1890, he presented his letter to one of Washington's most successful lawyers, James Hamilton Lewis, future Senator from Illinois.[15]

Through Lewis he met August Moore, a former Mississippian, and was hired to clerk in Moore's law office in return for a small salary and living quarters. Pittman read law under Moore's guidance, and in 1892 he was admitted to the Washington bar. Recognizing his great ability, Moore made him a partner the following year. But partnership did not mean prosperity. "We moved to Mt. Vernon in the northern part of the State where there were mines and saw mills," Pittman wrote. "Lumbermen had difficulty in selling anything and each case was a losing proposition." Finding Mt. Vernon "entirely too dead for a person of my temperament," Pittman gave part of his law library to a local judge, his office furniture to another attorney, and his "account books and promissory notes to the flames," and returned to Seattle in 1895.[16]

The nation was slowly recovering from the Panic of 1893, which would not reach its height in the West until 1896, and economic conditions in Washington did not improve. These were difficult years for a young lawyer. "I was receiving notes for my fees," Pittman wrote, "which were non-redeemable, while I was paying cash for my hotel bills." [17] When news of the Klondike discoveries reached Seattle, tales of easy money in the newly discovered gold fields, of overnight fortunes and boom towns, Pittman decided to leave his small practice and try his luck in the Far North.

In 1897, a year before the big gold rush began, Pittman sold his remaining law books to purchase a year's outfit, and headed for the Klondike. He sailed in July on the *Queen*, which was filled to capacity with gold-hungry stampeders, grubstakes, horses, and hay. By August more than four thousand gold-seekers had sailed from Seattle, but the *Queen* was one of the first steamers to reach Skagway Bay.[18] Skagway, being on the narrow neck of the Panhandle, formed an American bridge into Canadian territory. Within a few weeks of the world's hearing of it, the town had become a confused melee of swearing men and neighing horses, of rasping saws and yelping dogs.[19]

About seven hundred miles from Skagway lay the mining town of Dawson. To reach it, the prospectors had to cross Lake Bennett, north of Skagway, and then follow the glacial lakes and rivers down to the Klondike River and Dawson. The first forty miles to Lake Bennett was the most difficult part of the trip, crossing as it did a high mountain range. The old Indian trail could not have been worse; it was a series of quagmires and bogs from one end to the other, and so narrow, especially in the first twenty miles, that horses had trouble passing each other. The horses belonging to Pittman's party went down on the steamer *New Mexico,* he recalled. "We packed on our backs across the Skagway trail. . . . It was a motley crowd, bankers, lawyers, doctors, beggars, miners, pickpockets, and gangsters. Horses were dead all along the trail." [20] A member of that "motley crowd," Jack London, wrote that the horses died like mosquitoes and rotted in heaps from Skagway to Bennett:

They died at the Rocks, they were poisoned at the Summit, and they starved at the Lakes; they fell off the trail, what there was of it, and they went through it; in the river they drowned under their loads or were smashed to pieces against the boulders; they snapped their legs in the crevices and broke their backs falling backwards with their packs; in the sloughs they sank from sight or smothered in the slime; and they were disembowelled in the bogs where the corduroy logs turned end up in the mud; men shot them, worked them to death, and when they were gone, went back to the beach and bought more. Some did not bother to shoot them—stripping the saddles off and the shoes and leaving them where they fell. Their hearts turned to stone—those which did not break—and they became beasts, the men on the Dead Horse Trail.[21]

Within a month the trail became almost impassable, and by September all movement came to a standstill.

Upon reaching Lake Bennett, Pittman and his companion, Jim Lashua, whipsawed lumber in the sparse forests and built a boat which carried them the remaining 650 miles through a series of lakes and rivers to the Yukon, Dawson, and the gold fields. The two men sailed through Lakes Bennett, Tasish, Marsh, and Laberge into the Yukon River. Connecting Lake Marsh with Lake Laberge was Thirtymile

River, a swift, clear, beautiful blue stream, so treacherous that wrecks lined almost all of its brief course. Thirtymile narrowed to one third of its width as it descended into Miles Canyon, and rushed through like a millrace. The mile-long canyon is only a hundred feet wide with its walls rising a sheer hundred feet from the crest. The whirlpool in the center is so swift that two Swedes who were carried into the canyon by accident in the spring of 1895 spun around for six hours before escaping.[22] Below the canyon, Pittman and Lashua had to run White Horse Rapids, so named because the foam resembled white steeds prancing in the sunlight. According to Pittman's own account of his trip through the canyon and rapids:

We started down Thirty-Mile river in the evening and ran until after dark, looking for a good camping place. In the morning we were astonished to find that we were only half a mile above the canyon, and that by accident only we escaped going into it at night. A great many boats were landed in the eddy above it.

We tied up to the bank and went down to investigate. We found that while all were going through the canyon, none was running the rapids. The boats were being pulled out on the left bank just above the rapids and portaged for a distance of a mile to a point below the rapids. When we got back to the boat my partner said: "What do you think of the rapids?" When I told him that I had had enough of packing and was in favor of running them he was delighted.

We jumped in and shoved off. Jim took the twelve-foot oars and stood up and rowed the boat facing the bow. I grabbed the steering oar, and we swung into the canyon. I retain few distinct impressions, except that the walls of the canyon were flying by and that we were tossing violently. When we emerged from the canyon the water was swift but smooth until the White Horse rapids were reached, half a mile below. Jim stood the big oars up in the air, and with an arm around them rested peacefully as we drifted toward the rapids. Just before we reached them men ran frantically along the banks toward us, shouting, "The White Horse rapids are below you! Throw us a rope!"

Jim placed his hand to his ear and said: "Can't hear you. Whose horse?" They thought he was crazy and continued to shout: "The rapids! The White Horse rapids!"

We swung around the bend into the rapids. Jim dropped his oars into the water and began to work desperately. The spray was so thick that I could not see to steer, and had to rely on Jim for directions. As the bow swung one way or the other he would direct me by shouting: "To the right! To the left! Hard to the left! To the right! Steady as you are! Hard to the right! Hold her! Hold her steady!"

And we plunged over the falls at the end of the rapids in a wall of mist. The boat settled and trembled for an instant then shot out into smooth water.[23]

No further obstacles hindered the journey down the Yukon to Dawson.

The two men had reached the mouth of the Stewart River, eighty miles from Dawson, when the Yukon River froze. They built a cabin to store their outfits, killed a moose for food, and hiked to the town, arriving in September, 1897, eight months before the main onrush. Dawson, only one year old, was already the richest mining camp in the Yukon basin. Log cabins and canvas tents lined the main street and a polyglot crowd milled about day and night filling the saloons, dance halls, tent stores, and banks. Candles sold at $1 apiece; smoking tobacco was $7.50 a pound, oyster stew $15 a bowl; a copy of Shakespeare's complete works was $50. Pittman arrived in Dawson having only a Canadian dime in his pocket, and, as he wrote, with "drinks at $1 apiece, that's poverty." [24] When someone offered him $30 a cord to chop wood, he borrowed axes and a sledge and chopped. The money enabled him to lease a claim on Bonanza Creek and for two years he worked as a miner, exposed to all the hardships of the Arctic climate.

Because he had not served an apprenticeship of three years with a Canadian barrister or solicitor, Pittman was prohibited from practicing law in Dawson, but, nonetheless, he acted as the legal advisor of the group known as the Australians, who fought the dishonesty of Canadian government officers.[25] ("This does not include the Mounted Police," Pittman specified. "The Captain of the Mounted Police was judge, jury, and executioner. He punished the rich and the poor alike and preserved order.") [26] It appeared that clerks in the gold commissioner's office manipulated filings so that they gained title to valuable claims, causing a furor in Dawson. Through the legal efforts of the Australians the Canadian government replaced the corrupt officials.[27] This was Pittman's first experience with mining litigation, a field of law which eventually became his specialty.

In the latter part of 1898 Pittman met his future wife. While he was mushing alongside a creek near Dawson one day, an Indian driver tried to cross in front of his dog team. The two teams tangled and fought. Using his blacksnake whip, Pittman finally got his dogs back in line, but the two teams tangled and began to fight again. Just as Pittman was letting loose a string of oaths remarkable even for the Klondike, a pile of furs on the other sled stirred and an extremely pretty girl pulled down her cape and looked out. Pittman took one look, turned, and let his team, sled and all, slide down the icy hill into the creek.[28] The girl was Mimosa June Gates, whose brother Humboldt owned one of the richest mining claims in the Dawson area. In Nome, on July 8, 1900, Mimosa Gates became Mrs. Key Pittman. Federal Judge James Wickersham remembered her as "one of the most vivacious and beautiful young women in the town who married the most brilliant young lawyer at the bar of the court" in a ceremony presided over by the Episcopal parson and followed "by a gay marriage feast." [29]

In 1899, Pittman moved to the new mining camp of Nome, Alaska, which was located on a cape projecting into the Bering Sea some two thousand miles down the Yukon River from Dawson. Prospectors had discovered beach sands laden with gold, and extracted about $800,000 worth in six weeks. A stampede followed. Boats brought thousands of people from the United States to the new camp. Down from the Klondike and the interior of Alaska came additional thousands. The diggings were rich, they yielded millions and seemed inexhaustible. "It is going to be a wonderful camp," Mimosa Gates informed her brothers. "There has been at least twenty five boats in and gone bringing a great many passengers some of them were Whalers and it is within the last four days or so that the large passenger vessels have began to come, and there are lots of people here now. . . . People were wild here over the boats, as provisions were very scarce no fresh meat very little canned—scarcely any flower [sic] no milk and such things." [30]

By October, 1899, more than eight thousand people had settled in the Nome area, ready to face the severe Arctic winter. The Bering Sea froze solidly, cutting off all means of water communication, and to leave by land would have entailed a journey of some twenty-five hundred miles by dog team through a bleak and solitary land. "Furthermore," Pittman remembered, "we had nothing to do. The ground was frozen so that mining could not be carried on."

Set 8,000 husky, active, lively adventurous Americans to the task of amusing themselves and their neighbors and you are certain to have bizarre results. We had some. No one need pity us for our isolated condition. There are many of us who look back to that winter as the happiest of our lives.

Popular imagination of a new mining camp is rough, lawless and ignorant men assembled in a crude community, knowing nothing, caring nothing for, the gentler things of life. It is a wrong conception. Our colony at Nome was drawn from every walk of life. It contained some of the most cultivated and best bred people to be met in any society. Dress suits for evening affairs were by no means uncommon in Nome society, nor are they today. But we were all thrown, by force of our isolation and mutual dependence, into a splendid democracy, where the best, more than the worst, in us came to the surface. When Christmas approached a committee of representative citizens was solemnly appointed to take charge of organizing an adequate celebration. First a delegation was sent inland, equipped with dog sleds and provisions, to find a Christmas tree. No timber grows about Nome. The expedition had to journey 200 miles over the frozen snow before it found a tree that, in point of size and beauty, satisfied the members. It was a magnificent pine, some thirty or forty feet high. Carefully, to avoid injuring any of the limbs, it was hauled by dog teams 200 miles back to camp.

Out on the smooth ice of the Bering Sea, facing the town, a great pyramid of blocks of sawn ice was erected. This pyramid, rising tier on tier of blocks, was some thirty-five feet high. On top of it was erected an icy throne for Santa Claus, the tree was put up and most lavishly decorated.

On Christmas eve, the whole town marched out and massed itself in a great circle about the pyramid. It was an impressive sight. All of us, of course, were attired in furs, for the temperature was down to about 25 below zero. It was a still moonless night, but the glistening white ice and the aurora borealis furnished some illumination.[31]

The playwright Wilson Mizner vividly recalled this display and remarked that the festivities created a new attitude in what had been "the most irritable, competitive hell hole on earth." [32]

Nome had sprung up so rapidly that there was no authorized government and no charter to form one. To prevent lawlessness and to avoid the necessity of vigilante committees, the miners organized a "consent" government. Charles S. Johnson, United States District Judge for Alaska, had advised forming a municipal government for mutual protection until Congress passed appropriate laws, and on August 17, 1899, a mass meeting voted to consider his suggestion. Two weeks later, the seven-man committee appointed to draft a charter presented their proposals to the reassembled group. A motion made by one Francis McNulty to call the town Nome carried unanimously, whereupon Pittman moved "that the charter as amended be adopted." [33] This was a modern instance of "squatter sovereignty," in which the inhabitants agreed to the authority of a group of officials who undertook the task of preserving law and order and safeguarding the health of the community.

Pittman was appointed the first district attorney and served until the consent government expired in June, 1900, when the town became incorporated. Conditions in the new community were extremely favorable for dishonest administration, particularly in the abuse of power of attorney for locating claims. The new officials were "a bunch of crooks," who conspired to perpetrate one of the most audacious frauds in mining history. In July and August, 1900, the Pioneer Mining Company employed Pittman as an attorney in a suit against this corrupt government, an incident made famous by Rex Beach's novel *The Spoilers*.[34] (Newspapermen suggested that the young lawyer and the judge's niece were Key and Mimosa Pittman. Mrs. Pittman denied this. Key, she insisted, "never received any suggestion that he inspired any character in the book.") [35] After the ouster of the dishonest officials, the *Nome Daily Chronicle* commented that the city had returned to being a law-abiding camp, "one that can scarcely be equaled by any other mining community in the west. There have been any number of rows here, but they have generally been settled in the good old Anglo-Saxon way, and the worst wounds that have been on exhibition, after the scrap was over, have consisted of blackened eyes and bruised faces. That is as it should be." [36]

Pittman's legal training made him prominent in the politics of the new camp, and by 1900 the local newspaper referred to him as "the well known attorney." [37] Mining litigation was his specialty and his small office opposite Wyatt Earp's Dexter Bar became the center of a profitable practice—quick profit being a necessity in Nome with beer at $67.50 a barrel and a salt pork and sauerkraut dinner costing $1. In 1901, Pittman, with Albert Fink and Kenneth Jackson, two aggressive young lawyers, established the firm of Jackson, Pittman, and Fink and appeared in several cases before the Federal District Judge at Nome.[38]

True tales of the Klondike have been so embellished through the years that it is almost impossible to establish the original version. One of these stories involved Pittman and Wilson Mizner.

Pittman had shrewdly ordered several tons of coal shipped to him

during the summer of 1900; he had it piled in a mountainous heap behind his office and sold it at $150 a ton when winter came. His coal be-
came so valuable that he kept watch on it from his office window with
a shotgun over his knees. One winter afternoon Mizner came to Pittman's office with a sad tale. It seemed that Rose, one of the town's
doxies, was in the hospital and needed an operation. Mizner was trying
to borrow $200 from the bank but needed a cosigner on his note.
Pittman, familiar with Mizner's wiles, also knew "that on occasion the
Yellow Kid [Mizner] could be genuinely unselfish." He signed the
note. As Mizner dashed down the stairs, Pittman swiveled around in
his chair in time to see four of Mizner's friends "hauling away two
tons of coal on a sleigh." Later that afternoon, Pittman met Rose, the
supposedly ailing woman, at Tex Rickard's bar. When he asked about
the operation, she replied, "What operation?" And when the note fell
due a few months later, Pittman had to pay it. In less than five minutes
on a winter's afternoon, he had been bilked out of $200 and two tons
of coal.[39]

II

The Pittmans left Alaska for San Francisco in the autumn of 1901;
Mimosa had been ill and was advised not to remain in the Arctic for
the winter months. "We left on Lane's schooner, the *Barbara Hernster*
as a guest of Charley Lane and in company with Hoxey West and
many other of the old boys." [40] They intended to return to Alaska the
following spring, but news of a gold strike in the Tonopah area of
Nevada attracted Pittman to this virgin region. Leaving his wife in
San Francisco to await his call, Pittman set out for Tonopah in
March, 1902. "The stage was crowded and exceedingly disagreeable,"
he wrote Mimosa. "The occupants were a lot of common vulgar men.
Considerable building is going on and the city presents a very credit-
able appearance." [41]

The rush to southern Nevada had just begun but Jim Butler's discovery of Tonopah was already part of Nevada lore. In May, 1900, he
and his wife had been on a prospecting trip and had camped at the
foot of a hill in the central part of Nye County some fifty miles south
of Belmont. The next morning they found that their pack burros had
strayed. Butler set out uphill to find them, cornered them, and herded

them back toward camp. To speed their return trip, he picked up a rock and was about to hurl it at their rumps when he noticed it was mineralized quartz. Nearby was the outcropping. The Butlers gathered specimens and brought them to Tasker Oddie, district attorney of Nye County and future senator and governor of Nevada. Jim Butler offered Oddie a share in the mine if he would have an assay made. Oddie gave the specimens to Walter Gayheart, a mining engineer, who made the assay in return for part of Oddie's interest in the still non-existent mine. The analysis showed values of $80 to $600 a ton in gold and silver.[42]

For all practical purposes, Tonopah, as Butler named the new camp, was isolated from the rest of the world. No roads led to this undeveloped part of Nye, which, although one of the largest counties in the United States, in 1900 had a population of only 1,140. The nearest railroad connection was at Sodaville, sixty-three miles to the west, where a narrow-gauge railroad made triweekly connections to San Francisco about five hundred miles to the west, and to Salt Lake City seven hundred miles east. By the following year, nevertheless, claims were being made by the hundreds. Provisions sold at exorbitant prices, and water, freighted four miles by burro, sold for twenty-five cents a bucket. Only liquor seemed abundant. Tents were pitched helter-skelter in the shadow of Mizpah Mountain, and shacks dotted the sagebrush. The one hotel was the miserable Mizpah, where every whisper and snore could be heard over the house and where the rooms were so small that Pittman had to stand on his trunk to undress.

The Tonopah discovery, plus those at nearby Goldfield and Bullfrog, opened the southern Nevada area to a period of fantastic prosperity. Merchants and businessmen followed close on the heels of the miners, and soon their stores and offices were crowded side by side on what became the main street. Saloons were the first businesses established, and their number was popularly regarded as an indication of the prosperity of the camp. One year after the initial strike, Tonopah could boast thirty-two saloons, six faro games, two dance halls, two churches, and one school.[43]

Pittman discovered, as did the other newcomers, that a good deal of development work would be necessary to determine if the ores remained valuable at deeper levels. He was short on capital required for such an undertaking, but nevertheless he was so impressed by the town's need for a mining lawyer that he decided to stay. Although he had difficulty in raising $200 to build a two-room cabin, "I will succeed! I will succeed!," he promised Mimosa, who was in San Francisco recuperating from a severe asthma attack. "I am sorry that I have no money to invest for I know I could make a fortune. . . . I will soon be making money and then we can speculate." And a week later: "I am thinking of making our home in Nevada, and growing up with the country. I see many opportunities here both in law, mines and polytics [sic]. I feel very confident that I will be employed in most of the large suits, and the boys are even now talking of running me for the legislature. There will be a U. S. Senator elected at the next legislature and I could gain prominence there. (I have many schemes and am bending every energy to succeed.) . . . I will succeed and when I do I will make you the happiest woman on earth— . . . Nevada seems to offer the best opportunities." [44]

Pittman's reputation as a mining lawyer had preceded him: his rented frame bungalow office soon became the center of a "splendid business," which included the most important clients in Tonopah, and in a matter of months he developed an extensive mining and corporation practice. Successful in his speculations as well as his practice, by 1904—two years later—he was a wealthy man, an officer and stockholder in the principal mining and industrial companies of the state. "Things are looking much brighter. . . . The town has commenced to boom . . . the property is richer than ever—." And on his thirty-second birthday he asked Mimosa to project herself into the future. "Can you picture your thoughts, desires and disposition of five years hence— Do you think we will seek society of wealth or political position—or retirement, literary or art pursuits? . . . I feel confident of our success." [45]

III

Nevada had voted Republican since being admitted into the Union in 1864. On January 1, 1890, the Carson City *Morning Appeal* had raised the standard of revolt against the Republicans for demonetizing the state's chief product, the editor calling for a new party which would have the remonetization of silver as its principal platform plank. The Silver party was soon launched, and almost immediately it became a powerful force in local politics; thousands of voters aligned themselves with the new group, taking with them nearly all the Democratic and Republican politicians and office-seekers. Pittman joined the Silver party in 1902, explaining to a friend "that the increase of the circulating medium will be of benefit to every poor man in the United States, and to every man irrespective of his condition in the State of Nevada. No matter what may be considered as the dominant issue of the National Parties by the East, we know that favorable legislation to Silver is the most vital and important consideration." [46]

The Silver party swept the state in 1892, receiving almost two thirds of the vote. Four years later, the Democrats and Silver men agreed on most nominations and carried the election by heavy majorities with Bryan polling an unprecedented 81 per cent of the total —8,377 votes to McKinley's 1,938. Even after passage of the Gold Standard Act in 1900, this silver coalition continued to elect state officers on a ticket demanding remonetization of the white metal.[47] In July, 1902, Pittman was appointed a member of the state Central Committee. "I take the greatest interest in the Silver Cause and firmly believe that it is a subject of more interest to the people of the State of Nevada, and every poor man in the United States, than any other question of Public Policy." [48]

In January, 1904, William Jennings Bryan announced that bimetallism would not be the main issue in the forthcoming presidential campaign. The dominant questions would be the restriction of trusts, protection of labor, and honesty and morality in public office.[49] Pittman, who always had considered himself a supporter of Bryan, severed his relations with the Silver party and announced his intention of voting in the Democratic primaries. The Silverites, he emphasized in his letter of resignation, lacked a national organization and could not accomplish the reforms advocated by Bryan. "The Republican Party, by reason of the sentiments of its leaders will not, therefore I can see but one hope, and that is in the success of the Democratic Party." Others followed Pittman's lead and the Silver party faded away, its platform and membership absorbed by both the Nevada Republicans and Democrats.[50]

By 1904 more than twenty thousand people lived in the Tonopah area, with additional hundreds arriving each week. The gold and silver supply seemed inexhaustible; discoveries had been made practically everywhere. "Heard of a rich strike at Gold Mountain so determined to force the storm," Pittman related to Mimosa, who was again in San Francisco for treatment of her asthma. "The hail was as big as a hickory nut and the wind was fearful [but] the strike was bona-fide —In fact it is the biggest thing out of Tonopah. The free gold shows in all the rocks." [51] Two years later, Nevadans screamed themselves hoarse when the discovery at Round Mountain became the bonanza of all bonanzas with assays running over $400,000 to the ton.[52] The once insurmountable problems of transportation, fuel, water, and capital were slowly solved, and the hodgepodge of shanties gave way to frame buildings equipped with electricity and telephones. Tailors, milliners, clergy, actors, pickpockets, and the rest of the procession from the corners of civilization invaded Tonopah. Miners and mill workers replaced the speculators and gamblers as the town gradually emerged into a modern mining community.

Pittman's practice had grown with the area, and he was one of the most prosperous lawyers in southern Nevada, but he continued to strive for what he called "success." Although a wealthy man, he considered himself a failure: "Bryan at my age had been two terms in Congress and two years later was the nominee for President of the United States. I realize that I am not mature, not settled, not determined—I can see the change and look forward to the completion of the evolution." "My chief obstacle is procrastination," he confessed. "This I will try and overcome—I am not methodical enough. I am going to keep a diary for the purpose of watching my progress." [53] With boundless drive, Pittman pushed himself to his limits. Court opened at 8:00 A.M., and many a day he forced himself to remain until it closed at 9:00 P.M. His clientele by 1907, probably the most extensive in the state, included the Charles M. Schwab interests and the Southern Nevada Telephone and Telegraph Company.[54] He had extensive holdings in the principal mining companies of Nye County, including the Tonopah Extension, which could show a net profit of about $25,000 a month; [55] and he was a director in more than a hundred mining, banking, and utility companies. But he still considered himself inadequate—"I have failed you," he repeatedly told Mimosa—

and his life's aim—to make money and a reputation—impelled him on.[56]

Pittman's letters to his wife reveal a lonely man who craved love and who constantly sought companionship. He clung to Mimosa and fought desperately to hold her affection. "If you only knew how busy I am and what important matters I am attending to—all for you—all for you." Time and again he wrote of his two fears—losing her, and failure. "We will succeed . . . we must succeed." When Pittman suspected Mimosa of infidelity or when he lost a client or a case, he drank heavily, for which she admonished him. "I have taken nothing to drink since I left . . . I have not taken a drink down town," he protested. But, and perhaps rightly so, Mimosa repeatedly accused him of drinking and of unfaithfulness. He would respond with more protestations and pleas to bear with him: "I am earnest, and have no one but you." "Do not leave me. I need you. . . . [You are] strong, healthy, energetic, vivacious, fearless, enthusiastic, handsome, passionate, virtuous and affectionable, clean of mind and sound of judgment. You were endowed with every attribute to make a worthy man happy . . . do not leave me, I need you." [57]

After resigning from the Silver party, Pittman became a prominent Democrat and an executive member of the Nye County club. In 1908, he campaigned actively for the organization candidates, accepting speaking engagements throughout the state. He denied, at least publicly, any thought of personal political gain—"My sole desire is for the success of the whole Democratic ticket"—but he did not protest when the party leaders selected him to be one of five state committeemen-at-large.[58] Even though there was no free silver plank in their national platform, the Democrats carried Nevada for Bryan by about five hundred votes.

With the breakup of the Silver party, the Republicans now posed a threat to the Nevada Democracy. In 1909–1910, when there was talk of a new reform group, Pittman opposed the idea. Despite his protests to state politicians, the Socialist party was organized in July, 1908, and grew steadily, claiming 1,100 dues-paying members by 1912. The Socialist program called for the initiative, referendum, and recall, declaring "that with these in operation, the country can be no longer controlled by the corporations and grafters, but by the working man." [59] In repeated letters and talks, Pittman tried to discourage membership in this new third party, because he believed that all reform forces should unite with the Democrats as the only hope for national reform. "The insurgents of Massachusetts, New York and elsewhere are voting the Democratic tickets, and why in the name of God, should they not vote it in the State of Nevada?" [60]

In 1909, Pittman's friends began to ask if he would accept the Democratic nomination for United States Senator the following year. He carefully avoided saying no; instead he suggested that "our faction perfect our plans and be assured of control of the Executive Committee." [61] "To state that I would not desire to be elected to the United States Senate would not only be false but absurd," he confided to his friend Charles Sprague. "But, I do not intend to contend for such office or any other office until I am convinced in my own mind that I will win." [62]

Years afterward, Pittman recalled that his first serious thought of public office occurred at the Jim Jeffries–Jack Johnson prize fight at Reno on July 4, 1910, when his friend Governor Denver S. Dickerson asked him to run for the United States Senate as a "sacrifice candidate." * [63] Pittman accepted the challenge. Mimosa, elated at his selection, attributed it to fate and she was confident that Pittman had been "ordained to be in that place and do more than any other Senator has every done—You will not fellow in their tracks but advance things for humanity." She thought that if he lost, it might mean the end of a successful law practice, for they would be "dead broke"; and also if he won, victory might end their dreams of wealth and the sensuous pleas-

---

* The Manhattan [Nevada] Mail commented that "interest in the Jeffries-Johnson fight has waned to a great extent since the announcement was made that 'Tex' Rickard will referee the bout. . . . Rickard has had very little, if any experience as a referee, and the fact that he will be the third man in the ring at the championship go, will have a tendency to cause many to think twice before they place their bets" (The Manhattan Mail, May 28, 1910, 2:1) .

In later years, Pittman delighted in telling his Senate colleagues that he won his first nomination to that august body in a poker game on the night of the Jeffries-Johnson fight. The game, which included the state Democratic leaders, was steep, and the future Senator was $5,000 ahead. Pittman, according to his story, placed his winnings on the table and challenged the Democratic leaders to match this with the senatorial nomination. They accepted. Pittman won the hand and received the nomination. I have been unable to check the accuracy of this story, which is now part of Capitol lore.

hours persuading and cajoling the Nevadans. On the final roll call, Nevada, pledged to the unit rule, cast its six votes for the majority resolution.[38] Although the Platform Committee was upheld, the Democratic party had been split asunder over the resolution to condemn the Ku Klux Klan.

The balloting for a presidential standardbearer was anticlimactic and served further to widen the chasm in an already divided party. The Nevada delegates favored McAdoo above the other nominees. It was obvious, though, that none of the prominently mentioned men would obtain the necessary two-thirds vote and so Pittman opposed pledging the state to any candidate. "McAdoo will receive the votes of the delegation so long as it is practicable. But why label the delegation?" he asked his contingent. "The minute you label it you debar yourself from free and open conference with uninstructed delegations or delegations instructed for other candidates." Pittman had no doubt that the convention eventually would have to agree on a dark horse. When this occurred, he hoped to have "many friends in every other camp" and use his influence to obtain commitments for himself and his state.[39]

The first few ballots convinced Pittman that an absolute deadlock existed between McAdoo and Al Smith. He advised the former to honorably withdraw and retain his influence in the nomination of another candidate, but this suggestion went unheeded. When Pittman was absolutely certain that McAdoo could not be chosen, he joined a number of other Democrats in a behind-the-scenes effort to bring about a compromise. Meanwhile, the Nevada delegates, voting under the unit rule, continued to cast their six ballots for McAdoo.

Pat McCarran, a member of the delegation and Pittman's perennial rival, insisted that the Nevada state Democratic convention had endorsed Al Smith. In fact, he openly declared that the instructions of the state group were to cast only one courtesy vote for McAdoo. McCarran went out of his way to embarrass Pittman, who was conferring with Smith supporters in an attempt to break the deadlock, by repeatedly polling the delegation and putting the Senator on record against Al Smith.[40] Pittman refrained from a public showdown with McCarran but his private comments remain unprintable. He was more annoyed, though, at both Smith and McAdoo for acting "like dunces in not getting out of the race," especially after the first day.[41]

On the day before the final balloting, Pittman joined with the rest of his delegation in casting a unanimous vote for Smith so as to let McAdoo definitely know that his withdrawal was long overdue. After that, the Senator asked the Nevadans to support John W. Davis. Since a majority opposed his suggestion, they agreed temporarily to back Senator Thomas Walsh.

The McAdoo-Smith battle for the nomination represented more than a collision of personalities. Here on the floor of Madison Square Garden, the clash between urban "immorality" and rural "piety" had created a convention deadlock which would divide the Democratic party for years to come. John W. Davis was nominated on the 103rd ballot; there were a few cheers, lasting less than five minutes. The band played something that ended in the Star-Spangled Banner. Then it was over—the Democracy had found a candidate.

Immediately after Davis' selection, Frank Polk, Norman Davis, Pittman, and several other prominent Democrats met with the nominee to discuss a vice-presidential candidate. After several names had been mentioned, John Davis turned to Pittman and asked him to be his running mate. The Senator politely refused, indicating that a labor man was needed since Robert La Follette's independent candidacy would appeal to that group.[42] Several western delegates, nevertheless, appealed to Pittman, asking him to recant. He replied that his statement was irrevocable, but nonetheless the Alaskan delegation cast its six votes for him. A divided convention nominated Charles W. Bryan amid boos, hisses, and jeers and adjourned *sine die*.[43]

"Our Convention was a very unfortunate affair," Pittman informed his brother Will. "Intense bitterness was engendered between Catholics and Protestants." The Senator realized that Davis, whom he had not known before the convention, had a less than even chance of winning. La Follette, he feared, would draw more votes from the Democrats than from the Republicans. "If La Follette can carry seven Republican states, the election will be thrown into Congress. If thrown into Congress, Davis will be elected. If La Follette does not carry these states, then Coolidge will probably be elected." [44] Davis' victory would have been assured, the Senator told his friend Senator John Sharp Williams, had it not been for the religious row.[45] He considered the nomination of Governor Bryan a mistake, for it added dead weight to the ticket, the only benefit being that it kept "W. J. off of Davis' back, which, of course, is quite a relief." [46]

After the convention, Pittman was physically worn out and looked forward to an extended rest at Lake Tahoe. Much to his surprise, John Davis summoned him to New York during the first week in August to ask his advice on conducting the campaign. Pittman suggested several major speeches interpreting the main platform planks, and Davis seemed pleased. After several days of conferences, Davis asked Pittman to take charge of his personal speaking engagements and to accompany him on his main tour.[47] The Senator accepted. "Davis cannot do without me so I must stay—," he wrote Mimosa.[48]

John Davis delivered the most important talk of the campaign at Sea Girt, New Jersey, on August 22, 1924, his first major speech after being nominated. Before 35,000 Democrats, Davis condemned the Ku Klux Klan by name and challenged President Coolidge to join him in a similar declaration. This was a definite, specific repudiation of the Klan, going beyond the plank in the party platform and approaching the anti-Klan resolution so narrowly defeated at the national convention. By the middle of August, Democratic leaders had become convinced that the Klan was a liability rather than an asset, and they decided to wipe it off the political map. Several of Davis' advisors opposed this strategy, but he followed the suggestions as outlined by Pittman. "I advised Mr. Davis to denounce the Klan in his Seagirt speech. If the platform had contained the denunciation of the Klan that Davis made in his Seagirt speech, he would have obtained no credit as a candidate. . . . There is no doubt that Mr. Davis would have eventually denounced the Klan, but I felt the time to do it was in his first speech." [49] Party leaders, gratified at the favorable reaction to the speech, warmly congratulated Pittman for his strategy.

As the campaign progressed, Pittman realized that Davis' chances of victory were diminishing. His spirits were slightly raised, however, during the September tour through the West, which the Senator described as a "victorious march." [50] "I got into Davis' labor speech at Wheeling what I wanted," he told Mimosa. "I hope to get the material things in his Omaha speech." [51] Pittman thought, and confidentially wrote, that if Davis should be elected he would be his principal advisor on western matters, as well as his patronage chief for the area.[52] By October, however, the outlook for victory appeared dismal. "It is a shame he should have had forced upon him such a miserable organization," complained the Senator. "From the Chairman [Clem Shaver] down most of them are incompetent and inexperienced." [53] Reports from Nevada added to his despair. His friend Sam Belford bewailed that local Democrats were thoroughly demoralized and disorganized. "Davis is being universally neglected. It would not surprise me if he ran third in Nevada." [54] The verdict was decisive, as Coolidge received more than two million votes over his combined opposition, carrying with him a solid Republican Congress. Belford's prediction proved correct. Davis ran a poor third in Nevada —Coolidge received 11,243 votes; La Follette, 9,769; Davis, 5,909. Pittman, disappointed but certainly not shocked, agreed with Will Rogers that "the result was just as big a surprise as the announcement that Christmas was coming in December." [55]

In retrospect, Pittman attributed the "miserable campaign" and the stunning defeat to the bitter religious fight which had split the Democratic party. The Republicans, he thought, had convinced conservative Democrats that unless they voted for Coolidge, William Jennings Bryan would in some way become President. La Follette, on the other hand, had assured liberal Democrats that Davis was a reactionary. (To counteract La Follette's charge, Pittman composed a series of articles on John Davis for distribution in Nevada, concluding the final one by emphatically denying that Davis "had Wall Street views. He is a poor man and always has been.") [56] Undaunted by defeat, the Senator looked forward to the next election, certain that the only hope of the Democratic party lay in educating the liberal voters. "The tremendous endorsement of the Coolidge administration will make that administration arbitrary beyond imagination. There is only one hope of ever stopping it and that hope lies in the Democratic party." [57]

Years after the election, John Davis remembered that a rather rigidly pietistic friend once asked, "Did you say anything in the course of the campaign you didn't believe?"

"Oh, yes," Davis replied.

With a shocked expression, his friend inquired what that was. Davis answered, "I went around the country telling the people I was going to be elected and I knew I hadn't any more chance than a snowball in hell. . . . That's the only thing I can recall that I'd have to admit wasn't true." [58]

III

"Everybody has gone money crazy. No one cares anything about honesty in Government. All they desire is a boom in which there will be an opportunity to rob somebody. We will have a boom for a while and later on somebody will have to pay for it," said Pittman in 1924. In Washington, Democrats complained that thieves and bootleggers conspired with the chiefs of government bureaus and cabinet members. Republicans, on the other hand, kept cool with Coolidge. "The Republican Party, realizing its impotence and corruption, is attempting by every means to make Cal Coolidge out as a little God," contended Pittman. "His silence is not based upon wisdom but upon a knowledge of his ignorance and his fear of offending the big interests who own him." The Senator frankly admitted that both parties were in "chaotic condition." "Neither party has any policies, and some charge that there is a lack of principle." [59]

Most of Pittman's senatorial work between the presidential campaigns of 1924 and 1928 dealt with local issues. Arid Nevada had problems and needs wholly unlike those of other regions. The state's farmers, for example, had to change desert lands into productive fields, a process of which their eastern counterparts knew little. Some Nevada valleys have no rain for a year or more, and areas larger than Connecticut contain only a few score water sources. In parts of the state, the average annual temperature is around one hundred degrees, while in other sections, killing frosts come as late as May and begin again in September. Nevada, with a land area equal to that of all New England and Pennsylvania, had a population of but 77,000 in 1920. One could ride for days through its interior without meeting a person or seeing a house or finding a well. The assessed value of the state's taxable property in 1925 totaled only 199 million dollars. If Nevada was to undertake irrigation, reclamation projects, and rural road construction, federal aid was a necessity.

Between 1924 and 1928, Pittman introduced twenty-seven public bills, twenty-four of which were to help Nevada or Nevadans. Of these bills, four were reported out of committee, while only two became law. The administration, he reasoned, remained completely hostile to the West and supported long committee hearings to purposely delay legislation. The Senator bitterly criticized Secretary of the Interior Hubert Work, believing that with the approval of the President he intended to put the West on a business basis. Westerners "will be permitted to starve to death while they learn to do without eating. If Hamilton were alive today, he would be willing to serve Coolidge in any capacity on earth." [60]

In No. 27 of the *Federalist,* Alexander Hamilton wrote that the Senate would develop into a national body composed of men with great knowledge, reluctant to be tainted by factionalism and local prejudices. This was not Pittman's conception of a senator. Between 1924 and 1928, he rarely spoke on the Senate floor except to further the interests of his state. In June, 1924, for example, when a conference report on an appropriation bill omitted a Pittman-sponsored item for the Spanish Springs, Nevada, reclamation project, he conducted a one-man filibuster and prevented adoption of the entire report. When the Senate reconvened after the summer recess, every member of the Appropriations Committee grudgingly assured Pittman that they would stand by him in forcing the Spanish Springs amendment to the appropriations bill. The Nevadan eventually won out.[61]

Pittman excelled in obtaining subsidies for his state. When he introduced an amendment, he instructed Nevada's lone congressman to introduce the exact item in the House to avoid difficulty in conference committees. In 1926, following this practice, he secured a $50,000 appropriation for a survey of water storage and dam sites on the Truckee River in Nevada.[62] During the Sixty-ninth Congress (1925–1927), he ardently backed a controversial Long and Short Haul amendment to the Interstate Commerce Act which Senator William McKinley of Illinois labeled "one of the most pronounced pieces of class or sectional legislation that has ever been proposed in the history of the deliberations of this Chamber." [63] After a heated debate, the amendment failed to pass the Senate, but Pittman would not admit defeat. He consistently reintroduced it as a rider. Once the Nevadan angered Senator William Bruce of Maryland, who caustically commented that he remembered a time when "if the brains were out the man would die, and time was when, if a legislative measure were knocked in the head, it would gasp and give up the ghost. But that time seems to have passed." [64] Despite criticism from his Republican colleagues, Pittman, a master in the manipulation of amendments and riders, usually got what he wanted. In 1924, Nevada was one of the very few states which received more in subsidies from the Federal Government than it paid in federal taxes.

Pittman did not antagonize his Democratic colleagues by speaking on issues which did not affect his area. During the prolonged debates on Muscle Shoals he never asked for recognition to deliver a speech on any phase of the complicated subject and usually abstained from voting on all controversial amendments. When Senator Norris' bill finally passed the Senate in March, 1928, Pittman was reported as not voting.[65] The Senator did support the farm bloc in its demands for relief for agriculture. In return, they looked kindly at bills which benefited the inter-mountain region.[66] Through these tactics, the Senator obtained what he wanted for his state and constituents. "I have for years been declaring that the interests of the west and Nevada are peculiar, and that our first fight is for those interests," he wrote in 1928. "Some of my local Democratic friends even have feared that I was a Democrat first and a citizen of Nevada second. They are wrong. I am dedicated to the principles of Jefferson, and yet, if they do not apply to a given state of facts, I do not hesitate to adopt the remedy that is essential for the particular emergency." [67]

IV

By the beginning of 1928, the consensus among Democratic senators was that Al Smith's candidacy grew stronger every day. The drys failed to find a leading aspirant after McAdoo announced he would not accept the nomination, and many who had opposed Smith in 1924 now considered his selection as inevitable. As early as December, 1926, Pittman confided to Nevada politicians that there was no question in his mind that Smith would be the Democratic nominee. The drys, he thought, were in "a pathetic condition." [68]

1928 was also an election year for Pittman. Friends in Nevada expected him to have a difficult fight and so advised him. Twenty-five per cent of the state's miners were out of work because of the depression in gold and silver. Many cattlemen, who usually voted Democratic, were being forced into bankruptcy and saw their land purchased by sheepmen. In the 1926 elections most state incumbents failed to be re-elected, and the Democratic governor, James Scrugham, was defeated. Pittman, perhaps realizing that his political life was at stake, refused to be a delegate to the Houston convention, saying that he wanted to give other Democrats a chance to attend. The Senator really feared that another religious quarrel combined with the state Republican trend might cost him his Senate seat.[69]

Although refusing to be a delegate, Pittman still took an active part in the preconvention activities. At the personal request of Governor Smith, he secretly drafted a short platform for consideration at Houston. For months prior to the convention, the Governor's non-official advisory committee directed his strategy from New York. Headed by Judge Joseph M. Proskauer and Mrs. Belle Moskowitz, this energetic committee carefully publicized Smith as the most attractive Democratic figure available for the nomination. (Mrs. Moskowitz's political perception so impressed Pittman that he described her as "a political genius.")

In Congress, Governor Smith also had an unofficial advisory group consisting of Senators Peter Gerry, Robert Wagner, and Pittman, and Congressman Parker Corning of Albany, which decided questions of congressional strategy but only after conferring with Judge Proskauer and Mrs. Moskowitz. During the first week of May, the New York group asked Pittman to serve as permanent chairman of the convention. He declined in favor of Senator Joseph Robinson, who, he explained, as a Southerner would have more influence in allaying any attempt to disrupt the proceedings.

Pittman devoted considerable time to preparing the platform draft, firmly believing that it should be short and state only fundamental principles. "Al Smith will be the platform and we do not want to hamper him with all kinds of detailed declarations with regard to legislation, which after all is wholly for the consideration of and determination by legislative bodies. The most important thing to be done at the Convention, because, of course, Al Smith is going to be nominated, is the adoption of a platform that every Democrat can stand on, and a platform that will not embarrass Democrats anywhere in the country." Confident that Smith would be chosen, Pittman considered the greatest danger he faced was from any hasty, irresponsible actions by his friends. "The fight has for months been rapidly drifting in the right direction and our plan has been not to disturb that drift." [70]

On June 5, 1928, Pittman came to New York to confer with Smith's "inside advisors." Judge Proskauer emphasized that it was imperative for Smith's nomination to have the platform properly presented and debated before the convention, and informed the Senator that Smith wanted him to be chairman of the Platform Committee. Pittman at first declined, explaining his own political situation, and pointed out that he even had refrained from becoming a convention delegate. Proskauer urged him to reconsider, which Pittman did only after the Judge assured him that no minority resolutions would be introduced by any Smith delegate.[71]

Pittman and Judge Proskauer revised the Senator's first platform draft in accordance with suggestions made by Smith. The Governor had accepted Pittman's general plank on law enforcement with one immaterial alteration, and had made a few changes on the foreign relations declarations and one on the tariff. (Claude Bowers said that he attended a conference at which the platform was discussed. "Key Pittman had read the plank of foreign relations. . . . It was a good plank but couched in super-diplomatic language so that it didn't say anything that anybody could understand precisely. When he got through Smith, who had met Pittman for the first time that night, said in that gruff voice of his, 'Well, that may be all right, but who in the hell knows what it means? I don't know what it means. I finally got it, but it gave me a pain in the back of the neck. We've got to remember that all people are not college professors and don't belong to the Union League Club. We've got to put this in language they can understand. Let me try my hand.' . . . When he got through there was dead silence for a minute. One of the party—I think it was Proskauer—said 'Al, that's pretty close to the League of Nations,' and nothing more was said.") [72] Smith and Pittman agreed that the platform should allay the fears of fanatical groups and not interfere with the freedom of the candidate. When the convention convened on June 26, such a draft had been completed.[73]

The Houston convention assembled amid tranquility unusual for these quadrennial meetings of the Democratic party. Even the diehards had conceded Smith's nomination on the first ballot. The California delegation, which successfully led the anti-Smith bloc four years previously, joyously chanted:

We're from Cal
We're for Al.[74]

It is difficult to imagine two conventions more dissimilar than those of 1924 and 1928. While the delegates listened to nominating and seconding speeches, the Committee on Platform and Resolutions closeted itself in the Houston Public Library. For thirty-six hours they discussed the platform, line by line, word by word. Not once during the interval did Pittman appear at the convention. With little food and less sleep, he presided almost continuously. The usual procedure is to present the platform to the delegates before candidates are placed in nomination for the Presidency; but at Houston this was reversed owing to the paramount necessity of drawing up a platform with supreme care and the amount of time consumed in doing this.

As chairman, Pittman attempted to act as a compromiser between the opposing factions represented on the Platform Committee. When he appointed subcommittees, instead of selecting those who agreed with him, he shrewdly selected the leaders of opposing schools of thought. He had Senators T. H. Caraway and Carter Glass on opposite sides of the McNary-Haugen bill, for example, and the result was the adoption of the plank Pittman had previously prepared. He moderated between Josephus Daniels and Newton Baker on one side of foreign policy, and Cole L. Blease of South Carolina on the other. The result was a compromise—the platform omitted any reference to the World Court. "I think one of the best things in the world is to remain silent, if silence will help the cause," Pittman told the committee.[75]

The vital plank was prohibition. The big question was whether the Platform Committee could avoid a floor fight by agreeing to a statement which would satisfy the extremists. The Sub-Committee on Prohibition's proposal contained a provision recognizing the right of the people to amend and to repeal amendments to the Constitution. This was voted down by the full committee, touching off a heated argument between Governor Dan Moody, of Texas, who represented the "bone drys"; Senator Edward I. Edwards, of New Jersey, representing the "wringing wets"; and Carter Glass, who was satisfied with Pittman's general law-enforcement plank. The debate continued for several hours until finally, Senator Glass offered an amendment striking out the wordy preamble of Pittman's draft, contending that the statement without the preamble definitely did not commit either dry or wet to cease activities. The committee reluctantly acquiesced, with only Governor Moody dissenting.

Governor Moody, despite pressure to the contrary, announced that he intended to file a minority report. A delegate from Utah then arose to state that he would do the same, only his would demand repeal of the Volstead Act. Before the debate again became acrimonious, Pittman turned to Glass and asked if, under his amendment, Governor Smith would be expected to desist from attempts to modify the Prohibition Amendment. Glass reiterated that Smith, or any wet or dry, could continue any and all activities.The plank was intended to commit the party and its candidates to simple law enforcement. Glass promised Pittman that he would make the same statement to the convention, which he later did. Moody still opposed the plank but now agreed not to file a minority report. A floor fight had been averted.[76] (When the final prohibition plank was read to Smith over the telephone, he reportedly replied: "It doesn't *say* anything. It only dodges and ducks.") [77]

Great confusion reigned in the convention hall when the platform was ready for presentation. A one-hour recess had expired but the delegates were late in returning from a hasty dinner. Pittman, smiling whimsically, and immaculately clad in white flannel and blue serge, took his place before the microphones and began to speak. Several minutes elapsed before the weary delegates realized that the platform was being read. By this time, Pittman, too fatigued to go on, had given his papers to a reading clerk, and he sank into the nearest comfortable chair.

Suddenly, the gathering was galvanized into attention. The platform pledged to enforce the Eighteenth Amendment and all other provisions of the Constitution. There were no minority reports. There was no debate. In a matter of minutes, the platform unanimously passed amidst a thunderous ovation. That such unanimity could be secured on the platform after the schism of 1924 seemed a political miracle. The man responsible for this harmony still sat with apparent nonchalance in his comfortable chair. "If our ticket is successful," Joseph Robinson wrote Pittman, "it will probably owe more to you than any other individual who attended the Houston convention. You displayed masterful skill and diplomacy and succeeded in preventing the slightest division over platform provisions." [78]

Pittman's platform deliberately compromised controversial issues to avoid a floor fight. The vague phraseology did appear as a "dragnet"—which is what all party platforms are actually intended to be. The farmers practically wrote their own plank. The longest in the platform, it committed the party to liberal farm relief legislation. The platform spoke out for abolition of the "lame duck" Congresses; for Philippine independence; for a complete reorganization of the departments, bureaus, and boards in Washington. The broad statements gave Smith plenty of room to do in a national way the things he had done in New York. In the main, this was a progressive document. Although the delegates departed from Houston holding sharp differences of opinion just as when they came, they left without having had their views rubbed raw by violent friction.

The tariff plank, except for one suggestion from Smith, stood as Pittman had drafted it. It committed the party to support duties that "permit effective competition, insure against monopoly, and at the same time produce a fair revenue." This statement would have been sufficiently ambiguous had the plank not concluded with the pronouncement that "actual difference of cost of production at home and abroad, with adequate safeguard for the wage of the American laborer, must be the extreme measure of every tariff rate." With this, the Democratic position became almost indistinguishable from that of the Republicans. The plank represented the changing attitude of the party and marked the farthest departure that the Democratic party had yet made from its traditional tariff position. The growing importance of the industrial South had made it impossible for the Democrats to remain a strict low-tariff party.

Immediately after the Houston convention, Pittman spent five days in Albany, where he gave "valuable assistance" to Governor Smith in planning the campaign. It was slow, annoying, tedious work, and he repeatedly complained that local politicians did not seem to understand that there was also a national election to win. The situation improved with the appointment of John J. Raskob and the selection of an Advisory Committee, which Pittman had suggested. Unfortunately, the advisors became actively involved in the campaign. Speeches and letter answering occupied most of their day, leaving little time for them to think and plan the daily pragmatic strategy so necessary for a successful campaign.[79]

In September, the Senator returned to Nevada to begin his own fight for re-election. Many of his friends had cautioned that he was making a political mistake in being so closely identified with Smith. Pittman disregarded their advice and campaigned for the Governor throughout the state. In Elko, he called his talk "Al Smith, the Man." In Fallon, he assured the overflow audience at the Rex Theater that Smith favored a higher price for silver. The Hoover forces, however, appeared to have stronger arguments to use on behalf of their candidate. Republican literature told of how Hoover had tramped the hills of the West with a transit and level and plane table, while Smith had never been west of Denver. "Hoover will know more about the economic requirements of Nevada on the day of his inauguration," one Republican advertisement stated, "than the Governor of New York would know at the age of one hundred, if by chance he should reach that ripe old age." [80] Undaunted by the strong Hoover sentiment, Pittman personally paid many local Democratic newspapers to run Smith-Pittman political advertisements. He confidently admitted that he was engaged in his most difficult political fight since 1912, when he had been elected by only eighty-nine votes. "I will, of course, get the support of nearly all of the Catholics in Nevada," he told Senator Peter Gerry. "They only constitute about one-fourth of our Voters. On the other hand, I am receiving opposition from those who violently oppose Governor Smith on account of his religion." [81]

On Election Day, 1928, the Democracy suffered a most humiliating defeat. In addition to the breaking of the "solid South" and the loss of New York, the Far West, which had voted for both Bryan and Wilson, disowned Smith as it had Cox and Davis. The Governor carried only five of Nevada's seventeen counties—the total vote was: Hoover, 18,327; Smith, 14,090. Pittman, though, trounced his Republican opponent Sam Platt 19,515 to 13,414, carrying every county except Omsby and Douglas. "The fight was somewhat similar to that which confronted John W. Davis," the Senator wrote Belle Moskowitz. Smith had been "defeated through selfish reasons by those who should have been our friends, conspired against by the bootlegging interests and all of the so-called temperance societies, and fought almost as a unit by the Ku Klux Klan." He attributed the loss of Nevada to propaganda and rumors spread from house to house, and to the largest expenditure of money ever spent in a state campaign.[82]

V

Almost the last word said in the Senate before the adjournment of the special session of the Seventy-first Congress in November, 1929, was a remonstrance from the presiding officer. "No one in the gallery had the right to laugh," declared the Vice President.[83] Indeed, it had been difficult for many to refrain after months of pompous and repetitious oratory. In defense of this session, Arthur Macmahon has written: "Seldom, however, had a single session of Congress held greater interest for the observer of social forces. Seldom has the salutary role of the Senate in our present political complex been more convincingly demonstrated." [84]

In his message to Congress, which convened on April 15, 1929, President Hoover declared: "I have called this special session of Congress to redeem two pledges given in the last election—farm relief and limited changes in the tariff." [85] Almost immediately after the message, substantially identical administration farm bills were introduced in the Senate and in the House of Representatives and referred to the Committee on Agriculture in each body. The agrarian relief program favored by the congressional farm bloc, however, differed fundamentally from that advocated by President Hoover. The farm bloc, exponent of the subsidy principle, introduced the export debenture plan, calling for export bounties on specific commodities. Pittman favored this amendment which senators added to the administration's measure, but he did not take part in either the committee or floor debates. In the face of active and bitter opposition of the President to the debenture plan, efforts to have the House agree seemed futile and were abandoned. Pittman voted for the administration measure, which created the Federal Farm Board, although he was confident that time would convince the administration of the error in rejecting the debenture idea.

The second reason for calling the special session—tariff revision—was of far greater importance to the Nevadan. During the 1928 campaign, Pittman had stated that the Democratic party had abandoned its low-tariff policy because of the economic evolution in the United

States. "There is no doubt that the Democratic party's view has been in a state of evolution for the last twenty-five or thirty years," he explained. "There is no doubt that with the growth of the West and South from a previous agricultural country to sections of varied industries the theory of the low tariff has ceased to exist." [86] Both major party platforms favored revising the Fordney-McCumber Act, the Republicans in explicit language and the Democrats by inference.

On May 7, 1929, Representative Willis Hawley introduced the administration's tariff measure. During the next year and a half, the Senate Finance Committee and the House Ways and Means Committee took nearly 20,000 pages of testimony in public hearings on the bill. In the Senate, the rate schedules were gone over three times; first, while the Committee of the Whole dealt with quesions raised by the amendments from the Finance Committee; second, when individual amendments were considered in the Committee of the Whole; and finally in the Senate proper, where over a hundred reservations brought many matters previously decided to a vote again. Senator Simmons of North Carolina led the debate on behalf of the Democrats, setting the tone by explaining that "the Democratic Party . . . has advanced from the old theory of a tariff for revenue only, to the theory of a competitive tariff. Whatever may have been the former Democratic formula for measuring tariff duties or whatever may have been the interpretation of the meaning of that formula by its tariff legislation, the Democratic Party of the present day stands for a competitive tariff." "I concur in every solitary statement there," Pittman told his colleagues in commenting on Simmons' speech. "I think it is the clearest and most forceful pronouncement we have heard in years. I think it is in exact accord with the platform of the party." [87]

A tabulation of Pittman's voting on the 182 amendments which had roll-call votes shows that on only thirty-one of these, or 17 per cent of the time, did he vote with Senator La Follette's Republican insurgents in trying to prevent moderate revision from becoming "prohibitive super-protection," as Congressman Cordell Hull phrased it. On 105 votes, or 58 per cent of the time, Pittman was reported as not voting. The Senator's high abstention record certainly did not mean that he was not interested in tariff legislation. On the contrary, he introduced and consistently supported amendments which would protect Nevada industries. Through his amendments and riders, duties were raised on gypsum, clay, silica, silica sands, manganese, and tungsten. At one point, Senator La Follette declared that a Pittman amendment to raise the duty on silica sands had been introduced to solely benefit Nevadan interests without considering the entire industry. Pittman's amendment was defeated. Four months later, however, the Senator introduced almost the identical amendment, this time as an amendment to an amendment. His persistence ended in victory and a duty on silica sands was included in the final Senate bill. "The whole proposition is to protect the western section of this country," said Pittman.[88]

Pittman had good cause to be concerned about Nevada's industries. If Congress lowered the duty on tungsten ore by just five cents a pound, many mines in the state would be forced to close due to foreign competition. In a Nevada gypsum mine labor averaged $5 for an eight-hour day, while the wages paid across the Mexican border were only $1.21. Nevada could not compete with Mexican gypsum without a protective tariff. Silica sand, which is used in the manufacture of glass, was shipped from Belgium and delivered to the Pacific Coast for $4 a ton. Similar sand from Nevada could not be delivered to the same point for less than $9 a ton. A duty of at least $5 a ton was necessary for competition. Through months of fatiguing debates, Pittman successfully protected the industries of his state. Carefully studying each tariff amendment, he used his legislative ability to protect Nevadan interests. Operating from his office, he dispatched notes of encouragement to friendly senators and frantic pleas to others. Above his desk stood the great seal of his state with its motto: "All For Our Country."

VI

By December, 1930, Nevada had more unemployment in proportion to population than existed anywhere in the United States, with thousands of migrants on their way to California only intensifying this number. Available jobs declined to record lows, and the 1930 placement of male laborers fell to 51 per cent of the 1929 figures.[89] When the state reached the limit of its indebtedness road projects came to a halt, adding hundreds to the ranks of the unemployed. In addition, the price of silver fell from a high of 74¢ an ounce in 1922 to a low of 26¢ an ounce in 1931. Mines closed as owners could not sell their products for a price which would equal the expenses of production. Mining stocks with high-grade ore behind them plummeted as they failed to attract purchasers.[90] To make matters worse, the 1930 drought had caused heavy destruction to farm lands. Springs and water holes dried up, killing thousands of stock animals. The Salvation Army reported that it fed more people in Nevada proportionately than anywhere in the United States. A general curtailment of operations in mining, lumbering, and railroad activities caused many to just leave the state. For an area which was not industrialized and whose wealth lay in the soil, this was total depression. "Darkness is enveloping us," lamented Pittman. "No ray of light meets our weak vision." * [91]

The congressional election of 1930 marked the first Republican setback since 1916. When the Seventy-second Congress convened in December, 1931, the Democrats organized the House after twelve years of minority opposition. In the Senate, the administration held a precarious 48 to 47 plurality, but except for organization, this proved meaningless, since Republican insurgents opposed most Hoover policies. Not in many years had the Democrats returned to the Capitol so full of confidence and so ready to fight from the drop of the gavel.

The Senate Democrats quickly took advantage of Republican disunity. When the Republican insurgents announced their intention to boycott their regular caucus, the Democrats decided to accentuate the split. The Senate was scarcely organized when, on December 8, 1931, Senator Joseph Robinson nominated Pittman to oppose Senator George Moses of New Hampshire for president pro tempore. Moses, who had served in that position for six years, was a conservative Republican who had alienated the insurgents by calling them "sons of the wild jackass." Between December 8, 1931, and January 4, 1932, twenty-one ballots were taken. Each resulted in deadlock. The Democrats never wavered from their support of Pittman, but the thirteen insurgents would neither vote for him or absent themselves. On the fifteenth ballot, to emphasize that they opposed Moses personally and not a Republican president pro tempore, the insurgents switched

* Years later, Pittman wrote James Farley that the "rugged individualism of Herbert Hoover was too rugged, even for the pioneer folk of Nevada" (K. P. to James A. Farley, September 9, 1936, Nevada Folder, Box 300, Office File, Franklin D. Roosevelt Papers, Hyde Park, N. Y.).

their votes to Senator Felix Hebert of Rhode Island, a most conservative Republican. Back-scene negotiations were unable to break the
deadlock. By December 17, after the seventeenth ballot, Pittman
termed his fight as "hopeless." * He told John W. Davis that the voting would continue only to further deepen the rift in the Republican
party. "We are engaged in skirmish at the present time preparatory to
the great battle of 1932." [92] On January 4, 1932, after the twenty-first
ballot had been completed, both sides agreed that it was futile to
continue the election. In default of any other settlement, Senator
Moses continued in office under an 1890 resolution which stated that
the president pro tempore "shall serve until his successor shall have
been appointed."

As economic conditions worsened, congressional differences of opinion as to how to meet the emergency sharpened. "The remedies proposed by President Hoover," declared Pittman, "have offered no remedy, and conditions have gone from bad to worse and are still on the
downward course. Such remedies as have been suggested by him have
only gone to the extent that a narcotic would serve to one suffering
from appendicitis." [93] Some senators contended that the government
should cut expenditures and reduce taxes. The proponents of this
scheme held that lower taxes would stimulate private industry, confidence in capital would be restored, and conditions would improve.
Pittman shared the other main line of thought, which believed that
the depression could not be halted until the market price of commodities rose above the cost of production. Such a rise in commodity
prices could not take place until the demand for products increased
through a rise in purchasing power. Forty per cent of the purchasers
in the American domestic market were laborers and those dependent upon them. If individual industry could not afford to employ
these laborers, then the government had to hire them for economi-
cally sound public works until industry assumed its normal function
as the employer.

The Senate Democratic Policy Committee appointed Senators
Wagner, Walsh, Buckley, Robinson, and Pittman to draft a party
relief bill. On May 25, 1932, this unofficial group introduced their

* Pittman had been the Democratic nominee for president pro tempore of the
Senate in 1919, 1921, 1925, and 1927.

legislative program.[94] Their bill provided for $300,000,000 to be advanced to the states in proportion to population for the relief of the destitute with additional authority granted to the Reconstruction Finance Corporation to advance up to $1,500,000,000 for revenue-producing projects initiated by states, municipalities, and public corporations. Provision was also made for construction of $500,000,000 worth of federal works to be financed by means of a twenty-five-year bond issue and a sinking fund. "We are in a situation to-day far more serious than we were ever in," said Pittman in defending his measure.[95]

Broadened by the addition of nearly two score amendments, the Senate approved the relief bill on June 23, 1932, without a recorded vote. After prolonged negotiations with the House, the final conference report passed on July 9, 1932. The President responded with a strong veto message insisting that the measure framed by the Democrats would interfere with state control over the unemployment problem, violating "every sound principle of public finance and government." Hoover expressed his willingness to accept certain parts of the bill and no time was lost in formulating a new relief measure in accordance with his specific recommendations. The compromise passed the Senate on the last day of the session and was signed by the President on July 21, 1932.

Pittman thought that stagnation of international commerce and trade caused the economic collapse. Relief measures, such as the one he assisted in framing, would only alleviate the effects of the depression. The government, he believed, had to take steps to correct the decline in trade which had brought on the disaster. The Senator argued that differences in the exchange value of the money of countries remained the chief obstruction to commerce and trade. Over half of the people of the world, for example, used silver money alone and the United States had negligently permitted their currency to be so beaten down in value as compared to gold-standard money that the silver users could no longer purchase American products. "The inexcusable, unnecessary, and almost criminal causes for this silver money depression can be easily eliminated through the action of an inter-governmental conference. Trade barriers can be removed through reciprocal agreements and commerce restored. Then our purchasing power will return, industry will prosper, unemployment will cease, confidence will be reestablished, and Government aid will no longer be necessary." [96]

The 1920's were frustrating years for the Democratic party. The loss of three successive national elections, the lack of national patronage, and intra-party disagreements combined to splinter the Democratic oak of the Wilsonian years. By 1932, Pittman was one of only fifteen Democrats who had served continually in the Senate since Wilson's administration. Pittman and his colleagues yearned for another Democratic administration. If their party won, they would be the chairmen of the committees, the presidential advisors, the patronage dispensers. Under Wilson, for example, Pittman had been able to obtain a disproportionate amount of federal appointments for his small state. "If a Democratic President is elected," he wrote in 1930, "I should be in a position to have my recommendations again considered." [97] The Senator was convinced that to insure victory in 1932 a strong leader was needed, one who would be able to prevent another convention split. The 1930 elections convinced Pittman that this strong leader had emerged—Franklin D. Roosevelt.[98]

CHAPTER IV

"The Best Present
I Have Ever Received"

Silver is the economic issue of American politics which has transcended party lines since 1873. It might seem strange to have men take the metal from one hole in the ground only to have the government bury it in another. Yet, thousands of people depend upon this transfer for their livelihood and well-being. It was their prosperity that mainly concerned Nevada's Key Pittman during his twenty-seven years in the United States Senate. His record shows he specialized in matters affecting his own state, but his influence far outweighed the size and wealth of Nevada.

I

The defeat of Bryan in 1896, the passage of the Gold Standard Act in 1900, and the gradual return of prosperity shattered the Senate silver bloc. Between 1900 and 1916, it was futile for westerners to demand a return to the 16-to-1 ratio when the average commercial rate was about 36 to 1. During the World War, however, the demand for the white metal, particularly needed in purchasing jute and raw materials from India, proved a godsend to the miners. For many years the price of silver had averaged 60¢ an ounce, but war conditions drove it to more than $1.[1]

In April, 1918, an event in remote India revitalized the Senate silver interests and resurrected the quiescent question. Great Britain had been purchasing large amounts of war materials in India in order to support the Mesopotamian campaign. To meet these expenditures, the British government issued what were commonly called council

75

bills, which passed in India as rupee currency and which were re-
deemable on demand at their face value in silver, the common specie
of India. German propagandists, actively at work throughout the war,
tried to convince the Indians that the British banks lacked sufficient
reserves to buy back these council bills. An unexpected run on the
redemption agencies in 1917 verified this. The British managed to
meet demands for payment in silver up to the beginning of 1918, but
by that date they had practically exhausted their holdings. Redemption was then made in gold. By March, though, the entire specie reserve of the Empire had dwindled to about 34 per cent of the outstanding currency. Britain had to have relief since dishonoring the
bills would mean the collapse of the Mesopotamian campaign and a
possible revolt in India. The only reservoir of silver in the world am-
ple to meet the situation was in the United States Treasury. In its
vaults lay approximately 490,000,000 silver dollars, which had been
accumulated under the provisions of the Bland Act of 1878 and the
Sherman Act of 1890.[2]

In March, 1918, Britain appealed to the United States for financial assistance. Pittman related how he first learned of the Indian
situation:

I was sitting in my office one day in the early part of 1918 when I received
a telephone message from Mr. Raymond T. Baker, the director of the Mint.
He urged me to come down to the Treasury Department immediately to confer with regard to some very important business relating to the production
and price of silver. I had already made preparations for departing from Washington within 20 minutes after I received the telephone message. I stated this
fact to Mr. Baker and told him that I would return in two days' time and
would then take the matter up with him. He then called Mr. [Russell C.]
Leffingwell, the Assistant Secretary of the Treasury, to the telephone and
Mr. Leffingwell told me that it was not only a matter that affected the welfare
of the silver industry but that it was much more serious; that immediate action was necessary to prevent disastrous consequences to our success in the war.
I, of course, went immediately to the Treasury Department. There I found
Mr. Leffingwell, Mr. Straus, Mr. Baker and other representatives of the Government, the British ambassador and other representatives of foreign countries, giving instant evidence by their demeanor of the grave crisis that occupied their thoughts.

The British ambassador at once frankly stated the case. . . . He frankly
confessed to us that in a very few days the Indian Government would be

compelled to admit that it could not redeem these certificates unless a supply of silver could be obtained, with the result that there would be great disturbances in India. We all knew what a revolution in India would mean.[3]

The millions of silver dollars lying in the United States Treasury guaranteed redemption of the silver certificates issued against them. Congress, and Congress alone, had authority to authorize melting these coins and to supply the bullion to the British government.

Pittman had been working on a silver purchase resolution before the Indian situation became acute, and Senate leaders now gave him full charge of the emergency legislation. Motivated by a desire to help his country, the Senator also saw an opportunity to assist the silver industry. "Our mines would all be closed down if we could only receive the present world market price," he said. Senators and representatives from the silver-producing states, while keenly aware of the need for emergency assistance to Great Britain, were, nevertheless, deeply concerned with the replacement of the reserve to the full extent of its possible depletion. Their experiences with executive construction and administration of the Bland and Sherman Acts warned them against the consequences of ill-considered legislation. They made it a condition, therefore, both of their support and of the passage of the bill, that the complete replenishment of the funds must come from silver produced in the United States. No discretion whatever upon this subject was to be given to any official or department. The repurchase price of $1 an ounce was agreed upon after a conference between senators from silver-producing states, producers, and experts from the Treasury Department. In other words, the Treasury guaranteed to rebuy all silver that would be sold at the swollen war price.* When the House was informed of this, Representative Edward Platt of New York exclaimed from the floor that this was "a plain case of holdup by the silverites." [4]

Pittman described his bill as a war emergency measure when he introduced it on April 9, 1918. He requested that it be referred to the Committee on Banking and Currency, where senators and representatives of the silver states, together with Treasury officials, appeared

---

* The Treasury Department wanted the repurchase price to be 89¢ an ounce, the then current price of silver, which Pittman refused to accept (K. P. to W. C. Ralston, January 28, 1921, Silver Folder, Box 111, Key Pittman Papers, Library of Congress, hereafter cited by folder and box number).

to testify and to explain the importance of the Indian specie shortage. After a brief hearing, the committee unanimously approved the bill and reported it to the Upper House. Each member was told of the crisis situation and few speeches were delivered, but those that were made carefully guarded the prime purpose of the resolution. Much to Pittman's surprise and elation, both the Senate and the House agreed to the silver plan with only mild and unorganized opposition. On April 23, 1918, President Wilson signed it into law.[5]

The Pittman Act of 1918 became the first major silver enactment since 1890. Passed by Congress as an emergency measure, it was designed by its framer to assist the silver industry by establishing a temporary minimum price of $1 an ounce. The act authorized the Secretary of the Treasury to melt up to 350,000,000 standard silver dollars and to sell the bullion at not less than one dollar an ounce. Silver certificates equal to the number of melted dollars would be immediately replaced with Federal Reserve bank notes in small denominations. Of course, the repurchase section was the most important part of the act for the silverites. American mines produced approximately 74,000,000 ounces of the metal in 1915 and about the same for 1916, with an average price for those years of 59¢ an ounce. The Treasury was now to buy domestically mined silver at $1 an ounce until it replaced the exact amount of the melted coins. The Pittman Act therefore assured the miner of a minimum of $1 an ounce for at least four years. Thus, two markets for American silver existed: the world market and the government market. The unusual war demand for silver, 1917–1919, caused the world price to rise to an unprecedented $1.38 an ounce in 1919. "The outlook for silver is better than ever before and the prosperity of Nevada is assured," commented the *Reno Evening Gazette*.[6] In 1920, however, the high price for the year reached $1.37, but then sharply dropped to 60¢ an ounce.[7] The provisions of the Pittman Act, nevertheless, compelled the government to buy American silver at $1 an ounce.

By 1921, many congressmen began to ask why the United States was buying several million ounces of silver—the entire produce of America's mines each month—at thirty-five cents an ounce above the world market price. The answer was simple. The Pittman Act provided for such purchase. "The Act cannot be repealed because the Western Senators are unalterably opposed to such repeal, and the rule of unlimited debate existing in the United States Senate guarantees that it never will be repealed," boasted the Senator.[8] The actual cash loss on purchases under the act amounted to some $70,000,000, but the total cost far exceeded this sum. Sales to England amounted to approximately $259,000,000, and the repurchase of American silver replaced this. The metallic value of the dollars at the time of sale was approximately $200,000,000. Their value after repurchase, however, was approximately $60,000,000 on the open market, the difference representing an additional loss.[9]

The world price of silver dropped below $1 an ounce on May 17, 1920, for the first time since the passage of the Pittman Act, causing producers to begin selling to the government. Under the provisions, the Treasury purchased silver until July, 1923, when the 259,000,000 or so silver dollars sold to Great Britain had been replaced. During this period, the mining states experienced a false prosperity because owners speeded up operations to take advantage of the $1 price. Silver producers gratefully sold their entire output to the government, but they also realized that this temporary subsidy would soon end. Alarmed mining organizations flooded Pittman with petitions and resolutions urging him to have his act extended. A reluctant House stymied any joint action and the silver senators, perhaps in an act of desperation, decided to appoint a Commission of Gold and Silver Inquiry with power to investigate the causes for the depressed condition of these metals. Five senators were named to the commission, which had to report back to the Senate by January 1, 1924, the majority party selecting three and the minority two. The Republican members were Tasker Oddie of Nevada, chairman; Frank R. Gooding, Idaho; and Thomas Sterling, South Dakota; with Pittman and Thomas Walsh of Montana serving as the Democratic appointees. Oddie appointed Pittman vice chairman and a one-man subcommittee to examine the administration of the act bearing his name.[10]

In May, 1923, Pittman began an intensive investigation of how the Treasury Department had carried out his act.[11] Even before the hearings were completed, the Senator had concluded that the Treasury failed to enforce each provision in good faith, necessitating an extension for several months. He insisted that the Treasury Department still had to purchase some 14,500,000 ounces of silver. This amount, he explained, was obtained by melting "Pittman dollars" and using the bullion for subsidiary coinage, a permissible function under the Pittman Act. The Senator reasoned that this silver should have been purchased by the Mint at $1 an ounce. The Treasury Department rejected his interpretation and maintained that the terms of the act were satisfied when it returned to the Pittman dollar account the exact amount of silver which the Mint had used in emergency subsidiary coinage regardless of the repurchase price.[12] He also charged that foreign silver had been purchased by the Treasury and coined into "Pittman dollars" contrary to the act. When the Treasury Department stopped purchasing silver according to their meaning of the law, the world price of the white metal was approximately 65¢ an ounce. If the department acceded to Pittman's demands, this purchase of 14,-500,000 ounces at 35¢ an ounce above the market price would have meant an additional five- to six-million-dollar subsidy distributed to silver producers.

The Senator persisted in his charges but the Secretary of the Treasury considered purchases under the Pittman Act completed.* Pittman would not concede, assuring producers that there was sufficient evidence to force the Treasury Department to resume purchasing. He urged them to secure a writ of mandamus in the District Court at Washington, D. C., "to compel the Treasury to perform its ministerial duty" and he even suggested the precedents to be used in such legal action.[13] While these proceedings were pending, Pittman introduced a bill directing the Mint "to complete purchases of silver under the Act of April 24, 1918, commonly known as the Pittman Act." [14]

The Senator's bill, which was referred to the Committee on Banking and Currency, provided for the purchase of 14,589,730 ounces of silver at $1 an ounce. With the world market price averaging 67¢ an ounce and American mines producing approximately 5⅓ million ounces a month, Pittman's bill would have provided assistance for about three months at an apparent cost of some $4,800,000 to the government. Pittman and former Senator Charles S. Thomas, now representing the Western Association of Producers and Refiners of Silver,

---

* The Secretary of the Treasury was acting under a ruling made by the Comptroller General of the United States. Pittman called this decision "strained and free from any legal foundation." He appealed to the Comptroller General for a reconsideration, which was denied (see Comptroller General Folder, Box 137).

were the only witnesses called before the committee. Pittman had no difficulty in convincing his colleagues that the silver industry had been mistreated by the Treasury Department. Both he and Senator Thomas reiterated the old argument that the government would not lose money by resuming purchases but would actually gain some three million dollars as silver was coined at $1.29 an ounce.[15] The committee favorably reported the bill and it passed the Senate on May 29, 1924, over the repeated protests of Secretary of the Treasury Andrew Mellon.[16]

The House was not as kind to the silverites. Pittman's bill remained in committee as Congress adjourned for the summer. "There is no doubt that the bill will pass in December," the Senator predicted.[17] Unfortunately for the silver interests, their opponents blocked House consideration of the measure. Almost immediately after the next Congress convened, Pittman reintroduced his scheme, only to have it fail in the House again.[18] This time, however, defeat marked the final effort of the silverites to have the Pittman Act extended on their terms.

II

The depression in the silver industry was already in its third year when the stock market crash occurred. In 1926 the British Royal Commission on Indian Currency and Finance had decided to place India on a gold standard. To accomplish this, the vast silver hoard had been melted into bullion and gradually placed on the world market. In addition to Indian demonetization, other countries had found the debasement of their silver coins a ready means for obtaining funds to pay their war debts. In 1928 alone, Belgium, France, and Great Britain released some forty million ounces of silver.[19] This dumping of foreign bullion on the world market depressed the price and the metal declined steadily from a high of 73¢ an ounce in 1925 to a low of 25¢ reached in 1932, the lowest price on record. Mines throughout the West closed and thousands became jobless. Farming communities and towns dependent upon mine employment slowly went bankrupt. Nevada's production of silver decreased from 9,400,000 ounces in 1924 to 4,200,000 ounces in 1930. Twenty-five hundred miners were idle in the state in 1930—enough votes to defeat Pittman at the next election.

The Senator considered the price depression part of a world problem created by Great Britain, and the exclusion of foreign silver appeared to be the only feasible temporary solution. This could be accomplished, he reasoned, through a high tax. On May 16, 1929, he introduced an amendment to the tariff bill providing for a duty of 30¢ an ounce on imported silver, promising to use his every muscle and sinew to secure its passage.[20]

Pittman was considered the leader of the silver bloc in the Senate and he became determined, even fanatical, in his efforts to assist the industry. For him, the panacea to the world's economic problems was a rise in the price of silver and it is small wonder that his colleagues affectionately called him the "Silver Key." He saw almost every issue —from foreign policy to the price of cotton—affected by silver. In numerous speeches and articles he would repeat that American exports, especially to the Far East, had declined because of its low price. In China, for example, silver circulated almost exclusively as the medium of exchange, making it the world's largest purchaser, but by 1930, it remained the only major country still on a silver standard. Pittman argued that the unprecedented drop in the price had caused a proportionate rise in commodity costs, which led to a decrease in American exports to China. To remedy this, higher world silver prices would have to be obtained through international agreements. The immediate problem, however, was to stop foreign dumping in the United States.

"The fact that we cannot compete with the cheap silver is demonstrated by the steady fall in the price, the closing down of our mines and the decreasing production in the United States," he told Alben Barkley.[21] Pittman's tariff of thirty cents an ounce would not have eliminated all competition from abroad, but it would have increased the price of foreign silver, thereby assisting the domestic market. The Senator worked for one year, often with unreasoning zeal, to secure this duty. After months of meetings and conferences, Pittman's amendment received a favorable vote in the Senate.[22] "We have got to work on the conferees of the House. Hawley, of Oregon, is the man we must try and get with us. I think I can get the two Democratic members. If the House conferees agree to the amendment, it will be all right."[23] The House conferees, however, refused to agree and instead referred the amendment back to each body for a vote. The motion picture, jewelry, silverware, and smelting interests had combined to oppose this silver tariff, which would adversely affect their industries, and the amendment was defeated in the House on May 2, 1930, by a vote of 72 to 202. Pittman took this as a personal challenge and vowed to fight any tariff conference report which did not include his duty. "The only way I know to get something in a conference report you want is to defeat the conference report and keep defeating conference reports until you get into the report what you are entitled to," he told James Scrugham.* [24] Privately, though, he conceded defeat, indicating that he had been "working on another attack." [25]

Pittman launched his new strategy on April 29, 1930, when he introduced Senate Resolution 256, which authorized the Foreign Relations Committee, "or any subcommittee thereof," to examine and study conditions that may affect American commerce and trade with China. On the surface, this resolution appeared to be a routine request by a member of the Foreign Relations Committee, and the Senate unanimously passed it, appropriating $20,000 for the investigation. "While the resolution on its face does not indicate its primary purpose, still you and I know what the purpose is," Pittman confided to Frank Norcross. "Borah has offered to make me Chairman of a subcommittee in charge of this investigation. This will enable me to go to the bottom of the question. I do not want any publicity given to this matter, however, as I would then receive opposition. We have got to have patience." [26]

On June 11, 1930, Chairman William Borah, a Republican but from the silver state of Idaho, appointed Pittman, a Democrat, chairman of a subcommittee to conduct hearings pursuant to the Senate resolution. Other members of the subcommittee were: Senators Hiram Johnson of California and Arthur Vandenberg of Michigan, both Republicans; Claude Swanson, Democrat of Virginia; and Farmer-Laborite Henrik Shipstead of Minnesota. Perhaps Chairman Pittman revealed the real aim of the Commercial Relations with China Subcommittee when he tentatively listed the cities where hearings would

---

* Pittman considered the Guggenheim interests as being primarily responsible for the defeat of his tariff amendment in the House. The Guggenheims produced a great deal of silver in Mexico, while their principal business in the United States was smelting (K. P. to B. F. Nepheys, Jr., February 26, 1930, Silver Tariff Folder, Box 101).

be held—Los Angeles, Seattle, Spokane, Salt Lake City, Reno, and Denver. For the doubtful, Pittman made the object of the subcommittee clear on the first day of the hearings. "There have been numerous plans suggested to the Committee [to improve commercial relations with China]," he stated. "These plans propose that the United States should lend to the Chinese Government hundreds of millions of ounces of silver now stored in the Treasury as silver dollars." [27] After the hearings, Pittman told Claude Bowers that the purpose of creating the subcommittee was to study methods for "the removal of the causes that are destroying silver as a basis of credit and as a money in those countries where it is the only money." [28] For months, Pittman's senatorial colleagues did not realize that he was working to secure a rise in the price of silver for the American producer by treating the question as a world economic problem. Their ignorance of this delighted him.[29]

Charles K. Moser, Chief of the Far Eastern Section of Regional Information, Department of Commerce, appeared before the subcommittee as the first witness. Moser testified that the most serious cause for the decline in American exports to China was the devastating civil war, which had disrupted water and railroad transportation, forced heavy taxes, and seriously affected trade with the interior. He disqualified himself from discussing the silver issue as he frankly admitted that he knew "next to nothing about it." Nevertheless, almost all of Pittman's questions dealt with the depressed price, the resulting "Chinese silver crisis," and the feasibility of a bullion loan to China. The Senator followed the same pattern of questioning with other witnesses. When Captain Robert Dollar of the Dollar Steamship Line suggested stabilizing China's finances by establishing a gold standard, Pittman abruptly interrupted to question Dollar's financial knowledge.[30]

The hearings continued through August and into September, 1930. It became evident that the subcommittee would conclude that a shortage of silver in China caused by the low price was the main reason for the decline of American exports to that nation. The obvious remedy to the silverites was a long-term silver loan to China. Theoretically, China would return the silver to American exporters in exchange for their products. The United States, though, would replace the silver loaned to China by purchasing domestic silver with dollars.

This would aid the exporter, increase the money supply, and above all, raise the price of the metal. During the hearings, Pittman repeated over and over that he suggested such a loan only to improve the welfare of the destitute Chinese people. Starvation and unemployment would decrease as the Chinese government could afford to increase its payroll. Any gain to the American silver producer, he insisted, was of secondary importance.

Pittman realized that a silver loan could be of value only if Great Britain agreed to suspend its Indian monetary policy and he now began to talk and write of an international conference to be called to stabilize the price of silver and end the dumping of Indian bullion on the world market.[31] In an article for the *New York Times,* Pittman explained that he was "firmly convinced that trade and commerce would be facilitated and economic conditions throughout the world greatly relieved if there could be an agreement between governments as to the price at which silver should be exchanged for gold." [32] The Senator did admit to associates that his real aim in suggesting an international conference was to bring about a rise in the price of domestic silver. He confided to Charles Thomas that he felt "satisfied that we are winning out by tying it to our export trade." [33] "Our matter is progressing splendidly," he boasted. "Our great danger is that some enthusiasts may attempt to go too far and too rapidly in this matter. If it progresses logically, it will reach the ultimate goal of bimetallism, but we cannot talk of that now." [34]

Despite frequent statements by witnesses that the loss of American trade occurred principally because of the political unrest and fighting within China, Pittman's final report concluded:

> The chief cause for the abnormal and sudden decrease in our commerce with China during the latter part of 1929 and 1930 was the sudden great and unprecedented fall in the price of silver. Silver is the only money in China, and it is the sole measure of the wealth and purchasing power of the people.

The low price, Pittman continued, and its effect upon the international monetary exchange were the chief reasons for the depression in international trade.[35] He attached two resolutions to his report recommending that the government take action to support a silver program.

The first of these requested the President to enter into discussions with India, Great Britain, France, and other countries, "looking to the suspension of the policy and practice of governments melting up or debasing silver coins" and selling the specie on the world market. The resolution strongly suggested that the President call or obtain an international conference to secure an agreement "with respect to the uses and status of silver as money" which would eliminate the abnormal fluctuations in the price of the metal.[36]

Pittman's second resolution requested the President to determine the advisability of lending silver to China, and to consider melting American dollars stored in the Treasury for such purpose. The loan was to be made over a long period so as not to flood China with the metal. A pacified China, he thought, under intensive development could consume over half of the annual world mine production. He asked that his resolutions be referred to the Foreign Relations Committee. The first, which provided for an international silver conference, was eventually sent to the Senate and favorably acted upon.[37]

The second proposal, too much even for Pittman's committee, failed to be reported. The committee discussed the resolution long enough, however, for astonished Chinese financial officials to report that they had not asked for such a loan, had no desire for it, and would reject it if it were tendered.[38]

When the Foreign Relations Committee proved reluctant to report Pittman's silver loan resolution, the Commercial Relations with China Subcommittee met in an emergency session to determine its next move. On April 14, 1931, the subcommittee directed Pittman to proceed to China to continue the study of American commercial relations with that country. "The decision of the subcommittee was rather sudden," the Senator wrote Norman Davis. "It appears that the President is afraid to make any move in this or any other matter." [39] Pittman spent a little more than a month in China, ostensibly gathering first-hand information to support the subcommittee's initial report. Most of his time was occupied with social engagements and conversations with American merchants who agreed with the Senator's silver loan plan. Before leaving China, Pittman called a news conference to emphatically deny rumors that "the Foreign Relations Committee of the United States Senate represents the silver mining interests of the United States." [40]

"Am convinced now absolutely that silver problem affects disas-

1900. Key Pittman in his Nome, Alaska, law office

About 1910. Tonopah, Nevada

1912. Key Pittman (*standing*) and Mrs. Pittman (*extreme right*) campaigning at a Nevada mining camp

September, 1919. Senator Key Pittman

August, 1921. Senator Key Pittman

1924. *Left to right:* Democratic national chairman Clem L. Shaver, Senator Key Pittman, Democratic presidential candidate John W. Davis

April 25, 1924. *Left to right:* Senators Henrik Shipstead, Frank Brandegee, George Wharton Pepper, Claude Swanson, Key Pittman

May 12, 1930—Senate Foreign Relations Committee. *Seated, left to right:* Secretary of State Henry L. Stimson; Senators Frederick Gillett, Hiram Johnson; Chairman William Borah; Senators Thomas Walsh, Claude Swanson, Joseph Robinson, David Reed. *Standing, left to right:* Secretary of the Navy Charles Francis Adams; Senators Pat Harrison, Robert LaFollette, Jr., Arthur Vandenberg; Admiral William V. Pratt; Senator Key Pittman

February 5, 1939, cartoon. *Left to right:* Key Pittman, Franklin Roosevelt, Senator Hiram Johnson (isolation), Former President Herbert Hoover (GOP sage), Secretary of State Cordell Hull (reciprocal trade), Senator Gerald Nye (neutrality)

October 4, 1939, cartoon. Senators Key Pittman and William Borah

trously our trade with every silver using country," the Senator cabled Bernard Baruch upon his return.[41] Pittman became so concerned with trying to obtain a higher price for American silver that he failed to realize that China had reached the peak of her prosperity in 1931, when silver was at its lowest price. Chinese financial experts maintained that the low price of silver had been a boon to their nation, for China was a buyer not *with,* but *of* silver.[42] But Pittman was interested in raising China's "buying power" through an American loan, which would increase the price of the metal in America. The economic troubles which China would face under rising silver did not concern him. During 1932, the House Committee on Coinage, Weights, and Measures continued to study Chinese economics, but Pittman's resolution remained in the Senate Foreign Relations Committee.

As the depression grew worse, Pittman's proposal for an international silver conference received support from varied sources. Resolutions adopted by several state legislatures and commercial organizations urged such a meeting. Farm interests again saw silver as the vehicle through which the agricultural states might express their age-old demand for an increase in currency. Inflationists also joined the bandwagon. Even eighty-year-old "Coin" Harvey repeated his arguments, which had once served as the gospel of Populism.[43] President Hoover, however, refused to take the initiative in calling a conference, perhaps fearing that European countries would want to enlarge the agenda to include war debts and the tariff. "The West has received little and cannot look for much more from a Hoover administration," Pittman bitterly complained. "We are existing under a selfish and heartless bureaucracy." [44]

Pittman was not a silver radical or an inflationist, and he probably cared little about agricultural prices. He firmly opposed a movement started by William Jennings Bryan, Jr., calling for immediate bimetallism. "There is absolutely no chance of passing through Congress a bill for bimetallism," he wrote. "The East is exceedingly suspicious of every move we make and we have been able to progress so far only by reason of the fact that we have been dealing with the question from a monetary exchange standpoint." [45] Conscious of the strong prejudice in the East against bimetallism, Pittman carefully avoided alienating his colleagues by reviving "Bryanism." He sought a rise in the price of silver by connecting its depreciated cost with the continuance of the world-wide depression. In January, 1933, the Senator voted against a free-coinage amendment introduced by Senator Burton K. Wheeler. He had "begged" Wheeler not to introduce his bill as it "would turn the whole East against us." [46] The Nevadan opposed any rash or extreme action by silverites, fearing that this would only damage their cause. "There is a desperate need for the restoration of the purchasing power of silver money and I have sought the means that I have considered most expeditious." * [47]

III

In June, 1932, representatives of several European countries met at Lausanne, Switzerland to discuss war debts and reparations. The United States refused to participate, adhering to its traditional opposition to debate such problems. A world conference without the United States was incomplete, and Great Britain proposed that another economic and financial meeting be held in London to specifically consider "measures necessary to solve the other economic and financial difficulties which are responsible for, and may prolong, the present world crisis." [48] The new agenda would not include war debts and reparations, tariff rates, or immigration restrictions. With regard to silver, Secretary of State Henry Stimson informed President Hoover that "there can be no doubt that a serious effort will be made to cope with the problem." [49] On May 31, 1932, the United States announced its intention to participate in the proposed conference. Pitt-

---

* Pittman always argued that his actions on behalf of silver were unselfish. In defense of a silver purchase bill which he introduced in 1932, he told his colleagues:

I know that it has been charged that the object of this bill, like other legislation that has been introduced for the purpose of increasing the price of silver, was prompted by the selfish desire to benefit the silver mines of the United States. I want to say that if the purpose of the Act is accomplished it will have that effect to a certain extent, but such consideration is insignificant, and I could not expect any support from Congress on such ground at this time.

Pittman, nevertheless, had extensive holdings in several silver mines. Any raise in the price of the metal meant a personal financial gain (U. S. Congress, Senate, Subcommittee of the Committee on Banking and Currency, *Hearings, Purchase of Silver Produced in the United States With Silver Certificates*, 1932, p. 14) .

man was optimistic. "I think we have made considerable advance. In fact, I believe that the silver situation will be solved in the near future." [50]

During the 1932 presidential campaign, both parties advocated an international conference on monetary problems. Each adopted planks pledging to do something about the low price of silver, although the Republicans hedged by stating they would uphold the gold standard. When Franklin Roosevelt took office, he agreed to continue preparations for the World Monetary and Economic Conference. In April, he asked Pittman to serve as a delegate, an invitation which was readily accepted. For seven weeks Pittman attended technical preparatory meetings at the White House or the State Department, and on May 19, 1933, he announced that all nations which had sent representatives to Washington to prepare for the London conference had "agreed in principle" on the need to rehabilitate silver.

At no time did either the administration or Pittman seriously consider the Senate resolution sponsored by Senator Burton K. Wheeler directing the delegates to "work unceasingly for an international agreement to remonetize silver on a basis of a definite fixed ratio . . . of 16 fine ounces of silver to 1 fine ounce of gold." [51] But inflationist sentiment continued to swell in Congress. On April 17, 1933, thirty-three senators appeared willing to vote for a free-coinage bill; on April 26, the number grew to forty-one; by April 28 to fifty-three. Senators Wheeler and King announced that they found the feeling for remonetization at 16 to 1 "overwhelming." Roosevelt finally bowed to the inflationist sentiment of his party in the West and South by accepting the Thomas amendment to the Farm Relief bill, which conferred upon the President extraordinary control over the currency. If there had to be inflation, at least Roosevelt now had the power to regulate it. [52]

Secretary Hull led the delegation to the World Monetary and Economic Conference, which left for London on May 31, 1933. Former Governor James M. Cox of Ohio served as vice chairman. Other delegates, besides Pittman, included Senator James Couzens of Michigan, Representative Sam D. McReynolds of Tennessee, and Ralph W. Morrison, a Texas businessman. None of these men had ever attended an international conference. The cross purposes and the disagreements among them were evident even before their departure. Hull was interested in reciprocal commercial treaties and tariff reduction. Pittman appeared concerned only with silver and opposed any tariff cuts. (He later confided to H. V. Kaltenborn that the only reason he went to London was to "do something for silver.") [53] Raymond Moley noted that Pittman was "more sympathetic than any other member of the delegation to the increasingly unorthodox monetary views of Roosevelt." Representative McReynolds, chairman of the Foreign Affairs Committee, and like Hull an ardent low-tariff man, took the trip as a junket. "He made no pretense to expert knowledge of monetary problems," Moley wrote.[54] James Cox, a hard-money man, favored a low tariff while Senator Couzens, a soft-money man, favored a high tariff.[55] No one knew Morrison's views on any issue before the delegation sailed. Morrison, James Warburg recorded, "made no sense whatsoever on any subject [and] was a delegate because he'd contributed $50,000 to the Democratic campaign." [56] In addition, Roosevelt had failed to make his own position clear. Secretary Hull later lamented that:

> Few mistakes can be more unfortunate than for the official head of a delegation to a world conference not to have a chance to consult with the President on the selection of the entire personnel—or at least let the personnel have that distinct impression. Otherwise there is little sense of loyalty or teamwork on the part of some, and open defiance from others. This has been my experience. . . . I left for London with the highest of hopes, but arrived with empty hands.[57]

Delegates from sixty-six nations representing more than a billion people convened in London on June 12, 1933. The London *Times* described the conference as "the greatest and most representative gathering of statesmen that has ever assembled for common counsel." [58] Roosevelt, however, did not think that the United States delegation had to be thoroughly informed on the problems to be discussed or united upon methods for solving them. The President expected to determine important decisions himself and thought that the staff of experts which he had sent would prevent the delegation from making mistakes.[59]

Pittman apparently was given a free hand in the silver matter. He selected his own advisor, Edward Bruce, a lawyer and artist who held an exhibition of his paintings in London during the conference. Herbert M. Bratter, the silver specialist of the Commerce Department, had been overlooked in preference for someone whose knowledge and views would not interfere with Pittman. For the six-week duration of the conference, the Senator concerned himself with silver. At meetings of the Monetary and Financial Commission, he talked only about the white metal and sometimes the delegates went to sleep. Once Dr. Hjalmar Schacht of Germany waved his hands furiously as if he would do almost anything to have the Senator stop talking, shouting: "All right, we agree about silver." [60]

Except for silver, Pittman was useless at London. Throughout the conference, especially at crucial moments, he would get drunk. While in this condition, his favorite method of amusing himself was to pop the London street lights with his six-shooter. Secretary Hull and Governor Cox were outraged at Pittman's behavior. Warburg noted that Pittman "was really a wild man when drunk, but he was drunk so often that he was often wild. . . . If he ever got the idea that you weren't on his side, God help you because that was the end." * [61]

The Senator became chairman of a subcommittee appointed to discuss "the necessity of enhancing and stabilizing the price of silver." For these discussions, the committee was limited to representatives from the principal producing countries (United States, Mexico, Canada, Peru, and Bolivia), and those holding large stocks of the metal (India, China, and Spain). Only after weeks of negotiations and conferences did they reach an agreement. At points, the group was held together only by Pittman's sheer determination to obtain an international agreement. "I found that I could accomplish nothing in a committee because the debate would run wild. Consequently I gave a lunch each day in my apartments to little groups and through this method finally brought about the agreement." [62] In the end, Pittman got what he wanted.

On July 22, 1933, eight nations consented to Pittman's silver recommendation, perhaps the only accomplishment of the London Conference. The resolution provided: (1) that governments would abandon the practice and policy of melting up and debasing coins; (2) that

* On one occasion, Pittman chased a technical advisor down the corridors of the Claridge Hotel with a bowie knife. The advisor, who was suspected of inadequate enthusiasm for silver, bought a gun for future protection (Arthur M. Schlesinger, Jr., *The Coming of the New Deal* [Boston: Houghton Mifflin, 1959], p. 211). Professor Schlesinger does not cite his source for this anecdote.

each country would replace low-valued paper money with silver coins and would refrain from legislation which would depress the value of silver in the world market. Thus, the main causes which Pittman considered the principal reasons for the depression in silver were to be eliminated. India, China, and Spain, as large holders of silver, further agreed not to sell more than an aggregate of 35,000,000 ounces annually for four years. The United States, Mexico, Canada, Peru, and Australia, as large producers of silver, agreed to purchase a total of at least 35,000,000 ounces annually for four years. The United States' share of this allotment was 24,421,410 ounces annually, which represented 98.5 per cent of American production for 1932.[63] Almost singlehanded, Key Pittman had committed the United States to buy the yearly production of American silver for four years—an objective which silver producers had been agitating for since 1873. In reviewing the work of the conference, Secretary Hull correctly wrote that "few were interested in the silver agreement." * [64] The few, however, rejoiced at the results of the World Monetary and Economic Conference.

The London silver agreement, although unanimously adopted, had to be ratified by each of the eight countries before April 1, 1934. The text provided for government purchases of silver, but it made no mention of either unlimited coinage or of any fixed ratio with gold. Congress had adjourned in June and would not convene until January, 1934, but it appeared that the strength of the inflationists, who favored bimetallism and unlimited coinage, increased daily.

In April, 1933, Senator Wheeler's amendment to the Farm Relief bill to remonetize silver on the old Bryan formula of 16 to 1, failed 33 to 43. The vote, however, underestimated the growing strength of the radical silverites and inflationists. Many new senators favored Wheeler's amendment but had refrained from voting for a variety of

* The day Pittman was to bring in his silver proposal to the plenary session, he was completely out of working order. The previous evening, he had entertained two "ladies" who were later ejected by the hotel. Governor Cox had arranged for the British delegate to make Pittman's report for him. This he did after the meeting had been postponed for three quarters of an hour waiting for Pittman. Hardly had the arrangements been made with the British when the Senator arrived, still very much the worse for wear. According to Cox, the Senator made a rambling speech of forty-five minutes which was "an utter disgrace" (The Reminiscences of James Warburg, Oral History Project, Columbia University, p. 1248).

motives. Although not an inflationist, Pittman tacitly supported the Wheeler amendment for political reasons. The Senator's aim was still to raise the price of silver. He knew that a bill providing for the free and unlimited coinage of the metal at a 16-to-1 ratio could not pass the House, and the defeat would only obstruct his main goal. The cause of silver, he wrote, would be put back forty years by the advocacy of a free and unlimited coinage bill. "We have been hampered—and when I say 'we' I mean those who believe in silver as money—and harassed and obstructed, not only by the ignorant extremists who believe that only gold is money, but by the extremists who are ignorant of the history of our country, of the control of our Congress, and the attitude of a majority of our people towards silver." [65]

Pittman repeatedly urged Roosevelt to adhere to the London agreement by presidential proclamation. "The instrument is not a treaty, or even an agreement that requires ratification by the United States Senate," he advised Henry Morgenthau, Jr. "It is simply a written memorandum of an agreement." * [66] He cautioned Louis Howe that the alternative to immediate acceptance would be a "riot" led by Wheeler and his "radical bill." "The rest of the world is awaiting the initiative of Roosevelt," the Senator told Josephus Daniels. "I have had the matter up with him several times. I expect him to take some action very soon." [67]

In October, 1933, the President put the so-called "gold buying policy" or Warren theory into practice by starting large-scale purchases of gold which were designed to raise commodity prices to their 1926 level by depreciating the dollar. The aim was implied currency expansion. Roosevelt also attempted to split the silverites and inflationists by suggesting that if the silver senators would form a coalition with sound-money advocates to defeat printing-press inflation, they "could write their own ticket." [68] His bid for such an alliance failed to break

* In 1940, Pittman argued that the administration's reciprocal trade agreements had to be ratified by two thirds of the Senate. "If the Senate wants to abolish its constitutional privilege to ratify treaties, it can do so now . . . but I warn the Senate that the time may come when the precedent we thus establish may be used in a manner which we do not like, then we will regret it." Pittman was speaking against the metal trade agreement which he thought adversely affected the Nevada mining industry (*Congressional Record*, 76 Cong. 3 Sess. Vol. 86, Pt. 3 [March 25, 1940], p. 3332) .

the silver-inflationist unity. On the contrary, Senator Wheeler, disappointed that the Pittman agreement did not include remonetization, announced again that he would propose such a resolution when Congress reconvened.[69] By December, 1933, it appeared that Wheeler was almost certain of having his 16-to-1 bill passed. Once again, as with the acceptance of the Thomas amendment, Roosevelt found it necessary to compromise to prevent radical monetary legislation, and Pittman's silver agreement served as the measure. After considerable correspondence between the President and Pittman as to the amount the government should pay for the silver, the President, on December 21, 1933, directed the Secretary of the Treasury to purchase it at $64\frac{1}{2}¢$ an ounce and to comply with the London agreement. (At first, Pittman had asked for $80¢$ an ounce but agreed to accept $64\frac{1}{2}¢$. On the day of the proclamation, silver was selling at $43¢$. The President's proclamation, therefore, assured the American producer that the price for his product would immediately rise $21¢$ above the current market price.) Ratification temporarily split the silver bloc on the need for inflation and thus nullified Wheeler's proposed resolution to secure remonetization. Pittman enthusiastically described the President's action as the most constructive yet made to correct the monetary problem. "Locally, it will greatly relieve the mining situation and will bring happiness to millions depending on mining." [70]

The use of the proclamation in this instance is an interesting and unusual construction of presidential power. Professor Edward S. Corwin defines presidential proclamations as "simply announcements by the President over the seal of the United States, his own signature, and the countersignature of the Secretary of State, of the construction put by the executive department on specified acts of Congress." [71] Roosevelt's silver proclamation was without precedent, as it put into effect an international agreement without congressional approval. The President rationalized his action by citing as his authority a section of the Thomas amendment to the Farm Relief Act of 1933 permitting him to fix the weight of the gold dollar. After the President's announcement, William Phillips, then Acting Secretary of State, admitted that he was not sure if the proclamation constituted a ratification of the London agreement. Pittman explained to the President that at first the Solicitor of the State Department "concluded that the agreement requires ratification by two-thirds of the Senate. Subsequently in a discussion between Mr. R. [Walton] Moore, Assistant Secretary of State, the Solicitor and myself, the Solicitor agreed that the form of ratification set out in the agreement was sufficient." Pittman asked that the United States immediately give notice "to the other governments party to the agreement that our Government did on the 21st day of December, 1933, ratify the agreement by issuance of a proclamation." Pittman's interpretation was accepted by Roosevelt and Hull.[72]

The President's proclamation meant the virtual free coinage of American silver for the next four years. In Tonopah, Nevada, they danced in the streets in one of the wildest celebrations seen in that mining town. Bartenders fulfilled a long-standing promise of free drinks should silver ever reach 50¢ an ounce or more. "Girls climbed on tops of bars. They pulled their men after them. The town would have paraded, if there had been a town band. Joy reigned supreme." [73] In Washington, Tonopah's representative in the Senate described the proclamation as "the best Christmas present I have ever received. I am more than happy that it is also a Christmas present from the President to all the people of my State." [74]

CHAPTER V

"...Becoming Somewhat Opposed
to Roosevelt"

I

"I want to win. I am tired of being in the minority," Pittman wrote on the eve of the 1932 convention.[1] The split of 1924 had not fully healed, and talk of another deadlock haunted him. Adopting "Victory Through Unity" as his convention slogan, Pittman urged that the platform be as short as possible to avoid unnecessary controversy. "In fact," he suggested, "if a party should pledge itself to maintain the Ten Commandments and the Golden Rule and fundamental principles announced by Jefferson, every one would understand then the attitude of the party toward all public questions."[2] In an effort to prevent dissension, the Senator even agreed to accept a compromise silver plank.

Pittman was convinced that Franklin D. Roosevelt would be the strongest candidate. After Roosevelt had soundly defeated Al Smith in the New Hampshire and Wisconsin primaries in March and April, 1932, Pittman sought to provide Smith with a graceful exit from the preconvention scene. In an exclusive interview granted to Arthur Krock, the Senator deplored the "humiliating position" in which Smith found himself as a result of the zealous activities of his partisans. "There are times for all things and for all men," he observed. "Sometimes the man and the issue meet, as they did in Governor Smith in 1928. Another time the junction does not seem to be made, as in Governor Smith's candidacy this year, but that does not reflect on the man. . . . The whole matter is in the hands of his friends. They should no longer expect this great leader, who will always have a

96

powerful influence in our party, to further contest when he is not a candidate for nomination and will make no campaign."

Smith did not take kindly to Pittman's advice. Within twenty-four hours of the Senator's interview, he released copies of letters to supporters in California, Connecticut, and Pennsylvania again declaring that he was a presidential candidate. To his Connecticut backers he wrote: "It is an absurdity for anybody to state that I will repudiate the action of my friends. The truth is I will stay with them and every one who knows me will have confidence in that statement." [3]

The Senate completely occupied Pittman's time during the weeks preceding the convention. "We are constantly in committee meetings and conferences, while at the same time attempting to protect the interests of the Government and our State," he informed his friend William Boyle. "Conditions of the war were nothing like these." [4] Pittman had been selected by the Nevada delegation to serve on the Platform Committee but he decided not to attend the convention. "My presence in Washington is necessary," he explained to Homer Cummings.[5] (He told one confidant that he had a good chance of having a silver bill passed while many senators were absent from the Capitol.) [6]

Being eight hundred miles from the convention did not prevent Pittman from having a part in the drama unfolding at Chicago. The Senator and his colleague Harry B. Hawes of Missouri were both disturbed by recurring reports that a deadlock might destroy the party's chance for victory. The two decided to do something about it. During the first day of the convention, Pittman and Hawes hit upon a Roosevelt-Garner combination as the best way to avoid a repetition of the 1924 fiasco. They called Roosevelt at Albany to ask if he had any objection. "Senator, that would be fine," he replied, "the Governor from New York and the Speaker of the House from Texas—clear across the country." Hawes then wired Jim Farley:

GROUP BELIEVE WINNING TICKET WOULD BE ROOSEVELT AND GARNER STOP NINETY VOTES OF CALIFORNIA AND TEXAS WOULD ELIMINATE DISPUTE STOP AM ADVISED WOULD BE SATISFACTORY TO PARTY STOP SEE SAM RAYBURN TOM CONNALLY AND CHECK MY OWN IMPRESSION STOP BEST WISHES.[7]

After a hurried telephone call to Pittman and Hawes to confirm the cable, Farley scurried through hotel corridors to find Silliman Evans, second-in-charge of the Garner management. Evans promised to bring Sam Rayburn, Garner's convention spokesman, to Farley's apartment. In the meanwhile, Pittman and Hawes proceeded to send telegrams to hundreds of Democratic leaders in Chicago and throughout the country urging them to do their best to obtain a Roosevelt-Garner coalition. "Garner's vote would elect on first ballot Roosevelt and Garner and end all disputes. We have been in conference today and approved suggestions. Know it will be satisfactory to all interested parties," Pittman cabled to Scott Ferris of the Oklahoma delegation. "We know that all interested parties are agreeable," he wired to Arthur Mullen, Roosevelt's floor leader. To Tom Connally, both senators telegraphed, "We have had a talk with interested parties and we can say no more. All agree ultimate nomination of Roosevelt assured. All believe that strongest ticket will be Roosevelt and Garner. Since abandonment of two-thirds fight results will be determined on combination on President and Vice-President tonight." [8]

At eleven o'clock on the first night of the conclave, Farley met with Sam Rayburn in an attempt to convince him of the necessity of a Roosevelt-Garner combination. Rayburn made no promise, but he did make it clear that he opposed a repetition of the Madison Square Garden convention. Though nothing approaching a deal was made, Farley felt that "Texas was our best bet." These discussions occurred before the first ballot. In 1948, Farley wrote that "many persons have claimed they effected the understanding which turned the tide in our favor. As a matter of fact, the first move came jointly from Senators Key Pittman of Nevada and Harry B. Hawes of Missouri." * [9]

Pittman considered Roosevelt's election a foregone conclusion. "Looks like we are going to have a Democratic victory at the coming election," he told a cousin two weeks after Roosevelt's nomination. "I think it is the only salvation of the country." [10] After the convention

---

* Although the exact details of the political intricacies of the convention may never be known, it appears that Pittman was in personal contact with Garner and had an assurance from him that he would accept a Roosevelt-Garner ticket. Pittman apparently conveyed Garner's definite acceptance to Breckinridge Long, assistant floor leader for the Roosevelt forces, between 8:00 P.M. and 3:00 A.M., June 30–July 1, 1932. This was before the roll call for the first ballot had begun (see Breckinridge Long to K. P., July 5, 1932, Democratic National Convention, 1932 Folder, Box 149, Key Pittman Papers, Library of Congress, hereafter cited by folder and box number).

had ended, the Senator volunteered his services to Roosevelt by suggesting, with due apologies for his presumptuousness, the do's and don'ts of conducting a national campaign. "I want to relieve your mind immediately with regard to my interest in this fight. There is nothing that I want except your success. I have about the highest honor that I can hold. I neither expect nor do I want any change of position." Roosevelt thanked Pittman for his support and asked him to hold himself "in readiness for consultation." [11]

Pittman's campaign advice, although warmly received, was disregarded—for example his urgings to make the monetary question the dominant campaign issue. Pittman proposed that an advisory committee be created to assist Roosevelt, recommending that the group consist of Al Smith, Albert C. Ritchie, "Alfalfa Bill" Murray, Newton Baker, and John Davis. This obviously was aimed at enlisting the good will and cooperation of the wise old leaders of the party, but Farley's boundless energy and the creation of the "brain trust" nullified the need for such a committee.

At other times, the Senator urged Roosevelt to "do what Harding and Coolidge did, prepare now to use the radio to the fullest extent. The idea of personal contact is imaginary and not well founded. It has more drawbacks than it has advantages." When Roosevelt intimated that he might make an extensive trip through the West, Pittman warned that "it would be a great error to start across the country on a speaking tour." [12] He repeated his protests to Farley but to no avail. The Nevadan just did not grasp the personal magnetism of Franklin Roosevelt. The western campaign trip that Pittman strenuously opposed was a triumphant success.

Pittman joined the campaign train at Salt Lake City on September 17. The enthusiastic crowds amazed him. "Practically all the people at small places and for hundreds of miles around such places come to the meetings. They come as those seeking salvation. They were in distress and despair and were looking for hope and encouragement. They left knowing that happy days will soon be here." [13]

Throughout the trip, Pittman reiterated his high tariff and "do something for silver" arguments. "In Colorado, Montana, Utah, Idaho and Nevada the Governor will probably be asked about the silver question. The best thing he can do is to stand upon the Platform," Pittman advised Louis Howe.[14] Roosevelt did not disappoint the Senator. At Salt Lake City, he stated unequivocally that silver must be recognized as a monetary metal. At Denver and again in Butte, Montana, he assured his audience that, if elected, he would adhere to the Democratic plank which declared that the United States should call an international monetary conference to consider the rehabilitation of silver. Elated at these pronouncements and the enthusiastic response, Pittman confessed to Roosevelt that he had never thought that a political trip could be so successful.[15]

Pittman considered the western campaign an overwhelming success, yet, he nevertheless returned to Washington feeling dejected. Recommendations made by him were not being accepted. His detailed objections to the suggested Southern tour, which he deplored as "impractical," were ignored by Roosevelt's eschelon of advisors. The "brain trust" with their new socio-economic theories annoyed him. Always wary of the intellectual, especially college professors, he now realized that they were the policy formulators. His elaborate economic arguments had been passed over for "text-book solutions" and he frankly conceded to Raymond Moley, whom he had met for the first time on the campaign train, that Moley's "understanding of the political situation was indeed surprising . . . in view of the fact that you are a professor."

As inauguration day approached, Pittman understood clearly that, in spite of his lengthy recommendations to the President-elect, politicians of his school were being relegated to the second level. "Things are getting more confused here every day," he complained to Moley after a silver plan of his had been vetoed by the "brain trust." "The problem I have to decide now or in the near future, or at least before the special session, is whether I will work in the organization or work independently." [16]

II

During the now famous Congress of the Hundred Days, Pittman voted for the New Deal measures but took no part in debate except, of course, if a resolution affected silver. He was absent from many meetings of the Senate preparing for the London economic conference. Whenever a monetary bill was being discussed, though, the Senator sat at his desk ready to defend the interests of Nevada. (In 1932, the state's silver output was only 15 per cent of the annual average for the preceding twenty-nine-year period.) "I hope my friends will not gather the idea because I have been intensely working for silver that I have not been working for every other industry in the State." [17]

Within seven weeks after the convening of Congress, more than twenty bills had been introduced to expand the metallic base of the monetary system through an increased use of silver. The silverites and inflationists demonstrated their growing strength when Senator Burton Wheeler's amendment to the Farm Relief bill providing for free coinage at a ratio of 16 to 1 was defeated on April 17, 1933, by a vote of 33 to 44. Except for strong administration opposition, the Wheeler amendment might have been adopted. As a result of increased congressional demands that something be done to expand the currency system, the administration, perhaps realizing the political expediency of accepting limited inflationary powers, now agreed to a revised form of an amendment to the Farm Relief bill introduced by Senator Elmer Thomas. Roosevelt told James Warburg that he had accepted the Thomas amendment because "unless something of this sort was done immediately Congress would take the matter in its own hands and legislate mandatory law instead of permissive." [18]

The silver provisions of the Thomas amendment, as revised by Pittman to meet administration objections, gave the President power to put the United States on a free-silver basis. Another section made the metal, along with all other currencies, legal tender and permitted the government to accept it in payment of foreign debts. The bullion was to be credited at the rate of 50¢ an ounce, approximately 22¢ above the world price. This repayment clause expired six months after the passage of the act, but Pittman believed that it would cause an immediate rise in the price of all world silver by at least ten cents an ounce. The aggregate value of the metal to be accepted under this section could not exceed $200,000,000. "This country demands cheaper money without running the risk of excessive inflation," declared the Senator in speaking in favor of the amendment.* [19]

* For a discussion of the Thomas amendment, see Arthur Whipple Crawford, *Monetary Management Under the New Deal* (Washington: American Council on Public Affairs, 1940) , pp. 40 ff.

James Warburg noted in his diary that Roosevelt instructed Raymond Moley, James Byrnes, William Bullitt, Lewis Douglas, Charles Taussig, Pittman, and him-

The Thomas amendment temporarily satisfied Pittman and other moderate silverites. Although most foreign governments neglected to take the opportunity offered by the silver clause to repay at least a portion of their debt, the price of the metal did rise.* The 1933 high was 45¢ an ounce, a 14¢ increase over the previous year. But in Nevada the 1933 production fell to 1,148,621 ounces, a decrease of 155,744 ounces as compared with 1932, and less than in any year since 1899. The value of the output, $402,017, though, amounted to $34,186, more than in 1932 because of the higher price.

The great victory for the silver miner in 1933 was the London silver agreement concluded by Senator Pittman in July. On December 22, 1933, President Roosevelt ratified it and authorized the United States Mint to buy the yearly output of American silver until December 31, 1937, at 64½¢ an ounce. The London agreement had allocated some 24,400,000 ounces as the annual share of the United States, which was approximately the average yield of American mines. The President's proclamation, therefore, was highly favorable to the domestic owner, for it provided for the purchase of his entire production. Pittman predicted that the world price of silver would now rise above 64½¢ an ounce and this would eventually remove objections to the free coinage on a ratio of 16 to 1.**

---

self to redraft the Thomas amendment. This was done on the evening of April 19, 1933. "Because so many were present, Pittman, Douglas and I finally retired into Moley's bedroom with a stenographer and got it down. The result of all this is that from a position twenty-four hours ago which meant the practically certain beginning of uncontrolled inflation, we have now covered up the worst features of the measure to a point where there is very little danger that popular interpretation of the measure will bring an uncontrolled inflation, as would have been the case with the original proposal, and where the only danger lies in what the President may do with the powers conferred upon him,—an exceedingly narrow squeak, which clearly indicates that this is not the only time such crises will occur." (The Reminiscences of James Warburg, Oral History Project, Columbia University, pp. 512–513.)

* The total silver received from foreign governments amounted to only 22,734,824 ounces. At 50¢ an ounce, the value of this silver was $11,367,412. Inflationists and silverites had thought that the entire $200,000,000 of silver would immediately flow into the Treasury.

** Although the President's proclamation applied to newly mined silver, Pittman was successful in convincing the Secretary of the Treasury to accept silver extracted from mine dumps created prior to the proclamation (K. P. to Henry Morgen-

Many silverites and inflationists were not satisfied with the advances the white metal had made in 1933. Even though the entire United States production had been added to the monetary stocks, there were those who thought that the desired inflation would not occur. With his December proclamation, Roosevelt had hoped that he had split the silverites from the cheap-money advocates, thereby preventing them from uniting behind any radical silver proposal. In a special message to Congress on January 15, 1934, the President, while recognizing the importance of silver in the currency system of the world, stated that he was withholding any recommendations looking to further extension of the monetary use of the metal until the London agreement was given sufficient time to operate. "If all these undertakings are carried out by the governments concerned," he said, "there will be a marked increase in the use and value of silver." [20]

On January 26, 1934, in spite of the President's wish to delay silver legislation, Senator Burton Wheeler introduced an amendment to the Gold Reserve bill providing for the purchase of not less than 50,-000,000 ounces a month until 1,000,000,000 ounces were added to the monetary resources of the United States. (The total production of domestic silver in 1933 amounted to 23,002,629 ounces. The monthly purchase of 50,000,000 ounces was therefore more than twice the production of the previous year.) A stop clause suspended this buying program when 371¼ grains of silver equaled the buying power of 23.22 grains of gold, which is a 16-to-1 ratio. Legal-tender certificates were to be issued against this bullion, valid for all monetary transactions.

Pittman supported the Wheeler amendment on the Senate floor as "simply another method for the President to get more basic silver in the United States." [21] Privately, the Senator, who actually opposed such a radical program, predicted that it would never become law. Nevertheless, Senator Wheeler had requested Pittman to deliver a "strong speech," and it would have been inept politics for the Nevadan to have refused. Before the final vote, the President, in an unusual move, announced through Majority Leader Robinson that the Wheeler

---

thau, Jr., January 22, 1934; Henry Morgenthau, Jr. to Superintendents of the Mines, February 2, 1934; Depts.-Govt. Folder, Box 142; *Nevada State Journal*, January 29, 1934) .

proposal conflicted with his basic monetary policy. The administration stand defeated the amendment, but by the narrow vote of 43 to 45.[22]

Pittman also introduced his own amendment to the Gold Reserve bill on the same day Wheeler proposed his plan, and the Senate adopted Pittman's amendment without a debate or a roll-call vote immediately after the defeat of the Wheeler purchase scheme. At their next meeting, the House of Representatives passed the Pittman measure in a matter of minutes. The amendment, far less extreme than the Wheeler proposal, called for no additional purchases of silver. The principal clauses (1) authorized issuance of silver certificates in place of coin to those who tendered eligible silver to the mints; (2) empowered the President to issue certificates against any silver in the Treasury not already held for redemption of outstanding certificates. This extended the use of silver as the Treasury had not been permitted to coin the seigniorage earned by the government; (3) permitted the President to raise the seigniorage charges on foreign-mined silver; (4) allowed the President to reduce the weight of the standard silver dollar the same percentage that he might reduce the weight of the gold dollar; (5) authorized the President to reduce and fix the weight of subsidiary coins so as to maintain the parity of such coins with other currency. This clause guarded against disappearance of silver in the event of an increase in the world market price to above $1.29 an ounce, the "coinage value" of silver in United States subsidiary coins.[23]

On the surface, the passage of the Pittman amendment appeared a victory for the moderate silverites and for the administration, which favored discretionary power. Few realized that Pittman secretly planned a startling new purchase program and that his addition to the Gold Reserve bill was the cornerstone of it.

Pittman now initiated a series of conferences with representatives of the Treasury Department. His silver plan, as confidentially proposed to Secretary Morgenthau, consisted of having the President use his powers under the Thomas amendment to buy the metal until 30 per cent of the United States currency was silver. Pittman explained that in 1933 the metal backed only 12 per cent of the circulating paper money of the United States, while in 1900 it supported 30 per cent. According to the Senator, the government would purchase silver from anywhere in the world, place it either in the form of bullion or coin in the Treasury, and issue silver certificates for it. The government, he reasoned, would be able to issue $1,800,000,000 in new certificates without having the ratio of silver-backed currency to other currency exceed the 1900 percentage.

"Why not try this plan?" he asked Secretary Morgenthau. "It is within the power of the President, at any time, by proclamation, to terminate it. That is the reason why this plan has an advantage over any congressional legislation. An act of Congress is inflexible, and sometimes is hard to repeal in the face of a filibuster. A Presidential proclamation can be annulled at any time. Why argue upon the theory as to what may happen with regard to our currency or our exports or our imports when the matter can be determined by actual experience without any danger whatsoever?" Pittman pointed out that his amendment to the Gold Reserve Act had been designed to give the President every power to implement this in a flexible way. "No one can contend that such method of inflation is unsound because it is backed with intrinsic value that is recognized throughout the world." [24] The administration, however, rejected Pittman's presidential proclamation plan, fearing the charge of government by decree.

The Thomas amendment, the London agreement, and Pittman's amendment to the Gold Reserve Act had not satisfied those congressmen who still insisted on doing something for silver. This group comprised not only representatives from the mining states but also congressmen demanding agricultural relief and inflation. On March 10, 1934, the House Committee on Coinage, Weights, and Measures reported out, from among the many bills sponsored by this alliance of interests, the Fiesinger and Dies bills.

The Fiesinger bill proposed the immediate purchase of 1,500,000 ounces of silver. It lost out in parliamentary precedence to the more radical resolution introduced by Representative Martin Dies of Texas. The latter created a board composed of the President, the Secretary of Commerce, and the Secretary of Agriculture which would negotiate with foreign purchasers to sell American surplus agricultural products at the world market price. Payment was to be made in silver coin or bullion at an agreed value not to exceed 125 per cent of the metal's world price. The bill authorized the Secretary of the Treasury to issue silver certificates based upon the agreed value of the bullion or coin in payment for the products sold. Thus, the purchase of surplus agricultural products was encouraged by offering foreign buyers up to 25 per cent over the world market price for their silver, if they exchanged this silver for excess farm products. This fantastic scheme passed the House on March 19, 1934, by a vote of 258 to 112 and was sent to the Senate.[25]

The Senate Committee on Agriculture and Forestry undertook the work of drafting amendments to the Dies bill to incorporate the ideas of the silver bloc. As rewritten, it retained the farm-surplus plan but also provided for the nationalization of domestic silver at the market price and the mandatory monthly purchase of 50,000,000 ounces of the metal until either it reached $1.29 an ounce or the 1926 price level for commodities was attained. The committee reported these amendments to the Senate on April 10.

Administration officials expressed uneasiness at the proposed mandatory legislation, and a showdown with the President appeared imminent. Four days later, on April 14, the congressional silver bloc conferred with Roosevelt, who reasserted his opposition to mandatory silver legislation, insisting that the Thomas amendment had already given him the power to buy the metal. He expressed sympathy with the intentions of those who supported the Dies bill but declared that he preferred to work out another international monetary agreement before attempting any further national legislation. "In the case of silver you don't know one damn thing—Key to the contrary," the President impatiently said. "We don't know how much silver there is in the world. It may be 15 billion ounces—and we don't know where it is held." He pointedly reminded the senators that "things are going damn well at this particular time—don't forget it." The silver-bloc senators called such an international agreement futile before the United States had agreed on an affirmative national policy.[26]

At a follow-up meeting with Treasury Department officials, Pittman returned to his arguments of how a further rise in the world price of silver would appreciate the value of the money of silver-using countries and enable them to increase their trade with the United States. By using a series of detailed graphs, the Senator attempted to demonstrate to the department that United States exports and imports were connected to the price of silver. A rise or fall in the price of the metal, according to Pittman's curves, always preceded the rise and fall in American exports from one to six months. These remarkable drawings also demonstrated that Great Britain used the appreciation and depreciation of silver for the purpose of appreciating and depreciating the purchasing power of gold. Secretary Morgenthau remained uncommitted, although he did ask Treasury experts to give him an immediate report on the elaborate material submitted by Pittman.* [27]

In an effort to break the deadlock, the administration sought to weaken the determined silver movement by investigating speculation in the white metal. During the third week in April, the Treasury Department began publishing the names of all known hoarders, a list which covered twenty-six closely printed pages. The report revealed no senators or representatives but showed widespread speculative interest in United States policy. Indignant at the action, Pittman bluntly told Morgenthau that this was poor judgment, and senators were "getting a little impatient with statements emanating from the Treasury Department reflecting upon their motive with regard to silver legislation. They say that we heard none of this when our Government was assisting in raising the price of gold." Pittman reminded the Secretary that threatening the Senate would not help the administration and he suggested that "a little more cooperation and a little less coercion would facilitate everything." [28]

The administration proposed a series of meetings in the hope of breaking the stalemate between the President and the silver bloc. Pittman wrote that he had been called to the White House frequently and that he was doing everything in his power to keep Congress in harmony with the President. "I think we have got enough votes to pass the Dies bill as amended by the Senate, and I think the House would agree to it," he predicted. "But, if the President is going to veto it on account of the mandatory provisions to purchase 50,000,000 ounces of silver a month, then I know that we have not sufficient votes in the Senate to pass it over his veto." A compromise with the President, he thought, remained the only answer to the problem; any other course of action would be "idiotic if it were not malicious." [29] To the President, Pittman wrote that the Dies bill with the Senate amendments was an "imperfect act, which might be internationally

---

* Pittman delighted in refuting the "so-called learned" silver arguments of the "professors" of the Treasury Department (see for example K. P. to William S. Boyle, May 1, 1934, B-General Folder, Box 11) .

disturbing," and he advised a compromise with the silver group to avoid political embarrassment in the 1934 congressional campaign.[30]

After conferring with the President on May 2, Pittman told reporters that the White House might agree to a bill if silver adherents did not demand inflexible legislation. He described how they had discussed the possibility of restoring the metallic balance of the currency system to 30 per cent silver and 70 per cent gold, as it had been in 1900. The Senator said that the President indicated no opposition to such a resolution. On May 5, after continued conferences with leaders of the bloc, Roosevelt indicated that he was ready for compromise. Eleven days of further negotiations and bickering followed. Finally, on May 16, the White House announced that within a day or two the President expected to send a silver message to Congress. Pittman gleefully told reporters that "we are all very happy and there is no misunderstanding now."

"How about the bill itself?" he was questioned.

"It will be ready very soon," he replied. "I should say we have reached the stage where a lead pencil is all that is needed to write a bill."

When asked if he expected the silver recommendation to pass at the current session, the Nevadan offered to bet any of the reporters $90 to $10 that legislation satisfactory to the silver bloc would pass before Congress adjourned. His challenge went unaccepted.[31]

On May 22, 1934, in a special address to Congress, the President formally requested passage of a silver-purchase act. It is clear, he stated, that as part of the larger objective of improving the financial and monetary system, "we should move forward in broadening the metallic base of our monetary system." He then proceeded to outline the general features of the suggested bill. Immediately after the reading of the message, Pittman introduced the administration's program. In a rambling hour-long speech, he reviewed the history of the silver movement and the framing of the compromise measure. "I think that this bill is an excellent one," he told his colleagues. "I think it is a magnificent compromise. . . . I think that the President of the United States has been in sympathy with us all the time, even if some of his experts were not in sympathy with us; and I feel that we have won a great victory in getting the President of the United States to concur with us so far as he has concurred with us, although I know he had the antagonism of nearly every one of the Treasury Department economists." [32]

The final bill, which was prepared by the Treasury Department and entitled the Silver Purchase Act of 1934, declared it to be the policy of the United States to increase the proportion of silver to gold in the government's monetary stocks. The Secretary of the Treasury was authorized and directed to purchase silver at home or abroad at such times and upon conditions that he might deem reasonable, until the proportion of silver was one-fourth of the monetary stocks of the United States or until silver reached its coinage price ($1.29 an ounce). The total amount to be purchased to meet this requirement, assuming that the June, 1934, gold holdings remained constant, amounted to approximately 1,308,000,000. (In order to comprehend the importance of this buying program, it should be pointed out that the world production of silver averaged only about 170,000,000 ounces for the preceding three years.) [33]

The act, almost identical with the silver-purchase plan confidentially suggested by Pittman to Secretary Morgenthau on February 16, combined mandatory and permissive features. Its principal mandatory provision declared that it was the purpose of the government to build up the metallic monetary reserves to 25 per cent silver and 75 per cent gold. The purchase program to carry out this policy was mandatory as to declaration but highly discretionary as to method and time of purchase. The silver senators accepted this permissive feature under the impression that the buying would be carried out in good faith.

The Silver Purchase Act became the principal silver program of the New Deal. It passed the House on May 31 by a vote of 263 to 77, and was approved by the Senate on June 11 by a vote of 54 to 25. On June 19, the day after the second session of the Seventy-third Congress had adjourned *sine die,* the President signed into law the largest silver-purchasing program in the history of the world. After passage, Pittman announced: "I feel that the gold and silver question is settled as far as legislation is concerned." [34]

While the Senate silver leaders and the President were attempting to resolve their differences, Pittman, perhaps overwhelmed at the future prospects for the white metal, wrote to the President:

There is an ancient fable that runs something like this:
There was a breed of monkeys 'way back in the Malay jungle. There were

only a few of them and they had lived in a very small space during all of their generations. There was only one thing that they would eat, and that was a little pomegranate—a little golden pomegranate—. And then along came a big fire and destroyed the entire area where these golden pomegranates grew. The little monkeys were starving, and other monkeys did their best to get them to eat other pomegranates. There was a beautiful silver pomegranate, just as delicious as the gold pomegranate which all of the other monkeys in the Malay Peninsula had grown fat on; but the little golden monkeys would not eat anything but the little golden pomegranates. And today they are all dead.

To which Roosevelt responded:

I remember that fable about the monkeys and the pomegranates but the true story runs this way.

"It was perfectly true that the little monkeys got on very well with their little golden pomegranates. After the big fire destroyed the golden pomegranates the little monkeys discovered vast quantities of silver pomegranates. They liked them so well that they ate dozens and dozens and dozens of them and that is why all the little monkeys are dead today!" [35]

III

Pittman returned to Nevada in July, 1934, to face a bitter re-election fight. The Republicans had nominated the aggressive forty-four-year-old state engineer, George Malone. A former captain of the University of Nevada football team, Malone had won his popularity in planning state flood and reclamation projects. The Pittmans, who referred to Malone as "the Molly," were distressed at the prospect of a strenuous campaign and possible defeat. "Just imagine Key being forced to travel around and campaigning in every town and hamlet in the State!" wrote Mimosa. "We have always known Malone's character intimately, so it means a deadly fight." [36]

Pittman campaigned on his achievements for silver. His opponents had planned to make its low price their main issue, but because of the London agreement and the Silver Purchase Act, their thunder had been stolen. During the campaign, Malone charged that Pittman limited his interest to silver as a commodity and opposed remonetization. Pittman countered by circulating copies of his remarks made in favor of Senator Wheeler's 16-to-1 proposal. He also obtained a letter from Wheeler declaring that Malone "knew very little concerning the subject of remonetization of silver and its effect, either upon the foreign trade of this country or other nations." [37] In speech after speech made in town after town, the Senator told of his long and continuous fight for the white metal. Throughout the campaign, local problems replaced Roosevelt's national program as issues. Pittman had an almost perfect New Deal record, opposing the President on only one roll call—to override the veto of the Independent Offices Appropriations Act (March 28, 1934). During the campaign, however, he rarely referred to his national voting record except if a legislative act had benefited Nevada.

Pittman "ran scared," although there was never much doubt that he would be re-elected. "The same people, or their sons and daughters who voted for me in 1934, also voted for me in 1912 and in every election since," he remarked.[38] (In the last days before the election an anonymous article was circulated, libelously accusing Pittman of being a nabob in the pay of the Wall Street silver interests. Pittman intimated that his Democratic rival Pat McCarran was the author.) [39] More than 42,000 Nevadans went to the polls, the heaviest vote ever recorded in the history of the state. Pittman soundly defeated Malone 27,581 to 14,273. "A lot of people are after us and they might take a State with a small population like Nevada to try to pick off one of my friends," Roosevelt wrote Pittman during the campaign. "The machine gun bandits are at work. So far I think their aim has been pretty poor!" [40]

The congressional election of 1934 was a ratifying victory for the New Deal. Although pleased at the national results, Pittman also viewed them with skepticism. "A number of our newly elected Senators may have a tendency to radicalism," he told Joseph O'Mahoney. "Many do not understand what the new deal means. Some interpret it as a drift towards the labor party. Others visualize it as socialism." He wrote Alben Barkley he had been informed "that ambitious junior members of the Senate are attempting to organize what they term a new deal in the Senate. This revolutionary movement must be stopped." The safest program, thought Pittman, was to support "the President straight through to the end." "We must discourage factional fights within our party ranks." Democrats of experience had to lead or else "we will lose our anchor and drift in a storm of uncontrolled legislation and debate." * [41]

The opening weeks of the Seventy-fourth Congress did not proceed as smoothly as Pittman had hoped. The Democratic elders maintained control but the administration's program, especially the huge work-relief bill, became entangled in committee procedure.** During these weeks, Pittman was despondent and turned more and more to drinking. "There has been a great change in the attitude of Senators since we convened," he wrote to Roosevelt. "Patriotism and loyalty seem to have gradually surrendered to expediency and self interest. Apparently at the present time we have no such thing as a Democratic organization in the Senate. . . . Every dog is for himself and, like wolves, they will eat you up if you fall for a moment by the roadside." [42]

Harold Ickes noted that Pittman was obsessed with the political situation. "He told me . . . that the President was losing a good deal of ground." The Senator bitterly complained that Roosevelt consulted only three senators, Pat Harrison, Joseph Robinson, and James Byrnes, while others had not been able to see the President and had suffered a loss of dignity and prestige. [43]

In a disconnected letter to the President, Pittman detailed this Democratic discontent and loss of party solidarity, telling Roosevelt that most senators thought "defeat is inevitable, and every man must take care of himself." He attributed this attitude to a lack of patronage and to the "strange and peculiar persons [who] have become ad-

---

* Pittman was re-elected president pro tempore (*Congressional Record,* 74 Cong. 1 Sess. Vol. 79, Pt. 1 [January 7, 1935], p. 128). Senator Royal Copeland of New York had threatened to oppose Pittman. "Copeland had the nerve to tell me that because I was Chairman of the Foreign Relations Committee that I was not entitled to be President pro tempore. . . . I won't yield to him. He is not entitled to the office. I am entitled to the office and will fight for it" (K. P. to M. M. Neely, November 13, 1934, Miscellaneous—Official Folder, Box 21).

** During the first session of the Seventy-fourth Congress, Pittman spoke infrequently on matters other than the monetary question. He did, however, unequivocally support the New Deal. On roll call votes, he voted for the Emergency Relief Appropriation Act (April 5, 1935) ; Sustaining of the President's Veto of the Patman Bonus Bill (May 23, 1935) ; Social Security Act (June 19, 1935) ; Wheeler-Rayburn Public Utility Act (June 11, 1935) ; Wealth Tax Act (August 15, 1935) ; Guffey-Snyder Bituminous Coal Act (August 22, 1935) .

visors. . . . You have made generals in the conquered army your generals and these generals . . . are pulling into the army those of the defeated columns." Pittman's remedy was twofold. "Do what Napoleon did—and what you are so capable of doing—in inspiring loyalty, patriotism, courage and the spirit of self-sacrifice in the most lowly private." Every Democratic senator had to be taken into the President's confidence. "Most of them are brave and loyal men, but they don't know they are in the army." [44]

Pittman's pessimism did not carry over to the monetary issue. Several silver resolutions were introduced during the first session of the Seventy-fourth Congress, which ended in August, 1935, but none aroused his interest. Pittman appeared satisfied with the administration's execution of the 1934 Purchase Act. "I know of no more successful handling of any question than the handling of the silver question by the President of the United States." The Senator had every reason to be enthusiastic. The Treasury Department had been buying at least 50,000,000 ounces of silver each month, a figure equal to the maximum demand made by the most radical silverites. Production in Nevada had increased from 1,148,621 ounces in 1933 to 3,057,114 in 1934, a gain of 166 per cent. "Mining has a bright future," he predicted.[45]

By April, 1935, because of the energetic policy of the Treasury Department in carrying out the Silver Purchase Act, the world price had been pushed up until it equaled the 64.5¢ paid to the western miner. (The United States bought domestic silver according to the provisions of the presidential proclamation of December 21, 1933, *i.e.* 64.5¢ was paid to the American producer. Foreign silver was bought at the world market price under the terms of the Silver Purchase Act of June 19, 1934.) Since the administration agreed to guarantee American producers at least as much as the world price, it became necessary to raise the domestic price. Secretary Morgenthau favored a 5-per-cent increase to 71.11¢ an ounce, which would be obtained by lowering the seigniorage rate from 50 to 45 per cent.* Pittman suggested to Roosevelt that the rate be lowered to 25 per cent, which would have raised domestic silver to 96.75¢ an ounce.[46] On April 10, 1935, the President, agreeing

---

* Under the presidential proclamation of December 21, 1933, the seigniorage rate was 50 per cent. The further proclamations of the President were modifications of the 1933 proclamation. The Thomas amendment to the Farm Relief Act gave the President the authority to regulate American seigniorage.

with Morgenthau, reduced the seigniorage 5 per cent, thereby raising the price of domestic silver to 71.11¢.

Spurred on by speculators, now confident that the United States intended to raise the price until it reached $1.29 an ounce, the foreign cost continued to jump. Within two weeks of the President's proclamation lowering the seigniorage charge, silver on the London market reached 70¢ an ounce. "It was, in my opinion, a mistake for the Secretary to advise the raising of the American price of silver only a few cents an ounce," Pittman wrote Roosevelt. "I respectfully suggest that in your next proclamation you give a wider margin between the world price and the United States price so as to avoid the necessity of frequently issuing proclamations." Pittman now suggested that 65 per cent of the silver be given to the producer, the government retaining 35 per cent as seigniorage, raising domestic silver to 83.85¢ an ounce. The President again relied on Morgenthau's advice and on April 24, 1935, the seigniorage charge was reduced another 5 per cent to 40 per cent, raising domestic silver to 77.57¢ an ounce.* [47]

From this point on, Secretary Morgenthau began to administer the Silver Purchase Act more conservatively, and the Treasury Department now attempted to peg the price it paid for foreign silver in an effort to halt speculation. After the President's April proclamations, the department refused to buy foreign bullion at inflated prices, causing the world market to drop. Morgenthau apparently intended to fulfill provisions of the Silver Purchase Act by meeting the 1:3 silver-to-gold ratio requirement without driving the price of silver up to $1.29 an ounce. The radical silverites vehemently protested against this new program; many had voted for the act thinking that $1.29-an-ounce silver would be the logical result of the huge buying program. "The silver program is about as clear as mud," fumed Elmer

* After the Silver Purchase Act had been in effect one year, the Treasury Department announced that it had purchased some 445,881,231 ounces of silver. (Domestic purchases amounted to 31,036,590 ounces.) The total world production of silver, for the calendar years 1934 and 1935 respectively, was 190,859,421 and 215,949,585 ounces (*Annual Report of the Director of the Mint for the Fiscal Year 1935*, pp. 48–49, 86, 104; *Annual Report . . . for the Fiscal Year 1936*, p. 104). As the United States purchased more than twice the world output of silver, the silver currencies of the world were seriously disrupted. Everest deals with this problem in considerable detail (Allan Seymour Everest, *Morgenthau the New Deal and Silver* [New York, Kings Crown, 1950] pp. 79–134).

Thomas, who threatened Morgenthau with a Senate investigation.[48]

Pittman took no part in harassing the administration to pursue a more aggressive policy, and he did not sign a petition instigated by Senator Thomas demanding speedier action. The Nevadan, more interested in mining than bimetallism, was satisfied that the Treasury Department had been carrying out the Silver Purchase Act in a conservative and orderly manner. He labeled the radical silver senators a "small selfish group" and advised Senator Duncan Fletcher, chairman of the Committee on Banking and Currency, to pigeonhole attempts to amend the Silver Purchase Act. "It is being administered in a very intelligent and practical way by the Treasury Department." [49] (Pittman had extensive interests in silver mines and was part owner of a $5,000,000 venture in the old Comstock Lode area. Any rise in the price of silver, of course, favorably affected his personal finances.) [50]

When Senator Thomas threatened Morgenthau with an investigation, the Secretary induced Pittman to submit his own proposal for a senatorial silver inquiry committee.* On April 15, 1935, Pittman introduced a resolution creating a standing Special Committee on the Investigation of Silver, which passed without objection. With the Nevadan as chairman, the radical silverites were stymied in their efforts to examine the Treasury's administration of the Silver Purchase Act. The committee, though at all times a threat to the Treasury Department, remained inactive until February, 1939.

The United States continued to be the main support of the silver market during 1936, the Treasury purchasing almost the entire domestic output at 77.57¢ an ounce. Morgenthau, with the approval of the President, had ceased aggressive open-market buying policies, thus stabilizing the price of foreign silver at approximately 45¢ an ounce. By December, 1935, the Secretary had decided that the silver-purchasing policy was increasingly futile and realized that by buying up all the free metal in the world, the United States would eventually force every silver-using country to paper money.[51]

In Nevada the rise in the domestic price of silver continued to be

---

* Everest writes that Morgenthau asked George L. LeBlanc, a New York banker, to assist him. LeBlanc, who was considered the "one man who could reason with Thomas," went to Washington on the evening of April 14. LeBlanc succeeded in restraining Thomas from congressional action for one day, thus enabling Pittman to introduce his investigation resolution (Everest, *op. cit.*, p. 59) .

the main reason for the recovery of the state's mining industry, and Pittman told Morgenthau that he did not care what happened to the world price as long as American producers continued to receive 77.57¢ an ounce. In 1936, for the first time in seven years, the Senator did not introduce a silver resolution or amendment during a congressional session. When eighty-two members of the National Committee on Monetary Policy petitioned Congress in May to repeal all silver legislation, the Senator quickly denounced the academicians who signed the request. "I do not want anyone to take this as a reflection on professors," he told his colleagues. "Personally, I think they accomplish just as much good as any other artisan such as a plumber or brick mason accomplishes in his own line." Pittman, distrustful of all intellectuals, no less a group that referred to silver as a "base, dishonest, depreciated metal," advised the signers to stick to their classrooms and texts and leave the silver issue to him.[52]

Foreign price fluctuations now remained the narrowest on record, indicating the silver market's complete dependence upon United States support—foreign silver averaged 44.8¢ in 1937 while the government continued to purchase domestic silver at 77.57¢ an ounce. Pittman confidentially told Roosevelt that he was willing to "let up" on the foreign purchase if the government concentrated on buying only American-produced silver.[53] As 77.57¢ an ounce was an excellent commodity price for the metal, Pittman obviously was aiming at an increased American output which would be purchased by the United States.

To avoid antagonizing either the administration or any of his colleagues who precariously supported silver, the Senator continued to avoid taking stands on controversial issues. Pittman was one of the few senators who made no comment from the Senate floor on Roosevelt's court plan. "Both sides were unreasonably vain and bitter," he wrote. "I constantly attempted to act as an intermediary and a peacemaker." [54]

The presidential proclamation of December 21, 1933, authorizing the purchase of domestic silver at 64.5¢ an ounce, and the modifying proclamation of April 24, 1935, which raised the price to 77.57¢, were to expire on December 31, 1937.* Fear gripped the silverites.

---

* The purchase of domestic silver under the presidential proclamations should not be confused with the purchase of silver in the world market under the authority of the Silver Purchase Act of 1934, which was a permanent law.

The thought that the domestic price would fall to the world level horrified them. "If the coinage of American silver did cease at the end of the year," warned Pittman, "it would result in the closing down of mines all over the country, not only so-called silver mines but gold mines, lead, zinc, and copper mines, because the working of those mines depends very largely upon the silver content of the ore or the rock."

Pittman somehow arrived at the conclusion that the rise in the price of silver had removed 400,000 people from the relief rolls. Senator Alva Adams of Colorado carried this statement further by reasoning that the government annually spent at least $800 for each person on relief, a yearly total of $320,000,000 if the miners were unemployed. But the government had wisely kept them at work at the bargain price of $112,705,000, the expenditure from December 21, 1933, to June 30, 1937, for domestic silver purchased by the United States. "The American miner," said Adams, "wonders why there should be objections to paying a small additional price for American silver in order to encourage and develop the mining industry and secure the many and important incidental benefits to the general welfare of the Nation." [55]

In spite of the arguments put forth by the silver bloc for maintaining its high price, the President, on December 31, 1937, extended his 1933 proclamation for one year. By choosing to extend this proclamation without his 1935 modifications, Roosevelt automatically lowered the domestic price of silver to 64.5¢ an ounce.

The silverites vehemently protested but the domestic price remained at 64.5¢ an ounce throughout 1938. The output of silver declined sharply. In Nevada, production fell 10 per cent in quantity and 25 per cent in value from 1937 figures. The general curtailment in the mining of zinc, copper, and other base metals caused by past overproduction might have been responsible for this sudden drop, for most silver is mined as a by-product of these metals. Pittman, nevertheless, blamed the lowered silver price offered by the government.

In order to obtain more support for silver, the Senator designed a scheme to tie the metal to the farm problem. In September, 1938, he proposed that the government dispose of its enormous cotton carryover by trading abroad ten pounds of cotton for one ounce of silver. The farmers would be paid 12.9¢ a pound with the estimated 670,000,000 ounces of silver thus acquired. This would be done by issuing certificates against the silver received from abroad. The administration took no official action on his plan, although critics of the scheme pointed out that cotton was selling for 8¢ a pound and silver at 43¢ an ounce in the open market. The Senator's proposal, therefore, would have meant paying 80¢ worth of cotton for 43¢ worth of silver.[56] Roosevelt, always careful not to antagonize the chairman of the Foreign Relations Committee, chided Pittman for his constant concern for silver. "[Congressman James] Scrugham tells me they have found a manganese process and that at the next session we will pass a bill demonetizing silver and substituting manganese," teased the President. "That will give variety to our currency and a nation wide political issue! Not only will the United States Treasury be saved but so will Brazil. That is why the Chairman of the Foreign Relations Committee will introduce it and call it 'The Pittman World Currency Act of 1939.'"[57]

On December 31, 1938, Roosevelt issued another proclamation extending the purchase of newly mined domestic silver at 64.5¢ an ounce through June 30, 1939. As the President's monetary authority under the Thomas amendment expired on that day, a contest soon began in Congress as to the wisdom of continuing these powers. Senator John G. Townsend, Jr., of Delaware led the attack on the entire New Deal silver program. On January 4, 1939, he introduced Senate Joint Resolution 1, calling for the appointment of a special joint committee to investigate the silver program "in all its aspects, including its objects, its administration, and its effects, both at home and abroad." Listing fifty-two objections to the existing policy, Townsend recommended a suspension of foreign silver purchases until the special committee submitted its recommendations.

Townsend's resolution stipulated that the special committee consist of five senators and five representatives. The latter were to be appointed by the speaker of the House, the usual procedure, but the five senators were to be chosen by the Vice-President from the Committee on Banking and Currency. Of the twenty members of the committee, only two came from the inter-mountain area.

Pittman attempted to prevent the appointment of this possibly unfriendly silver committee by having Townsend and three other senators named to his old Senate special silver committee, which was now resurrected. Townsend, undaunted by the Nevadan's actions, introduced a bill repealing the Silver Purchase Act of 1934 and requested that it be referred to the Committee on Banking and Currency, pointing out that a federal grant to the Delaware rayon industry to supply a substitute for the silk threads found in paper currency would be as logical as continuing the subsidy to the domestic silver industry.[58] Pittman immediately countered with a resolution prohibiting the purchase of foreign silver except in payment for farm exports. The Nevadan's bill also raised the price of domestic silver to $1.29 an ounce.

Pittman's special silver committee began hearings on February 7, 1939. In session after session, the silverites seized every opportunity to enumerate the values of the white metal. At Pittman's suggestion, Walter E. Trent, a professional metal lobbyist, was employed by the committee. Trent prepared about forty of the most remarkable charts and graphs, and the confusing curves and statistics proved, at least to his and Pittman's satisfaction, a relationship between commodity exports and the price of silver. One of Trent's more fantastic charts portrayed "the financial embarrassment caused by the United States permitting the commercial price of silver to recede below its monetary value." [59] After two months of hearings, and the inclusion in the record of almost every act pertaining to silver and countless state, local, and private petitions demanding a higher price for the metal, the committee recessed.

Congressional attacks on the administration's silver program continued, with critics declaring that the purchases had become an endless subsidy. At the time the Silver Purchase Act was enacted, Treasury gold holdings were $7,834,000,000. In order to comply with the "ultimate objective of having and maintaining one-fourth of the total monetary value of the gold and silver stocks in silver," the required amount of silver that the Treasury had to have was 2,024,000,000 ounces. Deducting the 696,000,000 ounces then on hand left a balance of 1,328,000,000 ounces to be purchased on June 19, 1934, the day the bill became law. Four and a half years later, the original goal of 2,024,000,000 ounces had been attained and surpassed by over half a billion ounces. By December 31, 1938, however, the government's gold holdings had increased to approximately $14,500,000,000, raising the required proportion of silver in the monetary stocks to 3,740,000,000 ounces. After deducting the 2,575,000,000 ounces of silver that the government held on December 31, 1938, a balance of 1,165,000,000 ounces of silver still remained to be purchased! [60] Pittman asserted that the silver program was not a federal subsidy, but, on the contrary, the government had made an enormous profit through its purchases. The Senator remained steadfast in his belief that the monetary value of the metal was $1.29 an ounce and any purchase made for less than this amount made profit for the government.

After much debate and a variety of hearings, parliamentary maneuvers, and threatened filibusters, the silver question finally came to a head during the last days of June, 1939. After much compromising and a successful attempt by Pittman in linking the administration's Neutrality bill to the silver issue, the Senate, on July 5, by a vote of 43 to 29, adopted a conference report which had been approved by the House five days earlier. The President signed the bill on the following day. [61]

The new act continued the Treasury's power to purchase foreign silver by leaving most sections of the 1934 Purchase Act unchanged. Perhaps the most important provision for the silverites was the one making the purchase of newly mined domestic silver and its price a matter of law and not a temporary grant of power to the President. The price was set at 71.11¢ an ounce, a compromise, for Pittman had demanded $1.16. The silverites, nevertheless, emerged victorious primarily because of Pittman, who had used his position as chairman of the Foreign Relations Committee to extract grudging administration support. "It is not for a period of six months or even two years but forever," he jubilantly wrote. "I can assure you that it will never be repealed except by another Act that raises the percentage of silver that goes to the miner until the miner gets $1.29 an ounce." [62]

IV

Key Pittman was a professional politician. His job depended upon others who got the vote out, enlisted new party workers, and conducted the electioneering. The 30,000 or so regular Nevada Democrats had to be kept in good humor, for any serious defection or factional split might cost Pittman his Senate seat. The local situation compelled him to think of his obscure supporters who coveted petty political office. On one occasion, President Roosevelt, at Pittman's insistence, removed the Supervisor of Sewing Projects, W.P.A., for Washoe County when local Democrats accused her of "Republicanism." [63] The Senator had had no claim to federal patronage since 1921. With the long awaited Democratic victory in 1932, he expected sufficient jobs to reward the partisans and bolster his machine. The Nevada Democratic County Central Committee prepared a list of federal political offices within the state, cautioning Pittman that his control of the organization depended upon "an even break in the matter of appointments." [64]

The most important dispenser of political offices for Nevada was the Secretary of the Interior, whose patronage scope ranged from choosing newspapers in which to publish notices of the General Land Office to designating deputy marshals for the Boulder Dam project. Harold L. Ickes was unknown to Pittman before his selection. "I am trying to get acquainted with the new appointee in the hopes that I may have some influence in future appointments," wrote the Senator.* [65]

As early as May, 1933, Pittman was dismayed about the lack of patronage he had received. Dozens of letters from constituents indicated that Republicans still occupied local political offices. Pittman demanded a clean sweep. He composed lists of new appointees, submitted them to various departments, but received practically no action. "At Boulder Dam, where we have about 3,000 men employed everything is under Republican management," he complained to Jim Farley. "This condition I am informed, exists with regard to the entire public land system under the Secretary of the Interior. I do not know how a person would get an appointment under the Secretary of the Department of Agriculture. The thing is all wrong. We have got to take political power out of the hands of the Republican cabinet members. They are not interested in the political situation, and I think that goes for Morgenthau. . . . I say to you frankly that Democratic Senators and Democratic Congressmen are becoming very much discouraged." [66]

---

* In 1935, Gifford Pinchot, in a letter opposing the transfer of the Forestry Bureau from the Department of Agriculture to the Department of the Interior, wrote: "Ickes himself is straight, but the whole history of the Interior Department is reeking with politics" (Gifford Pinchot to Dr. E. Willis Kobler, July 9, 1935, Reorganization Forest Service Folder, Records of the Office of the Secretary of Agriculture, National Archives) .

Before leaving for the London economic conference, Pittman wrote Louis Howe that Republicans were still in charge of hundreds of reclamation projects throughout the West. "I have not been to Mr. Ickes with regard to the matter. Senator McCarran and Congressman Scrugham have. They certainly got no encouragement. How can you talk politics to the Secretary of the Interior or the Secretary of Agriculture? It would be just almost as easy, however, to talk politics to Morgenthau. All of these men apparently think that intelligence is confined exclusively to the Republican Party." The Senator suggested that some method be devised to overcome this "unfortunate situation" as senators and congressmen "are not only becoming discouraged but the outlook for success in the next election is becoming dark." [67]

When Pittman returned from London, he found that the patronage situation had grown worse. He thought Ickes, Henry Wallace, and Morgenthau, then head of the reconstructed Farm Loan Board, were Republicans at heart who ignored all partisan patronage pleas. "Farley is out on a limb," the Senator explained. "He cannot get any more from these departments than anyone else." [68]

Pittman finally appealed directly to the President. "I am a little nervous with regard to the political situation," he wrote. "Of course, you have no nerves and I am glad of it. It is obvious, of course, that you are undertaking a great nonpartisan movement and this has brought to your support over ninety per cent of the people of this country. On the other hand, when enthusiasm lags or the ship gets in the doldrums, it is the Democrats that take to the oars." Roosevelt promptly responded, conceding that there had been few appointments from Nevada, and asked Pittman to "dig up the names of one or two really first-class men." Three weeks later, upon Pittman's recommendation, the President promoted Judge Frank H. Norcross to the Circuit Court of Appeals, Ninth Circuit, and designated William Woodburn district judge for Nevada. [69]

The Senator had expected his main patronage to come from the Interior Department. Harold L. Ickes, however, attempted to select appointees who were relatively free from political influence. Pittman was furious. For twelve years, he had been promising minor political jobs to his loyal supporters, and the Interior Department payrolls appeared to be the solution. Ickes did appoint Justus Wardell, a Pittman backer, as P.W.A. regional advisor for Nevada, but with limited patronage authority. Washington continued to maintain a strict control over most local appointees. Ickes, to Pittman's disgust, insisted that merit be the basis for appointment.

Pittman castigated Ickes for his method of dispensing patronage, claiming that Republicans and Democrats hostile to himself were being placed on the payroll. "While you are a Republican," he chided, "you have accepted office under a Democratic President, in a Democratic Administration. No one that I know of expects you to be a Democrat, but they believe that you cannot support a Democratic President without supporting the whole Democratic Administration." The Senator insisted that Ickes' administrative assistant, Ebert K. Burlew, directed the patronage and that he had Republican leanings. "I have every reason to believe, and do believe, that he has that peculiar Republican obsession that only Republicans are capable," the Senator accusingly wrote. "Roosevelt had no desire or interest to establish a fusion party, nor to have you do any unusual political acts that would tend to the disintegration of his own party."

Ickes considered Pittman's remarks insulting and decided to reply in "a strong letter on the theory that if I permit some of these politicians to get the idea that they can shove me around, they will not only do it but others will join them in the exercise." Ickes, who feared no politician, concluded his ten-page response to Pittman, in which he answered each of the Senator's assertions, with the blunt peroration: "I am the dictator of patronage and I shall continue to be so as long as I am head of this Department." * [70]

This sharp answer undoubtedly surprised Nevada's senior Senator and the Senate's ranking member. "My letter was written in the friendliest spirit," he apologetically told the Secretary. "I assure you that I will cooperate in every way for the success of your Administration." [71] Pittman's quiescent response was perhaps motivated by Ickes' appointment of the Senator's friend and supporter A. L. Scott as an attorney in the Interior Department. The quarrel stopped, at

---

* In April, 1933, Pittman had persuaded Ickes to appoint the Idaho Democratic State Chairman, Theodore A. Walters, as First Assistant Secretary. Ickes later wrote that Walters, who died in 1937, did "me as much damage as he could with his political patron" (Harold L. Ickes, "My Twelve Years with F. D. R.," *Saturday Evening Post*, June 26, 1948, p. 36) .

least temporarily, but Pittman, nevertheless, despised Ickes. The Secretary, not to be outmatched by anyone, delighted in collecting anecdotes about Pittman's drinking habits.[72]

The Ickes-Pittman feud smoldered until 1937. In December of that year, the Secretary decided to reward his administrative assistant, Ebert K. Burlew, by promoting him to First Assistant Secretary. Burlew, a government career man, had been employed in the Interior Department since 1923. "I believe his advancement will be a deserved recognition of the merit system in our Federal Service," stated Ickes.[73] Burlew's appointment as Assistant Secretary was mainly a change of title rather than of powers, a compliment arranged by a grateful Secretary.

Pittman had differed with Ickes on many occasions—the administration of the Taylor Grazing Act, the names to be included on the Boulder Dam dedication plaques, and on patronage. Burlew's appointment, however, became the last straw. "I consider Mr. Burlew a subversive force in the Department of the Interior," the Senator told Roosevelt. "If he [Ickes] insists upon the appointment of Mr. Burlew he will cause you a lot more trouble, and God knows you have plenty of it now." Pittman's warning was too late. Ickes had insisted on Burlew's promotion and Roosevelt had agreed. "I think he made a mistake," Pittman wrote to his friend William Boyle.[74]

Pittman demanded that the Public Lands and Survey Committee conduct an investigation to determine Burlew's competency. The hearings, which began on January 11, 1938, became, for the most part, an investigation of the Interior Department. The Senator repeatedly accused the department of laxity and inefficiency and monopolized the questioning, which ranged from alleged wire tapping in the department to outright corruption in the Park Service. His opposition to Burlew was based upon charges of negligence, insisting that Burlew's laxity had cost untold loss to the government. Beneath these charges of inefficiency, however, lay the Senator's intense dislike for Secretary Ickes. In addition, Pittman blamed his patronage problem on Burlew, who was also personnel officer of the department.

As the hearings progressed, it appeared that anyone who had a grievance, real or imaginary, with the Interior Department came to Pittman. Ickes was "pretty mad about the whole thing." Pittman, he thought, was just "trying to make trouble for this Department." According to Ickes' account, Roosevelt said "something about sending for Pittman if Barkley couldn't do anything with him, but he hasn't done so. On the contrary, the cordiality he showed when he greeted Pittman at the musicale following the dinner to the Supreme Court gave Pittman an assurance of Presidential support, or at least of indifference to the fate of Burlew and Interior." [75]

The President did not interfere in this household quarrel. By bantering with both Ickes and Pittman, he avoided a public dispute with either his Secretary of the Interior or the chairman of the Foreign Relations Committee. At the end of the lengthy Burlew hearing, which resulted in over six hundred printed pages of testimony, opposition to Burlew dissipated, save that of Pittman. The Senate confirmed him on April 5, 1938, without a record vote. [76]

Pittman had patronage difficulties with other executive departments. It appeared that the administration managed to award political offices to almost "every ex-politician" who opposed the Senator. The President, though, remained reluctant to interfere.[*] [77] As late as 1937, Pittman complained to Jim Farley that "the Republicans are still eating at the trough of the bombastic non-partisan alliance." "I hope to God that the people will find that there is such a thing as a Democratic administration with regard to patronage." [78] "The Secretary of Agriculture, who is a good Republican and always claims to be a strong personal friend of mine, and yet his department has never given me any appointments," the Senator wrote. "Of course Madam Perkins has never given me any consideration. She also is a former Republican with very strong socialistic leaning." [79]

Pittman resented the "professors" who surrounded the President and upon whose advice the President relied. Tugwell's philosophy, he assured Sam Rayburn, "doesn't appeal to thinking people." [80] "I am still a kind of a last resort advisor to the President," Pittman informed Breckinridge Long. "Whenever the professors have led him into violent opposition to Congress, I have been called in with other intimate advisors to ascertain what's the matter and what may be done." [81] To counteract the "Harvard Clan," Pittman brought deserving Nevada boys to Washington, found them government jobs,

---

[*] Pittman complained to Secretary Wallace that he gave his endorsements "absolutely no consideration" (K. P. to Henry A. Wallace, March 8, 1938, Office File, 1–R, Franklin D. Roosevelt Papers, Hyde Park, N. Y.).

and had them work their way through a local law school. In letters of recommendation, he took delight in writing that the nominee was well qualified "even though he is not a graduate of Harvard University, which seems essential to appointment in some departments of our Government." [82]

V

During 1938–1939, Pittman had another heated public dispute with Secretary Ickes—the issue was the allotting of twelve square miles of the Boulder Canyon Reclamation Area to Nevada. Pittman planned to stand for re-election again in 1940. The Nevada Democratic party, however, was being ripped apart by an intra-party feud between supporters of Pat McCarran and Pittman. The two men, political foes for years, were contending for control of the Nevada machine.[83] Pittman needed an issue, something which would bring him attention back home.

In October, 1938, the Senator proposed that the Federal Government cede approximately twelve square miles of public domain to Nevada for a state park. The suggested land, located nineteen miles from Las Vegas, was situated on a narrow inlet of Lake Mead on the northern side of the lake several miles from the western end. Pittman told Ickes that he could "visualize many hundreds of families of modest means being possessed of small boats, and taking their families out on Saturdays and Sundays for boating, fishing, and recreation on this safe little inlet." [84]

Privately, the Senator considered the park idea a shrewd political move. Clark County, with its center in Las Vegas, always had been a Pittman stronghold. With the completion of Boulder Dam, Boulder City, begun in 1931 as a government construction camp, attracted tourists from all over the world. Airlines advertised direct flights to Boulder City, "the new recreation spot of the West," and in 1937, some 700,000 tourists visited it. Las Vegas, of course, also prospered from this tourist trade. The city attempted to recreate the Wild-West glamor of the past, which meant an increase in bars, gambling halls, and night clubs. The proposed state park, with a direct highway from Las Vegas, would have increased real-estate values and would provide a new tourist attraction. By sponsoring such legislation, Pittman was sure of strong support in Las Vegas, which would offset the unknown voting pattern of Boulder City.

The suggested park plan had the enthusiastic support of the Las Vegas City Council, the Chamber of Commerce, and leading businessmen of the community, and Pittman became the guiding spirit of the project. "Get a description that will be sure to take in all the land we want," he wrote to his friend Claude Mackey. "The amount requested can always be cut down by the Committee." The Senator urged that an Izaak Walton League and a yacht club be established in Las Vegas as Ickes "will bring the matter to a head quite quickly." [85]

Ickes opposed the Pittman park bill from the start. He intimated to the chairman of the Senate Public Lands and Survey Committee that supporters of the bill were backed by a "number of gamblers who formerly flourished [in Los Angeles and who] have betaken themselves to Las Vegas":

It is rumored that they have set about to monopolize the gambling concerns of that city. It is further rumored that they are heartily in support of this State Park because they want to extend their enterprises so as to be able to reach out for the tourists who visit Boulder Dam and Lake Mead. It would not be the first time that persons with ulterior motives imposed upon a Representative or Senator by persuading him to offer a bill that would create an objectionable special privilege without divulging their ulterior motives.

Ickes bluntly told Pittman that "there is no necessity to create a State park if there is no purpose to sell liquor and permit gambling." [86]

The enraged Pittman turned his wrath on the "dictatorial" procedures of the Interior Department. The federal lands in western states, he charged, were "rapidly becoming a barony of the dictator at the head of the Department of the Interior." [87] Pittman's intimate friend Breckinridge Long noted that the Senator "hates Ickes with a wholesome hatred, and it does seem that Ickes goes out of his way sometimes to make things disagreeable and difficult for those Senators up there in his management of the public domain." [88] In spite of Ickes' opposition and the delaying tactics of Senator McCarran, the bill creating the park passed the Senate on June 13, 1939.* [89]

---

* Pittman supporters accused McCarran of being in the pay of the Boulder Dam Tours Company, which was opposed to the park plan. (See A. T. McCarter to K. P., March 7, 1939, Ickes vs. Pittman—Las Vegas Wash, 1939 Folder, Box 74.)

Pittman and McCarran had been feuding politically since 1916. In 1939, during

"You might possibly slip it through over in the House," Pittman instructed Congressman Scrugham. When Scrugham hesitated and thought of framing his own bill, Pittman reprimanded him: "I insist that you go to the two-thirds of the Committee that you say are with you and have them join with you in asking for a meeting for the sole purpose of reporting out my bill." [90] The House agreed to Pittman's bill after being assured that there would be no liquor or gambling in the park or within six miles of the exterior boundaries of the area. It was sent to the President on August 3, 1939. "I will be shocked beyond expression if he does not sign it," remarked the Senator.[91]

Ickes was determined to demand a veto. He "told the President how anxious I was that he should veto S. 2 . . . and he said that he would." [92] On August 10, 1939, Pittman received an unsigned memorandum from the President informing him of the veto. "I would gladly sign the bill," the note stated, "if I did not greatly fear the precedent created thereby. If we once start this policy we will have to go through with it with national parks, national monuments, national forests, etc. etc." The Senator, who had been bombarding the White House with demands that the bill be signed, became enraged at the President's "casual action in this matter." "How happy some of your most intimate friends and admirers would be if you cleaned off the barnacles from the hull of your Administration," he indignantly responded to the Chief Executive. "The law of self-defense is still the supreme law, whether it be invoked individually, by governments, or municipalities. Jefferson, as I understand it, considered the protection of minorities essential to good government." [93]

Roosevelt told Jim Scrugham that he did not understand why Pittman was so interested in the bill, and he attempted to soothe the Senator's feelings by asking him to sponsor a compromise measure to create a Boulder Dam National Recreational Area. Such a proposal, the President wrote, would "provide the people of Nevada with the opportunity they seek in this reservation, and at the same time, protect the national interests." Pittman, nevertheless, vowed to reintro-

---

the height of the Ickes-Pittman wrangle, McCarran wrote the President to express his "high opinion" of Ickes, recommending that he be retained as Secretary of the Interior (Patrick McCarran to F. D. R., June 10, 1939, Folder 4865, President's Personal Files, Franklin D. Roosevelt Papers, Hyde Park, N. Y.) .

duce his park measure at the next session. "I have ascertained definitely that I cannot carry the State Park bill over the President's veto," he confided to his friend Claude Mackey. "That ends the question for the present—only for the present. I expect to, and I know I will, carry the thing eventually. No use discussing it. Results count." [94] To Breckinridge Long, the Senator commented that he had been thinking of resigning as president pro tempore because of his growing disagreements with the President. [95]

Pittman considered himself a New Deal Democrat, although his continued opposition to Interior Department policies affecting Nevada led him to become "rather individualistic," as he phrased it. "I hate to take this opposition to the Administration but when the Administration listens to a man like Ickes, it is necessary. I doubt if he will be in office after next January. We may get a human being in there then." [96]

As before, the Senator jealously guarded the interests of his state. When national policy clashed with Nevada interests, he almost always defended the latter. In January, 1940, for example, the administration requested a three-year extension of the Reciprocal Trade Agreement Act, which was due to expire on June 12, 1940. The act, Franklin Roosevelt told Congress, "should be extended as an indispensable part of the foundation of any stable and durable peace. . . . I emphasize the leadership which this nation can take when the time comes for a renewal of world peace. Such an influence will be greatly weakened if this Government becomes a dog in the manger of trade selfishness."

The administration strongly supported the Reciprocal Trade Act. A bitter Senate debate, nevertheless, took place with Pittman taking the lead in opposing the bill, maintaining that executive trade agreements were really treaties which required ratification by the Senate. In long, dull speeches, he contended that reciprocity was unconstitutional as it delegated legislative powers to the Chief Executive. [97] (Presidential proclamations affecting silver somehow did not fall into this category!)

Breckinridge Long noted that Pittman actually opposed the pending copper agreement with Chile and a beef agreement with Argentina as being harmful to Nevada interests. (Pittman had successfully pigeonholed a proposed animal products convention with Argentina in the Foreign Relations Committee for five years as Nevada cattlemen did not favor it.) Long felt that the Senator's opposition to the Trade Agreements Act was entirely political. "Pittman thinks that the political consequences will be very severe and that we will lose four or five, possibly as many as ten, Senators from the Middle West and West if cattle and copper are insisted upon, because the fight in the Democratic primaries will be intense and the losing opposition may vote with the Republicans." [98]

The Trade Agreements Act passed the Senate on April 5, 1940, by a margin of only five votes, with fifteen Democrats joining the opposition. "We were fighting a losing fight from the start," wrote Pittman. "We had three votes in the majority the night before the vote. The power exerted was too strong for us to hold these votes. You can understand the power when you realize that Schwartz of Wyoming and Schwellenbach of Washington voted against us. The fight is not ended. Believe me, I'll bring it up again. . . . It's not the end of the fight." [99]

It was the end of the fight. Pittman's health was failing. His stamina was gone. His temper had grown short, his speech blunt. No longer could he concentrate on the complexities of legislation. In his last year, the Senator still bitterly resented Harold Ickes and those who opposed silver legislation. What he resented the most, however, was the failure of the President to consult him. Senator Pittman, Long noted, had become "somewhat opposed to Roosevelt." [100]

CHAPTER VI

Compromise and Indecision

I

The chairman of the Foreign Relations Committee is the only member charged by the Senate with specific responsibilities. All official business is handled by or through him, and the importance of the group varies with his ability. Under Charles Sumner, as Henry Adams observed, it became a Department of Foreign Relations over which Sumner haughtily ruled. "The headship of the first committee of the Senate," wrote Sumner, "is equal in position to anything in our government under the President; and it leaves to the Senator great opportunities." [1] During the Hoover administration, one European news agency cabled its Washington correspondent: "Never mind Hoover statement. Rush comment from Borah!" [2] With less dominating chairmen, however, the executive branch is able to overshadow the committee.

With the Roosevelt landslide in 1932, the Democrats gained control of the Senate for the first time since 1918. Seniority made Key Pittman chairman of the Foreign Relations Committee. Slender, graying, now sixty-one, he had been a committee member for seventeen years. Pittman's principal interest when he came to Washington had been to do something for the mining interests, especially silver. His power in foreign affairs was a political accident because he had no particular interest in the subject but had sought appointment to the committee in 1916, an election year for him, to impress the people back home. Seniority and party organization combined to make him chairman at a time when the fascist powers threatened to destroy the European democracies.

Pittman described his "foreign philosophy" to several friends after officially being confirmed by the Senate—the summation being that diplomats should concentrate on finding solutions to vexing international economic problems. He envisioned the chairman as a mediator working to maintain harmony between the President and the Democrats. After the administration stated its policy, he believed it was his duty to obtain sufficient support in the committee to report the bill and then secure enough votes in the Senate to pass it. This would require compromise and Pittman thought of himself as the ideal conciliator. ("I would rather live and compromise than die for a principle.") [3] Thus, his theoretical conception of the chairmanship. The practical application, however, usually failed.

During his eight years as chairman, the Senator's addiction to alcohol grew progressively worse. He had a refrigerator installed in the committee room in which liquor was stored. At meetings or hearings he always had a glass before him and continually sipped whiskey. Pittman was a steady drinker—seven days a week, consuming more than a pint a day, telling his aides that his doctor recommended a certain amount of alcohol for his system. About twice a month, Pittman would "go out on a binge and get himself plastered." For days he would go without eating a substantial meal but kept right on drinking. When Washington hotels and bars refused to serve him, the Senator would whip out his silver pistol, which he almost always carried with him, and threatened to "shoot up" the establishment. At times like this his wife was the only person able to quiet him. When Pittman became intoxicated, she nursed him by pouring black coffee into him. The Senator would never quite reach sobriety when he would begin his regular drinking pattern again. Of course, in this physical condition, many of the intricacies and subtleties of foreign relations bypassed him. (One eminent psychiatrist, Dr. Adolph Meyer, applied the term "Promotion depression" to certain individuals who advanced to positions which they were not competent to handle and who developed depressive reactions because of their anticipated failures. These people drank "to enjoy relief from the necessity of living up to standards unnaturally high for them.") [4]

Almost immediately after taking office, the Roosevelt administration announced that it would seek congressional approval of legislation granting the President power to halt arms shipments to aggressor nations.[5] The State Department championed this embargo and Secretary Hull hoped that it would have the backing of Republicans as well as Democrats. President Hoover had recommended a similar resolution to Congress in a special message of January 10, 1933. The Foreign Relations Committee had reported favorably and the bill passed the Senate during the last weeks of the Seventy-second Congress. A motion to reconsider, though, blocked passage and the session adjourned without acting on it. After a careful study of all questions of law and policy involved in such an embargo, the Roosevelt administration decided to urge enactment.[6]

The resolution authorized the President to prohibit the export of arms and munitions to any country he might designate. This attempt to change the traditional policy of American neutrality sparked a long debate in Congress because no such sweeping discretionary power had ever been conferred on any Chief Executive. The basic issue was whether or not the President should have authority to apply embargoes against any nation or nations which he might name as the aggressor. Many legislators feared that this might inadvertently involve the United States in an unwanted war.[7]

The administration resolution passed the House on April 17, 1933, and was sent to the Senate, where it was referred to the Foreign Relations Committee. The senators, not inspired by the cooperative spirit of the first hundred days, ripped into the bill. Tom Connally frankly told the President that he should first learn "the general philosophies of each Committee member before plowing ahead" with the arms embargo.[8] After several acrimonious sessions, Pittman was forced to inform Hull that there were serious objections to the resolution, the most important being granting the President power to determine aggressor nations. The members had concluded, the Senator wrote, that the exercise of such discretionary authority, especially against Japan, might involve the United States in war. Pittman invited Hull to appear before the committee to answer questions and clarify the administration's proposal, but the Secretary chose to respond in writing.[9] Hull's response reiterated the peaceful intent of the resolution and he urged adoption without any changes. This defense did not satisfy a majority of the committee, who rallied behind Senators Hiram Johnson and Arthur Vandenberg, opponents of the discretionary measure from the outset, to amend the House resolution requiring the President to embargo arms shipments to *all* belligerents.[10]

Pittman now informed the President that his committee would not accept Hull's recommendations but would pass only a mandatory embargo. Roosevelt apparently gave his "reluctant consent," but Hull so strenuously opposed any amendment which would weaken the force of the original resolution that he strongly urged the President not to support another measure. At his press conference on May 29, the day before the Foreign Relations Committee was scheduled to report out the amended resolution, the Secretary stated that the committee's views did not conform to those of the President or of himself, and in order to avoid a prolonged controversy the administration had reluctantly decided to drop the issue for that session of Congress.[11]

Roosevelt's first legislative effort in foreign affairs failed. This was a major defeat as it involved the administration's initial attempt to have power granted to the Chief Executive for use against an aggressor nation. Hull wrote that the Senate's failure to pass the arms embargo "was a real disappointment." Perhaps, though, through this experience, both he and the President learned that the strong-willed, independent thinkers on the Foreign Relations Committee would not act as rubber stamps. Gradually the administration would realize the value of consulting and compromising with its members. This was the first encounter with the committee and its new chairman. Others soon followed.

While the New Deal domestic program rolled along in Congress with relative ease, the administration continued to have difficulty with the Foreign Relations Committee. Toward the end of 1934, Secretary Hull decided to press for passage of the World Court protocol in an effort to "help buttress the whole structure of whatever remained in the way of order under law." [12] The protocol had been ratified by the Senate in 1926, but with a reservation that the court should not have authority to give an advisory opinion in any matter in which the United States claimed an interest without this government's prior consent. Several member countries refused to accept this conditional association, which in effect voided the Senate's ratification. In 1932, the Foreign Relations Committee again reported for adherence with similar reservations. The Senate took no action and the matter automatically went back to the committee, where it was when Pittman became chairman. The Senator evinced little more than a lukewarm interest in the court, and until prodded by the State Department he found excuses to delay committee consideration. Writing

Carrie Chapman Catt in February, 1934, for example, he bluntly declared that hearings could not be held as he had too many other important committee meetings to attend.[13] On other occasions, the Senator told interrogators that he had difficulty in obtaining a quorum in order to decide when testimony on the court should be taken. The issue remained dormant until Secretary Hull, with the President's approval, decided to press for membership.

On January 3, 1935, Assistant Secretary Francis B. Sayre discussed with Pittman the possibility of ratification of the World Court protocols, stating that the President was now prepared to urge "clean-cut adherence." Roosevelt, Sayre said, was anxious to have the adherence resolution passed without any restrictive provisions, but the Senator replied that he strongly opposed all court advisory opinions. He suggested that the Secretary tell the President that it would be better, therefore, if he did not assume the leadership in the fight either in the Foreign Relations Committee or on the Senate floor, adding that Senator Joseph Robinson might be placed in charge of the resolution as he agreed with the administration's views. Pittman predicted a long and bitter fight. While he assumed that his committee would report the administration's measure, he seemed uncertain as to whether it could be brought to a final vote.[14]

Following this conversation with the assistant secretary, Pittman wrote the President detailing his position and asked Roosevelt to relieve him from presenting the administration's resolution to the Senate. Predicting certain defeat, he described Hull's proposal as being contrary to the 1932 Democratic platform, and that "failure to yield to the adoption of reservations that some of our leading Senators deem essential will bring about unfortunate results." After conferring with Pittman, Roosevelt did yield. On January 9, 1935, at the President's personal request, Senator Robinson attached the disputed advisory reservation to the State Department's resolution, which the Foreign Relations Committee promptly reported out by a vote of 14 to 7.[15] Assistant Secretary Sayre advised the President that the inclusion of this amendment would "now remove the ground for much hostility and opposition." [16]

On January 14, 1935, the Senate began a two-week debate of the World Court protocols and the adherence resolution. The case against the court was presented by Senate veterans—La Follette, Johnson,

Borah, and Shipstead—who knew their parts by heart. Hiram Johnson voiced the popular argument when he asked: "Why do we enter it? Not for America, not for our beloved Republic; we enter it to meddle and muddle, under an hysterical internationalism in those controversies that Europe has and that Europe never will be rid of." [17] Except for a few parliamentary questions, Pittman sat silently and watched Senator Robinson lead the administration's forces.

As the speeches continued day after day, the opposition successfully roused the passions upon which it relied. William Randolph Hearst proved his right to the title of America's No. 1 Isolationist. No attack on the court proved too preposterous to be printed across the front of his newspapers. In addition, Hearst maintained a Washington lobby which quietly cornered doubtful senators. "It was a magnificent piece of work you did," William Borah wrote Hearst. "The work of your staff here in Washington was everything that could be desired." [18] From Detroit, Father Charles E. Coughlin accused the President of "selling the American people to the World Court." Invoking Washington, Jefferson, and God, Coughlin pleaded: "Today—tomorrow may be too late—today, whether you can afford it or not, send your Senators telegrams telling them to vote 'no' on our entrance into the World Court with or without reservations." The priest spoke on January 27, 1935. By January 29, the day of the Senate vote, over 40,000 telegrams had been sent in response to his request. Messengers carted them by wheelbarrow loads into the Senate Office Building. Western Union hired thirty-five extra clerks, Postal Telegraph fifteen.* [19] Delay and debate had proved effective for the court's opponents.

When Senator Robinson took the floor for his final plea, he denounced the "unfair, unjust, unreasonable propaganda carried on during the course of this debate." Pittman, supposedly the administration's chief foreign affairs spokesman in the Senate, remained mute.[20] (Henry Stimson had written in 1932 that he thought Pittman unalterably opposed the court in any form.) [21] On January 29, the treaty failed to receive the necessary two-thirds majority, the final count being 52 to 36 in favor, Pittman voting in the affirmative. Roosevelt praised Robinson for his personal and political courage on be-

---

* Borah cabled Coughlin: "How deeply indebted we are to you for the great victory. Thank you again and again" (William E. Borah to Charles E. Coughlin, January 30, 1935, World Court Folder, Box 391, Borah Papers, Library of Congress) .

half of the cause of peace. "As to the thirty-six Senators who placed themselves on record against the principle of a World Court," the President continued, "I am inclined to think that if they ever get to Heaven they will be doing a great deal of apologizing for a very long time—that is if God is against war—and I think He is." And to Elihu Root, Roosevelt acknowledged that the "wind everywhere blows against us," but "in time we shall win the long fight." [22] Three weeks after the defeat of the World Court protocol, Pittman complained to the President that "no one today knows what is the foreign policy of our Government. . . . There is no leadership in the Senate. . . . I will make my sacrifice for you because I know the sacrifice you are making." [23] His letter went unanswered.

II

The approach of the Italo-Ethiopian War and the sensational revelations of the Nye committee, which held armament manufacturers and bankers responsible for the World War, aroused public interest in neutrality and in the regulation of the arms traffic. Some fifteen bills were introduced in Congress during the 1935 session providing for various types of restrictions on munition exports. The Neutrality Act of 1935 was finally framed from this maze of proposals.

Key Pittman, along with other congressional leaders, had been urging that "we keep out of somebody else's war." War in Europe was inevitable, he predicted, and America must remain neutral, even if it meant waiving some rights recognized by international law:

> We must remain neutral. Our government must refrain from making or doing or permitting any act that may be construed as an unneutral act. . . . We should not, in my opinion, enter into any monetary, financial or commercial treaties or agreements with any European power until the impending crisis is over.[24]

When Hitler announced his intention to increase the size of the German army, the Senator quickly warned his fellow Americans to avoid becoming involved, even obliquely, in European diplomacy.[25]

Pittman's personal interest in neutrality legislation was accelerated when the State Department informed him in April, 1935, that the Nye committee planned to investigate the subject. Fearing an intrusion on his authority, the Senator bluntly warned the department not to furnish Nye with any information.[26] "I should think it would be the duty of the State Department," he wrote to Wallace Murray, Chief of the Near Eastern Division, "in the event that the [Nye] Committee should call upon the State Department for any information . . . to respectfully decline to furnish such evidence upon the grounds that the resolution creating a special committee of the Senate does not grant such committee authority to make such investigations or report, but that, on the contrary the Committee on Foreign Relations of the Senate, a standing committee, has been granted such jurisdiction and authority." * [27] Secretary Hull brought Pittman's objections to the at-

---

* Secretary Hull explained that the Roosevelt administration initially approved the munitions investigation, expecting that a Democrat rather than an isolationist Republican would be made chairman. The appointment of Senator Nye, Hull wrote, was a tactical error for which he held Senator Pittman responsible (Hull, *The Memoirs of Cordell Hull* [New York: Macmillan, 1948], pp. 215–216; 398). The whole story behind Nye's selection is not known and this writer's letters to him asking him to explain his selection have gone unanswered, but Pittman appears to have had nothing to do with Nye's appointment. The initiative that led to the introduction of the resolution calling for an investigation of the munitions industry seems to have come not from the Senate isolationists but from a Miss Dorothy Detzer, secretary and professional lobbyist for the Women's International League for Peace and Freedom. Miss Detzer first approached Senator George Norris and asked him to sponsor a Senate investigation. He declined but recommended Senator Gerald Nye as "the best fitted for the task." Although Nye had already refused, she tried a second time. He consented and several weeks later he carried out his promise (Dorothy Detzer, *Appointment on the Hill* [New York: Holt, 1948], pp. 151 ff.). Senator Nye introduced his resolution calling for an investigation into the munitions industry on February 8, 1934, and asked that it be referred to the Committee on Foreign Relations. Three weeks later, Pittman received unanimous consent discharging the Foreign Relations Committee from further consideration of the resolution. Pittman requested that the resolution be referred to the Committee on Military Affairs, which the Senator said "should have jurisdiction over the proposed investigation" (*Congressional Record,* 73 Cong. 2 Sess. Vol. 78, Pt. 4 [March 1, 1934], p. 3447). The Committee on Military Affairs reported favorably on Nye's resolution and on April 19, 1934, Vice President Garner appointed seven senators—four Democrats and three Republicans—to the Special Committee to Investigate the Munitions Industry. Garner did not designate a chairman (*Congressional Record, ibid.,* Pt. 7 [April 19, 1934], p. 6896). At the first meeting of the committee, Nye was selected chairman (*New York Times,* April 24, 1934, 14:1). The reason why Democratic Senators Pope, Bone, Clark, and Sheppard agreed to the appointment of Nye is unknown.

tention of Senator Nye, who subsequently stopped preparations for his neutrality investigation.[28] In the meanwhile, the State Department had begun its own detailed study in June, 1934, two months before the Nye committee had started its munition hearings.

At the beginning of July, 1935, Senator Pittman reported out from the Foreign Relations Committee two bills written by Senators Nye and Clark. One prohibited the extension of credit and issuance of loans to belligerents; the other regulated the issuance of passports to American citizens in wartime. Roosevelt and Hull had asked Pittman to kill these resolutions and it was their understanding that Pittman agreed to do this. Both were surprised, therefore, when the Senator placed the two bills on the Senate calendar.[29] Secretary Hull, as Tom Connally recalled, "came running to the committee to plead with them to withdraw these measures. He promised to send over his departmental bill in its stead." After a bitter argument amongst the members of the committee, a majority voted to table the resolutions until they considered the Hull measure.[30] The Secretary explained the complicated nature of the issues involved in neutrality legislation and suggested that a subcommittee be appointed to confer with the department. At the next regular committee meeting, on Senator Hiram Johnson's motion, Pittman directed Senators Borah, Johnson, Robinson, Connally, and himself to meet with State Department representatives.[31]

These semi-weekly sessions began on July 30, 1935, and continued for about a month. Hull or Under-Secretary William Phillips attended each meeting at which the department confidentially explained the intricate problems of neutrality to the senators. Pittman, somewhat surprised at the complexity of the issue, invited Nye and Clark, as well as other senators who had introduced neutrality resolutions, to be present. From the very first, a fundamental difference existed. The State Department maintained that discretionary embargo power should be given to the President while a majority of the subcommittee thought that all legislation should be mandatory, fixed, and inflexible.

On July 31, the State Department sent Pittman and Congressman Sam McReynolds, chairman of the House Committee on Foreign Affairs, their draft of a neutrality bill but it soon became apparent to Hull that the Foreign Relations Committee would not approve any discretionary powers for the President. Finally, when an impasse was reached, spokesmen for the State Department told Pittman "that they preferred their discretionary section but that they would not oppose the section proposed by the sub-committee" if it were adopted by the full Foreign Relations Committee. With this assurance, the committee tabled the Hull neutrality bill on August 7.[32]

Hull reviewed the Senate situation with the President and urged him to personally request Congress to pass a discretionary arms embargo to be applied in the event of an Italo-Ethiopian war. In a confidential memo, he wrote that the world situation had made it imperative for the administration to make a vigorous effort to secure its enactment.[33] On August 19, the Secretary gave the President the State Department's draft resolution and a proposed letter addressed to Pittman stating that the President had come to the conclusion that passage of a discretionary neutrality resolution "would assist in the present efforts toward the maintenance of peace and, in the event of the outbreak of hostilities, would serve the best interests of the country." As a postscript, Roosevelt added: "I hope you will note that as drawn this is only a temporary emergency act to cover the recess period of the Congress. The Act would expire 30 days after Congress reconvenes." [34]

Roosevelt signed this letter but it was not sent. Instead, Steve Early telephoned Pittman to say that the President requested that a discretionary arms embargo resolution be introduced in the Senate. Pittman, evidently surprised by this move, doubted the wisdom of it. He told Early he was perfectly willing to introduce the resolution as an administration measure, but he felt confident that it would not receive the approval of the Foreign Relations Committee or a majority vote in the Senate. "The Committee has," Pittman continued, "with the exception of three votes . . . decided that any embargo upon the exportation of armaments, ammunition, war materials, etc. shall apply equally to both or all of the warring countries. I will not make any comment when I introduce the resolution if the President so desires, but I assure him that in my opinion it will not be approved by the Foreign Relations Committee and will not be approved by the United States Senate. I believe he is entitled to this information because I believe that the adverse report by the Foreign Relations Committee and the defeat of the resolution upon the floor of the Senate will do great harm to our foreign policy." [35]

In another conversation with Early that same day, Pittman told of a compromise bill which he was preparing and how he had been "trying to harmonize things and get away from that fool Munitions Committee. . . . I tell you, Steve, the President is riding for a fall if he insists on designating the aggressors in accordance with the wishes of the League of Nations. He had better have nothing than to get licked, and I assure you that is what he is facing. I will introduce it if he wants to take the licking. I will introduce it on behalf of the administration without comment, but he will be licked as sure as hell." [36] The President yielded to Pittman and chose to drop the issue.

On the following day, August 20, 1935, Senators Nye and Bone started a filibuster which they threatened to continue until the Senate passed some sort of mandatory neutrality legislation. Only the week before, Senate Majority Leader Joseph Robinson was asked if neutrality legislation might be considered at that session. "There is no chance," he replied. But as he spoke, senators were alarmed at the London and Paris dispatches. The isolationists twisted history as they recalled that twenty years previously, President Wilson, the State Department, and unofficial Ambassador-at-Large Edwin M. House had played Great Britain's game. Now they suspected that President Roosevelt, the State Department, and Ambassador-at-Large Norman Davis were ready to play that game again. The Senate peace men, therefore, proclaimed themselves ready to filibuster indefinitely until neutrality legislation was brought to a vote. "I cannot imagine Congress leaving Washington without meeting this issue head-on," Senator Homer Bone declared. "I do not wish to have my country again plunged into war, and I am willing to do anything to prevent that cataclysmic horror again overcoming this country as it did in 1917. . . . Of what use is it to settle utility issues or anything else of the like, when the peace of the world is threatened? I don't want to return to my State of Washington and look into the faces of mothers whose boys may be carrying muskets without adopting this legislation." One by one, other senators took up the cry. "We were sucked into that last war," stated Senator Arthur Vandenberg, "simply because we had no neutrality policy." [37]

In an effort to stop the filibuster, Senator Robinson assured Bone that the Foreign Relations Committee had authorized Pittman that very morning to draft a neutrality resolution. It was being prepared, he told his colleagues, and Senator Pittman would put an end to the filibuster within half an hour. When Pittman did not appear, several senators left the floor to find him and urge that he bring in his bill. To their consternation, they found that instead of writing, he had been drinking and was in no condition for work. They spent an hour trying to sober him while the filibuster continued. When the Senator appeared to be in condition to draft the resolution, they took him back to his office, and with the assistance of Senator Borah, he went to work. At this important point, when the administration needed a strong, forceful spokesman in the Senate, Pittman proved that he was not capable of withstanding the emotional pressures allied with leadership. At about six o'clock, Pittman was ready with his neutrality bill and pages assisted him to his seat. The Senator's bill and Robinson's promise that it would be considered at the earliest practicable moment put an end to the filibuster.[38]

Pittman framed a compromise measure. He designed the resolution, he said, to produce "a great deal of harmonization" among the different Senate factions, but he unintentionally gave the President a considerable measure of discretion. It provided that the President "shall" impose an arms embargo "upon the outbreak or during the progress of war." This in itself was a double-edged provision, for the mandatory embargo did not include all war materials but only implements of war, and these were not defined. The President "may" extend this embargo to other countries as they became involved in the conflict. The bill established a National Munitions Control Board to register munitions manufacturers and license their exports, something Secretary Hull had previously suggested and very much favored. (In including the National Munitions Control Board, however, the Senator mutilated the original State Department draft by leaving out important provisions, apparently at random, and by adding himself to the membership of the board.) Pittman's section prohibiting American vessels from carrying munitions to belligerents was a concession to Senators Nye, Bone, Vandenberg, and Clark. The resolution also gave the President power to withhold protection from American citizens traveling on belligerent ships, a provision which Senator Borah had demanded. Pittman's neutrality resolution, the title alone placating public clamor, satisfied neither those who demanded a mandatory resolution nor those who favored strong Presidential discretionary authority.*

A few hours after Pittman had introduced his resolution, a dismayed President summoned Secretary Hull, Assistant Secretary R. Walton Moore, and Representative McReynolds to a solemn White House conference. As he entered the White House, McReynolds shouted to reporters: "They can't jam unsatisfactory neutrality legislation down my throat." A reluctant Chief Executive, however, with the consent of his Secretary of State, accepted this mandatory arms embargo provided that it expired on February 29, 1936. The Foreign Relations Committee agreed to this time limitation, and on August 24, 1935, by a vote of 79 to 2, an otherwise languid Senate rushed through Pittman's resolution in twenty-five minutes. President Roosevelt signed the bill on August 31, and America's first attempt to legislate against war became law. Philip C. Jessup aptly characterized the act as a "hodgepodge of ideas scrambled together in the legislative frying-pan in the closing days of a hot session in Washington." [39]

The Neutrality Act was, to a large degree, a result of the feeling created by the Nye committee. What began as a campaign to remove the profits from war ended in an attempt to keep the United States out of war through appropriate legislation. After signing the bill, Roosevelt issued a press release so ambiguous and couched in moralistic platitudes that two eminent historians have reached diametrical conclusions as to what he meant. Charles Beard viewed Roosevelt's words as hewing to the isolationist line, while Basil Rauch called it "the strongest statement in favor of collective security the President

---

* For a discussion of this point, see John C. Donovan, "Congress, and the Making of Neutrality Legislation, 1935–1939" (unpublished Ph.D. dissertation, Harvard University, 1949), pp. 57 ff., and David M. Leach, "The American Approach to Neutrality" (unpublished Ph.D. dissertation, University of Rochester, 1959), pp. 235–317.

Senator J. Hamilton Lewis introduced a resolution which would have allowed the Executive complete discretionary powers (*Congressional Record*, 74 Cong. 1 Sess. Vol. 79, Pt. 13 [August 21, 1935], p. 13953). Senators Clark and Nye, on the other hand, believed it "an inescapable conclusion that the policy of the United States must be fixed *before* the declaration of a European war" (Bennett Champ Clark and Gerald P. Nye to K. P., August 18, 1935, Correspondence N Folder, Sen. 74A–F9 [123C], Papers of the United States Senate Foreign Relations Committee, National Archives (hereafter cited as F.R.C.).

made until the Quarantine Address of October, 1937." * [40] Perhaps, Roosevelt would have shrugged off both Beard and Rauch. He might have reminded them that the President is also the leader of his party and as such he cannot be a dogmatist. Roosevelt opposed some of the provisions of the Neutrality Act but he also saw much good to it. When Ambassador William Dodd wrote from Berlin that he wanted to resign as a way of protesting the action by Congress, the President answered that the act was by no means the "unmitigated evil" that Dodd thought it to be.[41]

Pittman's drinking habits sometimes caused the administration considerable embarrassment. While under the influence of alcohol, the Senator's actions usually were not guided by critical ability, but rather by a compulsive drive characteristic of a chronic drinker.[42] Alcohol often caused Pittman to act on rash impulse, failing to grasp the importance of what he was doing. In December, 1935, for example, reporters quoted him as saying that Japan's ultimate objective was the conquest of the world and that, if the movement continued, the United States would be forced into a defensive war in the Pacific. When asked about the statement at his press conference, President Roosevelt demurred, claiming he had not read it. Secretary Hull said he did not care to comment because he had not seen the complete text. Although administration officials preferred to ignore the statement, as they did the Senator's comment in August, 1933, that the Monroe Doctrine should be scrapped, the Japanese embassy cabled a detailed report to Tokyo. Ambassador Hirosi Saito told reporters that he planned no formal protest to the State Department, but he expressed considerable regret that the statement was made by the chairman of the Foreign Relations Committee, whose pronouncements had more than the usual force.[43] Harold Ickes recorded in his diary that the President deprecated Pittman's comments before a meeting of the full cabinet, saying that he could not understand why Pittman should have said what he did considering the position he held in the Senate. "Of course," Ickes concluded, "the explanation may be that Pittman had been drinking too much. This would not have been an unusual situation for him." [44]

* On the flyleaf of his copy of Charles Beard's *A Foreign Policy for America*, which appeared in 1940, Roosevelt wrote: "40 years' hard and continuous study has brought forth an inbred mouse."

III

The Neutrality Act of 1935 had been in effect one month when the State Department began to study ways to improve it. ("Judge Moore, Hackworth and I are hard at work attempting to draft another neutrality bill," wrote Joseph Green. "That is a thankless task of which I am thoroughly weary, but it has to be done. At present we are attempting to find the impossible compromise between what the Administration wants and what we can presumably get through the Senate.") [45] Secretary Hull did not think the 1935 act should be allowed to expire on February 29, 1936, without new legislation being passed, because he feared that the Italo-Ethiopian war would probably still be raging. Public opinion, more and more alarmed by warlike developments in Europe and Asia, insisted on neutrality legislation as a means, however fallacious, of keeping the United States out of war. "There was no longer too much to be hoped from Congress on Executive discretion," Hull noted. "The opinion of the public and of a large portion of Congress was running strongly to the view that, to permit the President to apply the Act as to one, all or none of the belligerents would push the nation into war." [46]

The State Department formulated a bill which continued the mandatory arms embargo but which prohibited the export of all other war materials to belligerents in excess of normal quantities. The resolution assigned the President discretionary power to determine what "all other war materials" were and what constituted abnormal quantities. On December 31, 1935, the President and Secretary Hull met with Pittman; Representative Sam McReynolds; Representative John O'Connor, chairman of the House Rules Committee; and Assistant Secretary R. Walton Moore to discuss the proposed administration resolution. Hull conferred with Pittman and McReynolds again on January 2, 1936, to review the details, and on the following day Pittman and McReynolds introduced identical neutrality bills. The Senator assured his colleagues that the administration intended to keep the United States out of war and definitely would not assist the League of Nations in any collective effort. [47]

Pittman announced that he favored the administration proposal without any reservations and did not see any reason for public hearings or for delay by the Foreign Relations Committee. "It is my purpose at the [next] regular meeting to ask for a vote on the report of this bill," Pittman naively told his close friend Pat Harrison. "I am satisfied that each member of the Committee will be well prepared to vote his opinion on the subject—in fact upon the whole bill,—as he would be after the most exhaustive hearings." A majority of the committee, predicted Pittman, would vote for the resolution.[48] Obviously, the Senator had not been reading Senator Borah's speeches, for he completely underestimated the independence of his fellow committee members and the strong opposition in the Senate to any presidential discretionary powers. After just one meeting with his committee, Pittman confided to Hull "that members are taking the matter far more seriously than they did at the last session. It is evident that there is going to be strong opposition." [49] The Senator, nevertheless, remained hopeful.

The administration bill, which granted discretionary power to the President to regulate trade with belligerents, met deadly opposition from a majority of the Foreign Relations Committee. Senators Johnson and Borah took the lead in opposing the bill, insisting that open hearings be held. Johnson told Pittman that the administration "had discarded a great volume of international law which had been evolved out of many long and bloody struggles and we are scrapping a policy which, in days gone by—'The Freedom of the Seas'—has been tenaciously clung to, and valiantly fought for by the American Republic." [50] After three weeks of intensive debate, the committee remained hopelessly deadlocked. Senator Vandenberg strode fiercely out of one session, smarting: "Neutrality goes 'round and around, but it doesn't come out anywhere." [51]

During these deliberations, the White House maintained a truckling policy toward Pittman, whose support, no matter how weak, was required for the passage of the discretionary bill. (Assistant Secretary Moore noted that Pittman jealously guarded his position and bitterly resented committee members who issued public statements on foreign affairs, which he thought belonged to his private domain. Early in the session, for example, an article appeared in the Hearst papers to the effect that Hull had insulted the Senate Foreign Relations Committee by requesting the chairman to call on him to discuss pending neutrality legislation instead of going up to the Capitol to see the chairman. The State Department traced the origin of the story to Pittman's office. The Senator was also indignant toward members of Hull's staff, who he felt "interfered in matters that were none of their business.") [52] Secretary Hull and Moore both advised the President that they considered it "highly important to show how confidently the Senator is relied on to lead what promises to be a bitter fight." * [53] Roosevelt agreed and wrote Pittman of his utmost confidence in the Senator's knowledge, judgment, and ability.[54] Differences of opinion were so broad and divergent in the Foreign Relations Committee, though, that reporting out of any neutrality measure would probably have sparked a filibuster on the Senate floor. By the first week in February, both Hull and Pittman knew that the administration had lost in its attempt to have any discretionary powers granted to the President.

On January 10, 1936, the committee began open hearings and the isolationists, led by Senators Hiram Johnson and William Borah, dominated the sessions. They inserted a provision in the bill specifically declaring that the United States did not surrender any of its rights under international law. Johnson called Professor Edwin Borchard of Yale University and John Bassett Moore, one-time justice of the World Court, to tell the committee that the neutrality resolution more likely would bring war than peace. Johnson, therefore, introduced a new obstruction into the neutrality debates—opposition to neutrality on the grounds that such legislation violated the traditional right of freedom of the seas. The other extreme on the committee, represented by Senator Arthur Vandenberg, thought it a necessity to embargo the exports of all goods to belligerents to prevent the United States from being dragged into war.[55] (Assistant Secretary

* Pittman thought little of William Phillips, who served as Under-Secretary 1933–1936. He doubted Phillips' "unselfish loyalty to anyone" except himself and considered his choice as Under-Secretary as unfortunate (K. P. to F. D. R., February 11, 1933, Roosevelt 1932–1939 Folder, Box 16, Key Pittman Papers, Library of Congress (hereafter cited by folder and box number). Sumner Welles succeeded Phillips. Pittman had advised against Welles' appointment. He thought that Welles was ambitious, aggressive, and filled with "youthful confidence," and that he did not fit into the State Department organization (K. P. to Cordell Hull, April 9, 1937, Secretary of State Folder, Sen. 75–F9–1 [105G], F.R.C.). In discussing the qualifications of another Hull assistant assigned to the neutrality problem, Pittman bluntly wrote: "I have nothing against the damn fool except that he is a damn fool" (K. P. to Hiram Johnson, September 23, 1935, Correspondence J Folder, Sen. 74A–F9 [123B], F.R.C.).

Moore held secret conferences with both Borah and Johnson to explain the administration's position. "Although he has softened a little," he reported to Roosevelt, "Johnson does not seem to be able to get rid of the idea that in some sort of fashion, if enacted, it might tend to link us up with the League of Nations.") [56] After six weeks of wrangling, Pittman finally realized that measures favored by either extreme could not pass at this session, and so he introduced a compromise proposal. His new resolution, which had administration approval, simply made minor changes in the existing law and extended it for fourteen months, ending May 1, 1937. The State Department reluctantly gave its endorsement after the committee informally agreed that it was impossible to report out any other measure. The Foreign Relations Committee thereupon unanimously adopted Pittman's compromise plan.

A heated Senate debate followed. Pittman repeatedly explained to his colleagues that his committee had been unable to resolve the basic questions of what constituted the "essentials of war" and what items, if any, should be enumerated; or whether all such questions should be left to the discretion of the President. Senator Homer T. Bone questioned Pittman's sincerity by reintroducing the administration's original neutrality bill, and Senator James Pope criticized Pittman for deserting his own measure, accusing him of railroading his compromise through the committee. Pittman defended his action by reminding his colleagues that "legislation is a compromise. . . . I am so anxious to save the existing law that I am unwilling to assert my own views unyieldingly and die with them if necessary." * [57] A majority agreed with him and his new bill passed on February 18, 1936. This represents, boasted the Senator, "the furthest advance ever made by any government in its efforts to protect its neutrality and to escape the dangers of war."[58]

* One slight change, however, was at least a little comforting to the administration. The phraseology in the old act, "that upon the outbreak or during the progress of war between, or among, two or more foreign States, the President shall proclaim . . ." was changed to: "Whenever the President shall find that there exists a state of war between, or among two or more foreign states . . ." This left it to the President to determine whether or not there was a state of war. The importance of this change became manifest the following year, when Japan waged an undeclared war against China, despite which the Neutrality Act was not applied (Hull, *op. cit.*, p. 467) .

IV

The Seventy-fifth Congress convened on January 5, 1937, and was in session only one day when the administration called upon it to insulate the United States against any international conflict originating from the Spanish Civil War, which had begun during the previous summer. Since the 1935 and 1936 arms embargo statutes did not apply to civil conflicts, the administration immediately imposed a "moral embargo." Certain exporters, nevertheless, applied to the State Department for arms export licenses. The President thereupon gave his support for an amendment to the Neutrality Act to cover the Spanish situation.

Roosevelt, Assistant Secretary Moore, Representative McReynolds, and Senator Pittman cooperated in framing the administration's resolution, which banned all shipments of munitions and implements of war to Spain. An emergency measure, it was to be disconnected from general neutrality legislation. At first, Pittman thought the Spanish problem should be considered along with the entire neutrality issue. Secretary Moore, realizing how much time might be consumed in such a debate, prevailed upon him to deal with the matter as an urgent measure applying only to Spain. After considerable urging, Pittman "finally agreed" but insisted on seeing the President. At a hastily arranged meeting, the Senator pressed for his own explanatory preamble "to tell the world that we will not be involved." Roosevelt acquiesced only after Secretary Moore assured him that the phraseology was ambiguous and "meant nothing." [59]

Pittman introduced the joint resolution in the Senate on January 6, 1937, requesting unanimous consent for immediate consideration without reference to the Foreign Relations Committee. In response to pointed questions, the Nevadan maintained that the resolution, which denied arms to the recognized Spanish government as well as to the rebel forces, did not aid Franco's army "as they control a number of ports and have just the same access to imports as does the Government of Spain." It is our duty, he told his colleagues, "not to think of either of the opposing forces in Spain but to think of our peace and our own country. Two forms of government are fighting in Spain in what is called a 'civil war,' but it is a fight of foreign theories of government . . . in which the opposing forces are aided and sympathized with by great, powerful governments who espoused one cause or another." * [60]

Several senators began to question the wording of the resolution, especially the vague preamble, and it appeared that a prolonged discussion might follow. Senator Vandenberg, for example, stated that it contained equivocal statements. Pittman, perhaps understanding the importance of prompt action, notified the President that he intended to withdraw his preamble as a "compromise move." [61] The resolution was then unanimously passed and sent to the House. Thus, both the Legislative and Executive branches of the government joined in singular harmony in believing that to keep aloof from the Spanish conflict was in the best interests of the United States. This resolution, though, only prefaced the neutrality debates of this session.

"I cannot see how Europe is to escape a war," Claude Bowers wrote Pittman from Madrid. "This continent is a madhouse just now and I am afraid it is headed for another war out of which anything may come." [62] To eliminate, as Pittman phrased it, "the chief causes which drag a country into war," the Senator introduced his own neutrality resolution on January 22, 1937. He framed the final version without having consulted either the White House or the State Department, but both the President and Hull were aware of the proposed bill. ("Generally speaking," Hull wrote in 1937, "the attitude of the Department the last two or three years has been more in the direction of permissive legislation as a policy than Congress has been disposed to follow. In those circumstances it is natural that the Department would not send over a bill of its own but would be disposed to look with more favor on proposed legislation in either House that might contain the smallest amount of purely mandatory and inflexible legislation.") [63] Pittman told his intimate friend Breckinridge Long that Roosevelt would support his plan, for he had discussed parts of it with him on several occasions. The resolution was introduced without prior endorsement, though, to prevent the charge that neutrality legislation had been prepared in concert with Great Britain. Walter Runciman,

---

* Pittman was reflecting American public opinion in this statement. A Gallup Poll on January 11, 1937, found that 22 per cent of Americans favored the Loyalists; 12 per cent the rebels; 40 per cent were neutral; and 26 per cent had no opinion (Hadley Cantril [ed.], *Public Opinion, 1935–1946* [Princeton: Princeton University, 1951], p. 807) .

president of the British Board of Trade, planned to arrive in Washington on January 23 and was to be a guest at the White House for several days. Had the bill been presented after Runciman's departure, some senators, Pittman thought, might have charged that it had been framed in cooperation with the British.[64]

Pittman's resolution continued the embargo on all arms and munitions in case of war. In addition, the President was empowered to withhold any other "articles or materials" from belligerents that he might deem necessary "to promote the security and preserve the peace or neutrality of the United States." The bill contained a "cash-and-carry" provision, meaning that American vessels could not carry goods of any kind to belligerents after the President proclaimed the existence of a foreign war, and full title of all items shipped had to pass to the buyer before they could leave the United States. The President would receive power to decide when the "cash-and-carry" provision would go into effect as well as authority to prohibit exports of war materials to factions engaged in civil war, a provision which fixed the loophole that had been found with respect to arms shipments to Spain. Pittman said the resolution contained his ideas, but ones that he had discussed repeatedly with Secretary Hull; and the President told the press that there was no difference between the State Department's neutrality position and the Senator's resolution.[65] Arthur Krock suggested, though, that Roosevelt really favored a wider grant of discretionary power to the Chief Executive but public opinion and the Senate isolationist faction would not permit this. The *New York Times* reported the Nevadan had persuaded the President and Secretary Hull that the resolution was "as far in the direction of discretionary leeway as could be put through Congress at this time." * [66]

According to press statements, the administration appeared to be taking a hands-off attitude on the neutrality issue. Both Chairman McReynolds of the House Foreign Affairs Committee and Pittman pointed out to reporters that the "cash-and-carry" bill had not been sponsored by either Roosevelt or Hull. Pittman undoubtedly did not consider it inconsistent with this statement to have State Department technicians present at committee hearings, ready to assist him wherever possible. Actually, the administration maintained a decided in-

---

* In January, 1937, 69 per cent of Americans were in favor of having Congress as opposed to the President responsible for neutrality policy. (Cantril, *op. cit.*, p. 966.)

terest. Hull and Assistant Secretary Moore "had a long session" with Pittman and "came to a pretty full agreement," while the State Department kept the President informed daily of neutrality developments in Congress.

Moore told Roosevelt that McReynolds "is perfectly willing to go along with us," but he suggested that the President confer with Pittman and urge him to prevent any objectionable neutrality legislation. "My thought is that if these gentlemen can be brought entirely into accord with your views, there is a certainty of defeating any undesirable legislation." [67] The President, a master at making others feel important, understood how to maintain Pittman's support. Roosevelt knew the proper moment to make a "confidential" remark to Pittman about his "junior colleague" or when to discuss the possibilities of raising the price of silver. Almost every morning during the 1937 neutrality debate, a handwritten message from the President—a ribald story or some observations for the day usually beginning "Key, have you heard this one?"—would be delivered to the Senator's office before his arrival. This attention elated Pittman, making him feel almost indispensable to the President.

On February 13, 1937, the Foreign Relations Committee held hearings on the general topic of neutrality legislation. Assistant Secretary Moore appeared before the committee to defend the general principles of the Pittman resolution and to outline what the administration hoped would be accomplished in any neutrality law. "The whole purpose is to make certain that when the goods leave this country," Moore explained, "there shall be no American interest in the cargo. In other words, 'You can come and get it.' Vessels belonging to other nations can come and get the stuff, but they have the entire responsibility and risk." When Senator Vandenberg asked Moore if the Pittman bill substantially met with his approval, the Secretary replied: "Yes . . . I have looked at Senator Thomas' joint resolution and as I understand it, he makes the arms provision permissive. . . . He has a more flexible joint resolution than the Pittman measure, looking at that one feature. Being a practical man, and my understanding being that in all human probability the Congress is going to retain that mandatory provision, I say the Pittman joint resolution would, as I understand it, be fairly satisfactory." [68]

After this one open session, the committee decided that it would not hold further hearings because the members felt that they were familiar with all points of view. Four days later, Pittman reported that the committee, after discussing various proposals ranging from the stringent Clark, Bone, Vandenberg, and Nye joint resolution to the discretionary bill introduced by Senator J. Hamilton Lewis, had reached "virtual agreement." The bill, he said, was a "revised version" of the resolution which he had introduced at the beginning of the session. Despite his statements to reporters to the contrary, the State Department had suggested several modifying provisions to the Senator and, in fact, wrote the final committee version "word by word, line by line." "I have been in close contact with Pittman from the start," Moore wrote to the President, "and this is the best the Senate can pass." [69]

On March 1, 1937, Pittman interrupted the debate on the President's court plan to ask the Senate to consider his Peace bill, which he described as "the most important legislation that has ever been submitted to this body." His resolution, he told his colleagues,

proposes an entire new peace policy for our Government. It goes beyond any legislation ever adopted in this or any other country; and yet I contend that nothing in this proposed legislation prevents free commerce with the world, except as we have heretofore restricted it in existing law, or is discriminatory, unneutral, or constitutes a surrender of freedom of the seas. The resolution reenacts the existing law providing for an embargo against the export of arms, ammunition, or implements of war to any belligerents. This act has already been construed by the State Department and the construction has been adopted and proclaimed by the President of the United States.

Senators Borah and Johnson opposed the "cash-and-carry" principle as a surrender of freedom of the seas—that historic doctrine which says that Americans have the right to wander at will through the firing lines of a war selling their goods and guaranteeing safe delivery.[70] Pittman answered these critics with a pragmatic declaration that there "is no such thing as international law, under my conception of the word 'law' ":

The customs at various times adopted by nations, and the settlement of damages occurring in war, and the moral and humane rules of conduct prescribed by philosophers for nations in their relations to each other, have been designated as the common law of nations. The fact that governments have been unwilling to agree to any codification of these so-called laws is sufficient evidence to me that they have no force as common law.[71]

On March 3, 1937, the Pittman Peace bill passed the Senate by a vote of 63 to 6.

After the Senate passed the resolution, a conference committee met to settle differences between the Senate and House versions. It appeared that supporters of more mandatory provisions planned to obstruct passage of the committee report. Pittman's handling of the neutrality bill at this point was a masterful piece of legislative engineering. He managed it simply by holding up the conference report until the old neutrality law was about to expire. With only two days left, he brought out a secret draft which had been worked out by the conference group. The measure passed in one afternoon.[72]

None of the factions which had engaged in the neutrality tug of war in the spring of 1937 appeared satisfied. Senators Vandenberg, Nye, and Clark, for example, wanted to make it obligatory for the President to put the "cash-and-carry" section of the law into operation immediately upon the outbreak of hostilities. The State Department and its senatorial friends wanted more discretionary power for the Chief Executive. The contending groups finally agreed to Pittman's measure, a combination of mandatory and discretionary provisions. "This has been the most active and most tedious session that I have experienced," the Senator wrote, "not by reason of work on the floor of the United States Senate, but by reason of sharp conflicts in Committees and before the various Departments of the Government." He hoped, though, that his efforts would result in "cutting that cable by which we were dragged into the last war." [73]

CHAPTER VII

"His Leadership Has Broken Down"

I

The year 1938 gave the barefoot German waifs of 1919 a chance to sport their recently acquired boots on the cobblestones of Austria and Czechoslovakia. The Anschluss, the Czech crisis, and Munich appeared but preludes to the conflagration of 1939. In the United States, Key Pittman emphatically opposed making any change in the Peace Act. "There is a strong isolationist feeling in this country," the Senator confided to his friend Joseph P. Kennedy. "It would be almost impossible to amend the Neutrality Act, so as to place any greater discretion in the President." [1] The bitter memories of the past war and the dread of a future one, suggested by the rubble of Madrid and Shanghai, helped to create a public opinion which was earnestly groping for peace. With the Czech crisis, this determination to avoid war took on a new impetus. Yet many Americans doubted that if a major conflict came, the United States could maintain its isolation.

Pittman's ambassadorial friends Joseph P. Kennedy in London and Joseph E. Davies in Moscow kept him continually informed of the rapidly deteriorating European situation. Kennedy predicted that a balance of power would be reached in Europe and that "no immediate war is in sight." Davies was not as optimistic. "This European situation is going 'hell-bent' for trouble," he wrote Pittman. "The outer walls of European democratic defenses have not only been levelled but have been handed over on a platter." [2] Both ambassadors continually advised Pittman that America should keep out of the European mess. Pittman responded that he was uneasy over what might happen if the three totalitarian governments continued unimpeded in their conquests. He opposed any rapprochement with Hitler but favored coming to some agreement with Mussolini to pull him out of

155

the Axis orbit, and he suggested to Kennedy that Chamberlain "buy" Mussolini. "The only way to buy a dictator of his type is to pay his price. It would be cheaper than war, or even the preparations for war. . . . Why not have him rejoin the League of Nations and then have the League grant him a mandate over all the former German colonies in Africa? In addition to this, lend him—from time to time— money, not all at once." * ³ Pittman thought his plan would prevent a general European war.

II

On May 2, 1938, Senator Gerald Nye introduced a joint resolution calling for the repeal of the Spanish arms embargo. Nye told his colleagues that he was "not prompted by the interest of either side involved in Spain," but motivated only by a desire to right an injustice growing out of the entire program—"an injustice which reflects upon our country because of the departure from age old principles." Nye's resolution would have allowed the lifting of the embargo in force against the Spanish government, but he also included a provision forbidding American ships from participating in the proposed traffic. The motion was referred to the Foreign Relations Committee.⁴

In March, 1937, just one year previously, Nye, taking notice of the thousands of Italian and German "volunteers" fighting in Spain, had introduced a resolution critical of the administration's embargo, inquiring of the Secretary of State if America's neutrality laws were "sufficient to provide an embargo against nations whose armed forces are engaged in active warfare in another nation where a state of civil war exists." Although the liberal press had acclaimed the resolution, the administration, through Pittman, expressed opposition to such a request. In justifying this move in 1937, Pittman maintained that "this matter should not be stirred up in this country when there is nothing that we can accomplish by stirring it up except to arouse hatred." On his motion, the Senate referred the Nye resolution to the Foreign Relations Committee, where it was shelved.⁵

---

* Before Italy's invasion of Ethiopia, Pittman had characterized Mussolini as "the greatest man in Europe" (K. P. to Breckinridge Long, April 15, 1935, L Folder, Box 13, Key Pittman Papers, Library of Congress, hereafter cited by folder and box number).

When Nye's 1938 resolution came up for discussion in the committee, Pittman asked Hull for advice. The Secretary replied that even though the Loyalist cause looked dim, the United States had to maintain absolute neutrality toward Spain because of the unusual events which had surrounded the civil war. "In view of the continued danger of international conflict arising from the circumstances of the struggle," he said, "any proposal which contemplates a reversal of our policy of strict non-interference would offer a real possibility of complications." For this reason, the Secretary opposed the Nye resolution.[6] Pittman agreed to call a special meeting of the Foreign Relations Committee for the following morning and in less than thirty minutes the members, by a vote of 17 to 1, decided to postpone Nye's resolution indefinitely. "This is a black page in our history," Harold Ickes recorded in his diary.[7]

Claude Bowers later remembered that in March, 1939, Pittman had told him: "I am afraid we made a mistake in Spain," adding that at one time he thought the embargo would keep other nations out of the conflict and localize the war.[8] In 1937 and 1938, however, the Senator sanctioned the administration's policy. On the same day that Nye introduced his 1938 resolution, Pittman confided to Joseph P. Kennedy: "The fight over this resolution—if there is a fight—will add another grief to the Democratic Congressmen who are running this year." As late as January, 1939, when the State Department again considered lifting the Spanish embargo, Pittman told Hull that the Foreign Relations Committee had voted unanimously to drop any consideration of such legislation, explaining that the conflicting avalanche of telegrams from constituents convinced senators that they were on "too hot a spot to sit with ease" and the sooner they could get off it by avoiding the issue, the happier they would be.* [9]

III

During the summer and autumn of 1938, the Roosevelt administration smarted under a series of daily lashings from the Nazi press as relations between the two countries worsened. On December 22, Pitt-

* Pittman reported on January 25, 1939, that the Senate Foreign Relations Committee had received 35,000 letters dealing with the Spanish embargo during the preceding week.

man summoned reporters to his office and handed them this terse statement:

1. The people of the United States do not like the Government of Japan.
2. The people of the United States do not like the Government of Germany.
3. The people of the United States, in my opinion, are against any form of dictatorial government, communistic or fascistic.
4. The people of the United States have the right and power to enforce morality and justice in accordance with peace treaties with us. And they will. Our government will not have to use military force and will not unless necessary.

In less than one hundred words, Pittman summarized what the administration had been saying between the lines of diplomatic notes totaling thousands of pages. German newspapers quickly denounced the Senator. The Berlin daily *Zwoelf-Uhr Blatt* implied that relations between Berlin and Washington had reached their lowest point "thanks to the organized agitation of these American Ickeses, Pittmans, Baruchs, LaGuardias, Wises and Untermeyers." The *Deutscher Dienst* accused the Nevadan of a "carefully timed and brutal disturbance of the Christmas peace" while the Berlin *Lokal Anzeiger* declared that Pittman belonged to "the Ickes group"—a statement which must have amused the Senator. While German press comment was interspersed with such phrases as "rupture" and "abrogation of German-American relations," both German and American officialdom kept their silence.* [10]

Administration officials had become more critical of German policy during the last months of 1938. Secretary Harold Ickes had assailed Americans who accepted decorations from Hitler, and Under-Secretary of State Sumner Welles found cause to insult the German chargé d'affaires. On January 4, 1939, President Roosevelt took the lead by warning that the United States was in danger of attack. "There are many methods short of war," he told Congress, "stronger and more effective than mere words, of bringing home to aggressor governments the aggregate sentiments of our own people. . . . Events abroad have made it increasingly clear to the American people that dangers within

* *Time* magazine suggested that Pittman's comments might have been inspired by the White House, which was forced to maintain a more discreet policy (*Time*, January 2, 1939, p. 6).

are less to be feared than dangers from without." [11] It had become increasingly clear that the Roosevelt administration had decided to throw its influence into the balance on the side of the democracies by aiding them with American arms and munitions. Pittman gave his enthusiastic endorsement to the President's address and now began to suggest "methods short of war."

Pittman saw the changing trend of European events, especially the Munich agreement, as sufficient reason to start defense preparations and to revise the arms embargo provision of the 1937 Neutrality Act,* although he seriously doubted if "the extreme and foolish pacifist sentiment" in the Senate would grant the President additional discretionary power.[12] He now thought there would be a war in Europe before the summer. Breckinridge Long noted in his diary that he waged $10 against the Senator's prediction. "I bet him $10—date line May 5—entered it on his calendar, May 5 page: 'I owe Breck Long $10 on war bet.'" Long observed that Pittman had been drinking heavily and that his statements on the European situation were "rather belligerent." "Thinks we ought to help England and France prepare," wrote Long. "He is against Germany. . . . He wants to help them [England and France] build up armament so there will be no disparity between them and the Fascist Powers and so nobody will dare war. . . . He thinks Welles, the President and his own utterances have made Hitler think the U. S. is against him and that he will be more careful." [13]

Almost immediately after the President's "methods short of war" speech, Secretary Hull suggested to Pittman that the State Department prepare a resolution repealing the arms embargo, which the Senator would introduce. Pittman disagreed and emphatically declared that he had to draft any revised neutrality legislation because an administration measure would be interpreted as the first step toward lifting the Spanish embargo. He again told Hull of the isolationist strength in the Senate, adding that the desired goal could be achieved only by careful planning. His political judgment appealed to Hull, who acquiesced.[14] Pittman advised Roosevelt that no administration resolution be introduced until the Foreign Relations Committee had discussed the various bills presented by other senators. "It is evident

* Although the "cash-and-carry" section expired on May 1, 1939, the arms embargo and other sections were to continue unless Congress changed the law.

that there will be quite a contest between the proponents of the various bills. The merits and demerits of such bills will be very clearly exposed. After this process is ended I may be able to bring about a satisfactory compromise in the Committee. My position as a compromiser would be weakened if I presented bills and resolutions at this time." Pittman appealed for a free hand in the Senate as an administration proposal would "probably receive the united attack of all those holding divergent views." Roosevelt, he cautioned, had to remain reticent—at least until he could suggest something a majority of the committee could agree upon.[15] The President, perhaps also aware of the animosities aroused by his domestic policies, agreed to entrust the embargo revision to Pittman.

During January, February, and March, 1939, the President concentrated on his rearmament program. Following Pittman's advice, he refrained, at least publicly, from suggesting changes in the Neutrality Act. (When William Bullitt telephoned Roosevelt "to make a ringing denunciation" of Germany's attack on Czechoslovakia and urged the President "to go to Congress and demand the repeal of the Neutrality Acts," he was surprised that Roosevelt appeared "none too keen to follow these recommendations.")[16] Pittman and Hull, in the meanwhile, privately discussed revision but the Senator could not be persuaded to support the State Department's plan to free the Executive from all mandatory neutrality provisions. There was not "the slightest prospect of any measure being adopted giving the President authority to impose an embargo against an aggressor only," he informed Hull. Pittman also backed away from Roosevelt's suggestion of outright repeal of all neutrality legislation as being an impossible feat. Furthermore, the Senator became exceedingly apprehensive that any major changes in the neutrality law would reopen the controversial issue of American policy toward the Spanish civil war, causing the project for revision to be lost in a partisan debate.[17] "He seems to have less definite views of what sort of neutrality program is feasible," recorded Carlton Savage, Hull's assistant. "He does not want it to be known that he is giving consideration to any special plan."[18]

Pittman and Hull finally agreed on the general terms of the new bill. The "cash-and-carry" section would be renewed. Arms, ammunition, and implements of war would no longer be embargoed in the event of a war but were now made part of the cash-and-carry section.

There would be, therefore, no distinction between arms and other exports, and under this new plan any nation could come to the United States and buy whatever they pleased—from bullets to wheat, but they had to take title to the property in the United States and assume the risks of transporting it to its destination. Pittman assured Hull that he could get these modifications through in the Senate. (Jay Pierrepont Moffat recorded in his diary that Hull's views were never clearly defined and that he would repeatedly resort to vague statements and generalities, making it "almost impossible to pin him down" to specific details.) [19]

On March 20, 1939, Pittman reopened the neutrality debate by introducing his Peace bill of 1939. It was clear to all that if this resolution passed, Great Britain and France would benefit in the event of war, for they controlled the Atlantic. After Pittman presented his bill, the administration realized that cash-and-carry might operate to the advantage of Japan because the President was required to apply the act within thirty days after a war began. "The more I think the problem through," Roosevelt told Hull, "the more I am convinced that the existing Neutrality Act should be repealed *in toto* without any substitute. I do not mind if you pass this word to Senator Pittman and the leaders." Pittman appreciated the objection to the way his bill would work in the Pacific, but he rejected the President's "impractical suggestion" of repealing the entire Neutrality Act.* [20] To meet this objection, Pittman introduced a supplemental bill giving the President power to embargo exports and imports to and from nations violating the Nine Power Treaty. For tactical reasons which the State Department did not understand, the Senator carefully stated to the press that he had drafted the Peace Act without consulting the President, the Secretary of State, or any other member of the administration.[21] One reporter for the *Washington Post*, almost clairvoyant in his analysis, perceived the sharp cleavage in the Senate and predicted a "gigantic battle" on Capitol Hill.[22]

Pittman's Foreign Relations Committee began public hearings in

---

* Pittman later wrote that "the President and the Secretary of State both at all times favored the repeal of all domestic legislation and the reliance on international law" (K. P. to Charles C. Conroy, September 7, 1940, Correspondence C Folder, Sen. 76A–F9 [122L], Papers of the United States Senate Foreign Relations Committee, National Archives, hereafter cited as F.R.C.).

April on a series of bills which ran the gamut from outright repeal to mandatory legislation depriving the President of virtually any discretion in administering a neutrality act. The Senator had opposed open hearings, fearing that the administration's position would be damaged. In fact, he had assured Hull that only executive sessions would be held, adding that he would keep the department "fully advised of the views presented and of the apparent attitude of the Committee." His motion to this effect, though, failed, 11 to 8.[23] From this point the Senator began to find the going more difficult than he had expected. The isolationists on his committee had been strengthened by the addition of Senator Bennett Clark in April, 1939. The administration had not wanted Clark appointed to the committee, but the Senate clung to its tradition of seniority in selecting him for the vacancy. By the end of April, Pittman's early optimism about neutrality revision had begun to fade. "I fear," he wrote to Henry Stimson, "that the division among the leading peace societies in the country will tend to prevent any legislation at all." [24] On May 8, Pittman went to the State Department to persuade Hull to cancel his appearance before the Foreign Relations Committee, claiming that the isolationists planned to ask embarrassing questions. "The Committee is out of hand. The isolationists might even win," confessed the Senator.[25] Hull followed Pittman's judgment and did not testify. He continued to meet with individual senators, though, to explain his position. One week later, Pittman shocked Hull by completely reversing his previous pledges to the administration. "The situation in Europe," he now wrote, "does not seem to induce any urgent action on neutrality legislation." [26]

At the end of April, 1939, after almost a month of hearings prolonged by the isolationists, Pittman confided to Bernard Baruch that he was confident that ten of the committee's twenty-three members would vote for his neutrality resolution. "I am sure that two more will come to me." [27] The hearings concluded on May 8, but Pittman was unable to obtain the two additional votes necessary to report out his measure. "The neutrality situation seems to be going from bad to worse," wrote Moffat. "Confusion is worse confounded. The Secretary has had a series of talks with a group of Senators but has gotten nowhere. Pittman's leadership has broken down." [28] The cash-and-carry provisions of the 1937 act had expired on May 1, but the isolationist group remained strong and stubborn. Senator Borah thundered that the European democracies were "contending for the realization of their imperialistic schemes and not the destruction of Nazism"— while Senator Shipstead, another committee member, echoed these sentiments, declaring that "if we are going to do any missionary work, let's do it in the United States." [29] The committee remained hopelessly deadlocked. Reluctantly, Pittman admitted defeat for his resolution and asked the administration to suggest an alternate plan.

Roosevelt had entrusted the neutrality revision program to Pittman. During the four weeks of hearings, the President had avoided antagonizing Congress with advice on the subject. By the beginning of May, though, the White House realized that Pittman could not obtain a favorable report on any administration resolution. The Senator's new advice to the President was to "keep quiet" and avoid further neutrality discussions, so that Hitler would "be left in doubt as to what our Government would do" in case of war.[30] Roosevelt, on the other hand, wanted to make it crystal clear to the dictator that American aid to the democracies would be available. Wilson had erred in 1914, he thought, in not stating early enough where the United States stood, and he did not want that to happen again. On May 10, 1939, the State Department attempted to salvage the situation by supplying Representative Sol Bloom, the new chairman of the House Foreign Affairs Committee, with a suggested draft of a neutrality bill. After discussing it with Roosevelt, Bloom agreed to sponsor this resolution, which granted the President more discretionary power than did the Pittman bill.

On May 19, 1939, Roosevelt broke his silence and told House leaders that every effort should be made to eliminate the arms embargo from the Neutrality Act. Repeal of the embargo, he told the congressmen, "would actually prevent the outbreak of war in Europe, or if it did not prevent the outbreak of war, the elimination of that provision would make less likely a victory for the powers unfriendly to the United States." [31] By requesting complete repeal, the President asked for more than the Pittman and Hull agreement, which had placed arms, ammunition, and implements of war on a cash-and-carry basis. Majority Leader Rayburn and Speaker Bankhead warned Roosevelt that his proposal would be defeated. Pittman cautioned the President to first determine what legislation could pass Congress and then decide which bill he wanted to support. Roosevelt, nevertheless, decided to make the fight for outright repeal. "I am pushing the Neutrality matter," he informed Moore, "and I hope you will see as many people in the House and Senate as you can." * [32]

The State Department prepared a new resolution which incorporated Roosevelt's recommendation to eliminate the arms embargo and sent it to Pittman and Sol Bloom. "If we go in for embargoes on exports," Hull wrote to Pittman, "the logical thing to do would be to make our embargo all-inclusive. Modern warfare is no longer warfare between armed forces only; it is warfare between nations in every phase of their national life." "It is my firm conviction," the Secretary continued, "that the arms embargo provision of the existing law should be eliminated." [33] The following day (May 28, 1939), Representative Bloom and Pittman introduced a joint resolution, which had no provision for cash-and-carry and which gave the President wide latitude in deciding when and how the act would be applied. In a remarkable statement to the press, Pittman predicted that a majority of his committee would support the "basic principles" of the Hull recommendation. "Naturally," he stated, "I am in agreement with the Secretary's proposals because they are substantially in line with my own." [34] The Senator avoided giving his definition of "substantially." Privately, Roosevelt had canvassed senators, concluding that chances of passage appeared dim and that action by the House should precede any consideration by the Senate. [35]

After a month of acrimonious debate, the administration forces in the House failed to muster sufficient votes to repeal the arms embargo. Once again, the administration, plagued by endless difficulties, turned to the Senate. At a press conference on July 4, Roosevelt announced that he hoped the Senate Foreign Relations Committee would reconsider neutrality revision "in the interest of preventing war." Pitt-

---

* Jay Pierrepont Moffat wrote in his diary: "The Secretary has seen now dozens of Congressmen and Senators and the general burden of their story is that no one knows what would happen if the measure came on the floor. In fact, the feeling is so fluid that the Legislature has been likened to a flock of sheep in a pen where if one sheep jumped out in a given direction all the rest would immediately follow after. The only trouble is no one could calculate just which side of the pen the first sheep would jump out" (Jay Pierrepont Moffat Diary, May 25, 1939, Houghton Library, Harvard University).

man agreed to present the legislation to his committee. Hull's assistant, Carlton Savage, reported that "the Senator appeared to feel convinced that there was really no doubt of favorable action by the Committee at tomorrow's meeting, and therefore it would be inadvisable for the Secretary to submit any further statement." [36] (Roosevelt did what he could to have the committee report favorably on the State Department's proposal. He wrote Senator Pat Harrison, for example, expressing surprise at a rumor that Harrison was leaving Washington before the committee acted. "Pat, old dear," pleaded the President, "do please don't! I need you here on lots of things, including the next big thing on the calendar—the Neutrality Bill—and I do hope you will help me to get it out on Saturday and put it through.") [37] In spite of Pittman's renewed optimism, the Foreign Relations Committee voted 12 to 11 to defer consideration of all proposals to revise the 1937 Neutrality Act until the next session of Congress. Senators Gillette of Iowa and George of Georgia, who were not isolationists but whom Roosevelt had attempted to purge in 1938, voted against the administration and for postponement. The decision of the committee, wrote Pittman, "was quite disappointing." [38]

Refusing to acknowledge defeat, Roosevelt took the initiative in an attempt to break the deadlock between Congress and the Executive by calling a meeting of both Republican and Democratic Senate leaders at the White House on July 18.* The President opened the discussion by observing that prayer might be in order: "Our decision may well affect not only the people of our country, but also the peoples of the world." After three hours of talking, the senators present agreed that no neutrality legislation could be passed at the present time despite the large Democratic majority in the chamber.

"Well, Captain," Vice President Garner said turning to Roosevelt, "we may as well face the facts. You haven't got the votes, that's all there is to it." The President, lying back on his sofa, smoking his cigarette, nodded between puffs.[39]

The impasse between the Executive and Legislative branches could not be broken. Congress adjourned in August, leaving the munitions embargo on the statute books. Pittman lamented that he had more

* Present at the conference were: the President; Vice-President Garner; Secretary Hull; and Senators Pittman, Barkley, Borah, Austin, and McNary.

confidence in the will of God than in the philosophy of modern states-manship.[40] Four weeks later Europe was at war.

Pittman's vacillation and lack of leadership in the Foreign Relations Committee had been disappointing to the administration. His principal interests, regardless of conditions in Europe, remained Nevada and silver. In May, 1939, the Senator had forwarded to the President some Japanese paper bills being circulated in north China, two hundred of which he said equaled sixteen cents in United States money. He took the occasion to deliver a little homily on silver, to the effect that so long as China had used silver for money there had rarely been a bank failure.[41] In June, Pittman told his Senate colleagues that the government's silver-purchasing program since January, 1938, had been responsible for an increase in unemployment in the mining industry. The Senator asserted that Secretary Morgenthau's policy of lowering the price at which the government purchased silver from 77.57¢ to 64.5¢ an ounce was responsible for this situation.

The Nevadan challenged his colleagues to go out West to see a ghost town. "You will see 100 men and their wives and two or three hundred children living there, not a mill running and not a smelter running, and you wonder why they stay there—you wonder why they live there. Well, while those mines were running, these men built their homes, their children have been born there, their schools are there, they know no other home." [42] Pittman's panacea, once again, was to raise the price of silver.

"I understood your speech perfectly, and, of course, I know the problem in the seven States—employment, etc.," Roosevelt wrote Pittman. "On the larger question is the deeper problem of what we are headed toward if we continue to pile up silver and gold in the Treasury. For the silver we are already paying a straight subsidy of twenty-three cents an ounce over the world price—a larger proportionate subsidy than we are paying to wheat and cotton growers. And back of it all, the rest of the world does not seem to want our silver but they do want to send their silver to us. That is why I am inclined to the belief that our own subsidy to our own domestic silver producers is plenty high at sixty-four cents." [43] Roosevelt sent this note to Pittman on June 27, 1939, three days before the House failed to repeal the arms embargo. Between June 27 and July 5, the day on which the Senate Foreign Relations Committee began reconsideration of neutrality legislation, the President withdrew his opposition to a rise in the price of silver. According to Secretary Morgenthau, the President told him on June 23 that he intended to make a deal with Pittman in order to expedite Senate action on the repeal of the mandatory arms embargo from the neutrality law.[44] On July 5, the Senate, after being bantered by White House spokesmen, accepted a conference committee report which raised silver to 71¢ an ounce. Morgenthau later wrote that Roosevelt was forced to "buy" Pittman's support for repeal of the arms embargo by agreeing to the higher price for domestic silver, especially since Pittman told him: "We have got 18 votes—and what are you going to do about it?" * [45]

During the neutrality debate, a reporter asked Pittman if he believed that isolation was possible for this country.

"It's according to what you mean by that damn word," the Senator replied.

"If you mean, 'can we keep out of war?' Yes, if we are willing to give up enough of honor and material advantage for the sake of avoiding trouble. But if you mean by isolation that we shall draw up in a shell like a clam, No! Emphatically, No. We cannot afford not to take part in the affairs of the world in which we live." [46]

For six years, Congress had attempted to formulate a plan for the United States to follow in the event of a European war. Yet in September, 1939, when the talked-about war finally began, a majority of Americans thought that the neutrality laws needed revision. The President took the lead. "Roosevelt appeared to be a different man," Tom Connally noted. "He now spoke with sureness about foreign affairs and kept a firm grip on the reins as he detailed what he wanted from Congress." [47] Never again was Roosevelt to be defeated by the isolationists on a major foreign policy issue.

Congress convened in special session on September 21. Since its last meeting neutrality had been transformed from the realm of theory into reality. The President assumed the initiative. He told Congress

---

* Breckinridge Long noted that Pittman's motive in demanding a rise in silver was political—to insure his reelection in 1940. (Long Diary, July 6, 1939.)

In *F. D. R. His Personal Letters,* edited by Elliott Roosevelt, Mr. Roosevelt stated that his father agreed to a higher price for domestic silver in order to gain Pittman's support for repeal of the arms embargo (Elliott Roosevelt (ed.) , *F. D. R. His Personal Letters, 1928–1945* [New York: Duell, Sloan and Pearce, 1950], II, 898) .

that the arms embargo "is wholly inconsistent with ancient precepts of the law of nations" and he asked for repeal. "I give to you my deep and unalterable conviction . . . that by the repeal of the embargo the United States will more probably remain at peace than if the law remains as it stands today." The speech, although based on a State Department draft, had been completely rewritten by the President, with considerable change in order and emphasis.[48]

Once more the administration gave Pittman a free hand in framing and directing neutrality revision. Hull recalled that the Senator

insisted on being the sole guiding spirit of the legislation. At about the time Congress convened, he telephoned me and said rather arrogantly he hoped his committee would not be embarrassed by any indiscreet utterances from the Executive "end of the Avenue." He was also concerned lest anyone in the State Department give opinions to any other Senator.[49]

When Roosevelt again suggested outright repeal of all neutrality laws to Pittman at a meeting in the President's office on September 20, 1939, the Senator replied: "If you try that you'll be damn lucky to get five votes on my committee." * The Senator remained unenthusiastic about accepting advice from the State Department. Instead, fourteen Democratic members of the Foreign Relations Committee, headed by Pittman, set to work behind locked doors to hammer out a neutrality resolution which would repeal the arms embargo and pass the Senate. Republican members and Senator Clark of Missouri were not invited to express their opinions or shown the confidential working draft which Pittman, Connally, and Thomas of Utah had completed. "I don't think they would be interested," commented Pittman.[50]

Almost one week to the hour after the President had convened Congress in special session, the Foreign Relations Committee, by a vote of 16 to 7, approved and sent to the Senate the Pittman resolution, which followed Roosevelt's request by repealing the arms em-

---

* The whole problem of neutrality was discussed in a very general way at this meeting, which was attended by leading congressional leaders. Strong differences of opinion prevented agreement on a united bipartisan policy. The White House issued a press release only after each participant was satisfied that the statement was evasive and noncommitting (see minutes of "Very Confidential Conference of President and Congressional Leaders on Neutrality," September 20, 1939, Box 263, 1–P, President's Personal Files, Franklin D. Roosevelt Papers, Hyde Park, N. Y.).

bargo but which substituted a strict cash-and-carry system for all commerce with warring nations. Pittman asserted that it aimed to "preserve the neutrality and the peace of the United States and secure the safety of its citizens and their interests." In 1937, the Senator had included an arms embargo in his Peace Act and now, in September, 1939, he led the fight against it. "I have made a great many mistakes since I have been in the Senate, and frankly I admit it," he told his colleagues. "I really thought at one time that the embargo was going to be more effective than it was. I can't think it can be effective when there are just a few manufactured things like guns and ammunition in it and you have oil and gasoline and iron and steel and everything that makes ammunition out of it." [51]

Debate began in the Senate on October 2, with Pittman as the first speaker. The galleries were filled to capacity as an important chapter in American history unfolded. Obviously worn, he mustered his oratorical skill for an assault on the arms embargo, contending that it "was unneutral and unfriendly since it prevented Great Britain and France from obtaining the arms their control of the seas would ordinarily have made possible and thus, in fact, aided Germany." He discussed the various provisions of the resolution in detail, showing how each embodied the aim of the administration—to keep America out of war—and carefully avoided reference to the real purpose of the act—all possible aid to England and France with a minimum of risk.

For almost four weeks, a resolute minority led by Senators Borah, Vandenberg, Nye, and Clark campaigned against any change in the embargo. At the end of this momentous debate, in which nearly seventy senators put more than 1,000,000 words in the *Congressional Record,* the Senate adopted the Pittman resolution by a vote of 63 to 30. During the great debate, Roosevelt complied with the admonition laid down by Pittman and James Byrnes: "Stay out of the neutrality fight." This was regrettable for the Senate isolationists, who would have welcomed a rousing White House statement, which probably would have scared off crucial administration votes. (At one point, the State Department ignored a Pittman amendment liberalizing the shipping clauses. Although Hull found it "none too satisfactory and full of illogicalities," he thought that it would be a mistake to ask the Senator to correct it, considering the "attendant dangers" of such a move.) [52] House approval quickly followed and the President signed the bill on November 4, 1939. "No one could have striven more constantly or more effectively than you have," Hull wrote to Pittman. "I thank and congratulate you for the magnificent results in which your leadership played so large a part." * [53] Thus, the policy of forbidding arms exports to warring powers came to a rather ignominious end, the more so because it was abandoned in the midst of a European war the fear of which four years earlier had been responsible for its adoption.

IV

During 1940, the pressure of work began to show on Pittman, now sixty-eight. "I am as weak as a sick cat," he wrote to a friend. "I have been under the weather ever since the special session of Congress. . . . I am run ragged here with all kinds of troubles." [54] In March, Breckinridge Long recorded in his diary that he was shocked to see Pittman. "He is a sick man, for the time being. His cheeks are sunken, and he has lost a lot of weight. The sight of him really distressed me. He is suffering with some stomach ailment and I begged him to go to the Mayo Clinic." [55] The Senator rejected Long's suggestion and remained in Washington, where his work, assignments, and drinking continued.

By 1940, Roosevelt had charted his course for the Second World War. He became the undisputed captain as well as navigator. Pittman's advice, in spite of his senatorial position, was now completely disregarded. Many of the Senator's statements, in fact, embarrassed the administration. During the period of the "phony" war in the West, for example, Pittman sharply criticized Great Britain's policy of searching American ships and censoring American mail. The Senator, relying on international law—a concept he had castigated in defending his 1937 neutrality law—suggested economic retaliation against Great Britain for violating American rights. "We are suffering some losses and annoyances through the arbitrary action of Great Britain in carrying our vessels into her ports for search for contra-

---

* Pittman characterized Hiram Johnson as being "a complete isolationist and at the same time believes in standing on international law. The only difference is he believes in keeping out of war while at the same time fighting for your rights on the high seas" (K. P. to Virginia Pittman, October 23, 1939, P. Folder, Box 46) .

band," he stated. Much to the pleasure of the German government, the Senator warned Britain that "such illegal acts invite retaliation." [56] This was but one of a series of intemperate statements made by the chairman of the Foreign Relations Committee.

Early in 1940, Roosevelt sent Under-Secretary Sumner Welles as his personal representative to Germany, Italy, France, and England, instructing him to ascertain the views of the four governments toward the possibilities of concluding a just and permanent peace. The President carefully briefed Welles not to consider any temporary armed truce.[57] While Welles toured Europe, Pittman, without consulting the White House, proposed a thirty-day truce. "It is inconceivable that the warring powers should refuse an armistice to prevent calm discussion of the alleged causes of war and the objectives of such war." [58]

Pittman's plan received a cool reception in London, and the French government regarded it as inopportune. The President, irritated by the statement, summoned Breckinridge Long, now a special assistant in the State Department, to his office and handed Long two telegrams from the Paris embassy. They related to Pittman's suggestion and the adverse reaction of French officials. Long recorded in his diary:

The President read them aloud very carefully and slowly. He then asked me to see Pittman, because he and I were such intimate friends and because he realized that the President and I were close friends. He thought it would be better than for him to see him himself. He asked me to say to him first that any suggestion of a truce or an armistice was asinine. The British would not agree to an armistice if the blockade was to be suspended. The Germans would not agree to an armistice unless the blockade was to be suspended. However, during an armistice, for thirty days or longer, and with a suspended blockade Germany would proceed to restock with needed materials and the consequence would be that the war would be that much longer and that much more difficult.

The second was to tell Pittman a story. The story almost verbatim as related by the President follows, and I have translated it into the first person singular:

"In August 1918 one morning I had breakfast with Clemenceau. A few days before that the French had pushed the Germans back in front of Amiens from the five-mile line to the twelve-mile line, near Rheims the French had pushed the Germans farther back. The American troops in the Argonne had penetrated the German lines, and in the Chateau Thierry section after two weeks of hard fighting the American troops had pushed the Germans out of

Belleau Wood and had them on the retreat. So when I met Clemenceau that morning I said, 'Everything looks fine. You are doing very well.' The old gentleman replied, 'It looks fairly well, but it does not mean much yet. We cannot win this war and we cannot fight in the winter, so we shall not beat Germany until spring. However, these are details. It is not that we shall hang the Kaiser. And it is not that Germany shall be defeated. It is none of these things. These are all details. There is only one important thing I have striven for all my life. It is that one thing I hope to live to see. The important thing is this: The day a truce is signed with Germany there will be a lot of babies born in France. Those babies will have an allotted life of three score and ten. During their lives I want them to live without an attack from Germany. Since the days of Charlemagne in 890 no child has been born in France to live its allotted life of three score and ten without trouble with Germany. It is for that I fight this war. That is the important thing!' "

The President said, "You tell that to Pittman."

Pittman, Long noted, was in a depressed mood. He was highly critical of England and France and said "that there was hardly a man on the floor of the United States Senate who would stand up for them." Pittman thought that the Allied powers were "sullen, defaulters, and double-crossers." [59]

On April 9, 1940, the "phony" war came to an end. Denmark fell in one day; Norway in one month. On May 10, German troops invaded Holland, Luxembourg, and Belgium. In a prepared statement, Pittman declared that the British policy of appeasement was responsible for the invasion of Holland.[60] On June 5, the battle for France had begun. In two weeks, it ended. On June 25, as Great Britain prepared, as Winston Churchill said, "to defend every village, every town, and every city," Pittman expressed the opinion that it was futile for England to continue the fight. "The probability of Hitler's domination of Europe is evident," he told reporters. The British Ministry of Information quickly issued a statement describing Pittman's comments as being "in complete disagreement with British views." [61]

The Senator's irresponsible statements continued. Harold Ickes recorded in his diary a luncheon conference that he had with the President on June 27, 1940:

The President was quite worked up by a call that he had just had from Senator Pittman. He insisted that the President send "orders" to the English fleet to proceed to American harbors. The President told Pittman that he could not "order" the English fleet to do anything, but Pittman was insistent. According to the President, he was almost maudlin; he pawed the President, much to his disgust. While I was with him, the President sent for Steve Early. He was fearful that Pittman might have said something to the newspapers that should not be printed, but it appeared that Pittman was either too drunk to do that or not drunk enough.[62]

"You are right about the war situation," Pittman wrote to a friend in June, 1940. "It couldn't be worse. It keeps me busy all the time trying to prevent action on all kinds of crack-pot schemes." [63]

On July 25, 1940, Pittman formally announced that he would stand for re-election. He told Breckinridge Long that this would be his last campaign.[64] In October he left for Nevada to fight for his sixth term, feeling confident of re-election. The campaign, although short, proved strenuous. The Senator tired easily and often, returning many an evening completely worn out to his small suite in Tonopah's Mizpah Hotel. During the last weeks of the contest, he drank very heavily and was in an almost continuous stupor. Four days before the election, he entered Reno's Washoe Hospital. On November 5, his fellow Nevadans re-elected him by 6,000 votes over his Republican opponent, Sam Platt. But Pittman was dying. Just after midnight on November 10, 1940, his heart gave way.

Notes

NOTES TO INTRODUCTION

1. Eduard Beneš, *Democracy Today and Tomorrow* (London: Macmillan, 1939), pp. 210–211; see also Chapter VI

2. Walter Lippmann, *Public Opinion* (New York: Harcourt, Brace, 1922), p. 247. See also James MacGregor Burns' excellent chapter "The Congressman and His World" in his *Congress on Trial* (New York: Harper, 1949), pp. 1 ff.

NOTES TO CHAPTER I

1. Alfred B. Pittman to K. P., February 1, 1933; K. P. to Alfred B. Pittman, February 7, 1933, Key-Pittman Genealogy Folder, Box 1, Key Pittman Papers, Library of Congress (hereafter cited by folder and box number). See also K. P. to Frank N. Pittman, February 7, 1932, Key-Pittman Genealogy Folder, Box 1

2. K. P. to Mrs. C. C. Pittman, September 25, 1939, Key-Pittman Genealogy Folder, Box 1

3. K. P. to F. S. Key-Smith, May 4, 1934, Key-Pittman Genealogy Folder, Box 1

4. K. P. to Boutwell Dunlap, April 29, 1929, Pittman Family Folder, Box 1

5. *The War of the Rebellion: Official Records of the Union and Confederate Armies* (Washington: U. S. Government Printing Office, 1886), Series I, XVII, Part I, 392; XXIV, Part II, 421

6. *In and About Vicksburg* (Vicksburg: Gibraltar, 1890), p. 105; *The Vicksburg Evening Post,* January 12, 1934

7. J. S. McNeily, "Climax and Collapse of Reconstruction in Mississippi, 1874–76," *Publications of the Mississippi Historical Society,* XII (1912), 320 f.

8. *Mississippi Reports,* LV, 725, 751

9. Vail Pittman to author, January 22, 1960

10. Waller Raymond Cooper, *Southwestern at Memphis, 1848–1948* (Richmond: John Knox, 1949), pp. 54, 56, 67–68, 76, 78

11. Transcript of Record of Key Pittman, in possession of author

12. Cooper, *op. cit.,* pp. 72–74, 163

13. *Annual Catalogue of the Southwestern Presbyterian University, 1890–91,* p. 36

14. Cooper, *op. cit.,* pp. 76–77, 80

15. *New York Times,* May 21, 1939, Sec. VIII, p. 22

16. *Los Angeles Times,* December 17, 1913

17. K. P. to Jo Hubbard Chamberlin, January 19, 1940, Correspondence C Folder,

Sen. 76A–F9 (122L), Papers of the United States Senate Foreign Relations Committee, National Archives (hereafter cited as F.R.C.)

18. Ethel Anderson Becker, *Klondike '98* (Portland: Binfords and Mort, 1949), p. 3

19. See Pierre Berton, *Klondike Fever* (New York: Knopf, 1958), pp. 146–151

20. K. P. to Jo Hubbard Chamberlin, January 19, 1940, Correspondence C Folder, Sen. 76A–F9 (122L), F.R.C.

21. Jack London, "Which Make Men Remember," *The God of His Fathers and Other Stories* (New York: Doubleday, 1913), pp. 79–80

22. Berton, *op. cit.*, p. 280

23. Statement of K. P., "Yuletide in Frozen North," December 21, 1913, Biographical Data Folder, Box 1

24. *New York Times*, November 11, 1940, 12:7. See also Tappan Adney, *The Klondike Stampede* (New York: Harper, 1900), pp. 465–468

25. Sam P. Davis (ed.), *The History of Nevada* (Reno: Elms, 1913), II, 1076–1077

26. K. P. to Jo Hubbard Chamberlin, January 19, 1940, Correspondence C Folder, Sen. 76A–F9 (122L), F.R.C.

27. Russell A. Bankson, *The Klondike Nugget* (Caldwell, Idaho: Caxton, 1935), pp. 263–270

28. *San Francisco Chronicle*, May 10, 1937, p. 9

29. James Wickersham, *Old Yukon: Tales, Trails, and Trials* (Washington: Washington Law Book, 1938), p. 410

30. Mimosa Gates to Humboldt and Eddie Gates, June 3, 1900, Personal Correspondence, Mrs. Key Pittman, 1898–1903 Folder, Box 53

31. Statement of K. P., "Yuletide in Frozen North," *loc. cit.*

32. Edward Sullivan, *The Fabulous Wilson Mizner* (New York: Henkle, 1935), pp. 132–133

33. Wickersham, *op. cit.*, pp. 400–401

34. K. P. to George D. Kilborn, August 13, 1910, Political Correspondence, August 1910 Folder, Box 3. See William W. Morrow, "The Spoilers," *California Law Review*, IV (January 1916), 89–113

35. Mimosa Pittman to Bettie Larimore, March 9, 1927, Box 52

36. *Nome Daily Chronicle*, September 20, 1900, 2:1

37. *The Nome Weekly News*, September 5, 1900, 4:6

38. *Alaska Reports*, I, 305, 339, 346

39. Richard O'Connor, *High Jinks on the Klondike* (New York: Bobbs-Merrill, 1954), p. 234

40. K. P. to *The Arctic Chief*, June 9, 1912, A-Personal Folder, Box 25

41. K. P. to Mimosa Pittman, March 28, 1902, Personal Correspondence, Mrs. Key Pittman, 1898–1903 Folder, Box 53

42. Jim Butler to Thomas Wren, November 19, 1902, in Thomas Wren (ed.), *A History of the State of Nevada* (New York: Lewis, 1904), pp. 149–150

43. See Russell Richard Elliott, "The Tonopah, Goldfield, Bullfrog Mining Districts, 1900–1915" (unpublished doctoral dissertation, University of California, Berkeley, 1946)

44. K. P. to Mimosa Pittman, April 4, 1902; April 11, 1902; Personal Correspondence, Mrs. Key Pittman, 1898–1903 Folder, Box 53

45. K. P. to Mimosa Pittman, April 2, 1904; April 19, 1904; September 19, 1904; Personal Correspondence, Mrs. Key Pittman, 1904–1905 Folder, Box 53

46. K. P. to Thomas Worburton, July 7, 1902, Political Correspondence, May 1902–March 1903 Folder, Box 2

47. Wren, *op. cit.*, pp. 88–89; Davis, *op. cit.*, I, 426–433; James G. Scrugham (ed.), *Nevada* (New York: American Historical Society, 1935), I, 411, 431

48. K. P. to J. C. Humphreys, July 6, 1902, Political Correspondence, May 1902–March 1903 Folder, Box 2

49. *The Commoner,* January 29, 1904, 3:1–3; February 19, 1904, 1:1–2

50. K. P. to Nate Roff, March 12, 1904, Political Correspondence, February 1904–December 1907 Folder, Box 2; Jeanne Elizabeth Wier, "The Mystery of Nevada," in Thomas C. Donnelly (ed.), *Rocky Mountain Politics* (Albuquerque: University of New Mexico, 1940), p. 110

51. K. P. to Mimosa Pittman, April 19, 1904; September 22, 1904; Personal Correspondence, Mrs. Key Pittman, 1904–1905 Folder, Box 53

52. *Tonopah Miner,* June 16, 1906, 3:2

53. K. P. to Mimosa Pittman, September 19, 1904; July 8, 1905; Personal Correspondence, Mrs. Key Pittman, 1904–1905 Folder, Box 53

54. See the Tonopah Office Files, 1902–1915, Boxes 114–117, and the Legal File, 1902–1915, Boxes 118–123. These files contain correspondence, bills, and receipts which illustrate Pittman's successful legal practice. See also Bessie Beatty, *Who's Who in Nevada* (Los Angeles: Home Printing, 1907), p. 72; *Tonopah Miner,* June 16, 1906, 4:1

55. *Tonopah Miner,* June 25, 1910, 1:3; July 9, 1910, 1:3–4

56. See K. P. to Mimosa Pittman, May 14, 1909, Personal Correspondence, Mrs. Key Pittman, 1908–1910 Folder, Box 54

57. K. P. to Mimosa Pittman, July 8, 1905, Personal Correspondence, Mrs. Key Pittman, 1904–1905 Folder, Box 53; K. P. to Mimosa Pittman, June 2, 1908; May 8, 1909; June 7, 1909; Personal Correspondence, Mrs. Key Pittman, 1908–1910 Folder, Box 54

58. K. P. to Sam Davis, August 22, 1908, Political Correspondence, January–October 1908 Folder, Box 2

59. Davis, *op. cit.*, I, 457–458; *The Manhattan* [Nevada] *Mail,* April 8, 1911, 1:1

60. K. P. to Sam Davis, April 28, 1910, Political Correspondence, January–June 1910 Folder, Box 2

61. K. P. to Sam Belford, December 2, 1909, Political Correspondence, 1909 Folder, Box 2. See also *The Manhattan Mail,* May 7, 1910, 2:2–3

62. K. P. to Charles S. Sprague, April 27, 1910, Political Correspondence, January–June 1910 Folder, Box 2

63. K. P. to H. D. Dickerson, April 19, 1937, U. S. Marshall Folder, Box 16; K. P. to John Hix, July 19, 1939, Newspaper Folder, Box 39

64. Mimosa Pittman to K. P., July 8, 1910, Personal Correspondence, Mrs. Key Pittman, 1910–1913 Folder, Box 54

65. K. P. to Mimosa Pittman, July 10, 1910, Personal Correspondence, 1908–1910 Folder, Box 54

66. *Tonopah Miner,* July 16, 1910, 8:1–2 (see also *The Tonopah Sun,* July 13, 1910, 1:1–2). The following issues of the *Tonopah Miner* are the sources of the information and quotations in the remainder of this paragraph and the next two paragraphs: November 5, 1910, 4:1 (see also *The Manhattan Mail,* July 16, 1910, 2:1); July 6, 1910, 4:1; August 20, 1910, 8:1–4; September 10, 1910, 4:1; October 22, 1910, 8:1; November 2, 1910, 4:1; November 5, 1910, 4:1 (see also *The Manhattan Mail,* November 5, 1910, 2:1–2); October 15, 1910, 4:1

67. Senate Joint Resolution No. 3, *The Journal of the Senate of the Twenty-fifth Session of the Legislature of the State of Nevada,* p. 29. See also George C. Perkins to K. P., February 12, 1911, Political Correspondence, 1911 Folder, Box 4

68. K. P. to R. J. Mapes, November 18, 1910, Political Correspondence, November 1910 Folder, Box 4; K. P. to Charles S. Rosener, November 18, 1910, Political Correspondence, November 1910 Folder, Box 4

69. *Tonopah Miner,* January 7, 1911, 4:1

70. *The Clark County Review,* July 27, 1912, Editorial Page

71. George Springmeyer, "History of the Progressive Party in Nevada," in Davis, *op. cit.,* I, 453–457

72. *Tonopah Miner,* September 7, 1912, 5:1–5

73. *Tonopah Miner,* November 2, 1912, 4:1

NOTES TO CHAPTER II

1. K. P. to M. E. Jepson, July 3, 1916, J Folder, Box 7, Key Pittman Papers, Library of Congress (hereafter cited by folder and box number). Boxes 64–68 contain Pittman's correspondence with Executive Departments 1912–1918 on behalf of his constituents

2. K. P. to Mimosa Pittman, February [n.d.] 1913, Personal Correspondence, Mrs. Key Pittman, 1910–1913 Folder, Box 54

3. K. P. to Mimosa Pittman, February 22, 27; April 5, 12, 1913; *ibid.*

4. Woodrow Wilson, *The New Democracy: Presidential Messages, Addresses, and Other Papers (1913–1917)*, edited by Ray Stannard Baker and William E. Dodd (New York: Harper, 1926), I, 1.

5. *Congressional Record,* 63 Cong. 2 Sess. Vol. 51, Pt. 15 (September 2, 1914), p. 1460; *ibid.,* Pt. 13 (August 5, 1914), p. 13319; *ibid.,* Pt. 2 (December 19, 1913), pp. 1487–1488; *loc. cit.,* 64 Cong. 1 Sess. Vol. 53, Pt. 8 (May 4, 1916), p. 7412; *ibid.,* Pt. 13 (September 2, 1916), p. 13655

6. *Loc. cit.,* 63 Cong. 1 Sess. Vol. 50, Pt. 4 (August 21, 1913), pp. 3572–3584; *Reno Evening Gazette,* June 26, 1913

7. *Congressional Record,* 63 Cong. 1 Sess. Vol. 50, Pt. 3 (July 26, 1913), p. 2802; K. P. to J. T. Goodin, April 17, 1916, Go Folder, Box 7

8. Woodrow Wilson to K. P., May 28, 1913; K. P. to Woodrow Wilson, May 29, 1913; as quoted in Ray Stannard Baker, *Woodrow Wilson, Life and Letters* (New York: Doubleday, 1931), IV, 122–123

9. See Arthur S. Link, *Wilson: The New Freedom* (Princeton: Princeton University, 1956), pp. 304–314

10. *Washington Post,* April 10, 1914

11. *Gardnersville Record-Courier,* April 24, 1914; *Carson Appeal* [Carson City, Nevada], April 6, 1914

12. *Carson News* [Carson City, Nevada], April 10, 1914

13. *New York Times,* September 4, 1913, 8:2; *Sparks* [Nevada] *Tribune,* December 5, 1913

14. *Congressional Record,* 63 Cong. 1 Sess. Vol. 50, Pt. 6 (October 7, 1913), pp. 5483–5495

15. M. M. O'Shaughnessy, *Hetch-Hetchy: Its Origins and History,* San Francisco, 1934, p. 51

16. *San Francisco Examiner,* December 6, 1913, 2:7

17. K. P. to N. P. R. Hatch, July 23, 1915, H Folder, Box 7; K. P. to Mimosa Pittman, January 3, 1915; December 13, 1915; Personal Correspondence, Mrs. Key Pittman, 1914–1915 Folder, Box 54

18. K. P. to Franklin Leonard, July 21, 1916, L Folder, Box 8. See *Congressional Record,* 63 Cong. 1 Sess. Index, p. 270; *ibid.,* 2 Sess. Index, p. 352; *ibid.,* 3 Sess. Index, p. 144

19. K. P. to Raymond T. Baker, February 18, 1915, B-Personal Folder, Box 25

20. *Oakland* [California] *Tribune,* August 3, 1913. See also *Carson News,* February 20, 1914; *Goldfield* [Nevada] *Tribune,* February 5, 1914; *Sparks Tribune,* February 5, 1914

21. K. P. to J. T. Goodin, June 10, 1916, Go Folder, Box 7; K. P. to Mimosa Pittman, February 16, 1916, Personal Correspondence, Mrs. Key Pittman, 1916–1921 Folder, Box 55

22. *Congressional Record,* 64 Cong. 1 Sess. Vol. 53, Pt. 11 (July 7, 1916), p. 10539

23. K. P. to Vail Pittman, July 21, 1916, Pi Folder, Box 9

24. K. P. to James T. Boyd, April 11, 1916, Bo Folder, Box 6

25. K. P. to H. W. Huskey, August 18, 1916, Hu Folder, Box 7

26. K. P. to Peter Breen, April 20, 1916, Br Folder, Box 6; K. P. to C. C. Emerson, May 19, 1916, E Folder, Box 7; K. P. to J. T. Goodin, June 10, 1916, Go Folder, Box 7

27. See for example *San Francisco Examiner,* October 23, 1916, 16:1; October 31, 1916, 20:1; November 3, 1916, 20:1; *Nevada State Journal,* October 27, 1916, 4:1; *Reno Evening Gazette,* November 1, 1916, 4:1–2

28. *Nevada State Journal,* August 15, 1916, 4:1. Sam Platt, Pittman's Republican opponent, owned the *Reno Evening Gazette,* the second state-wide newspaper

29. K. P. to Mimosa Pittman, February 14, 1916, Personal Correspondence, Mrs. Key Pittman, 1916–1921 Folder, Box 55

30. *Congressional Record,* 63 Cong. 2 Sess. Vol. 51, Pt. 5 (March 19, 1914), pp. 5101–5102

31. *Carson Appeal,* March 24, 1914

32. *Nevada State Journal,* August 14, 1916, 6:3; August 23, 1916, 4:1; August 24, 1916, 8:4–5; *Reno Evening Gazette,* October 31, 1916, 3:1–7

33. K. P. to Frank Reber, August 26, 1916, R Folder, Box 9; *The Seattle Daily Times,* December 21, 1916, 21:6

34. K. P. to Norman Hapgood, September 10, 1916, H Folder, Box 7. See for example Go Folder, Box 7 and R Folder, Box 9

35. Speech of K. P. at Tonopah, October 11, 1916, Speeches, Articles, and Remarks, 1916–1917 Folder, Box 160; K. P. to Mary Harrington, August 23, 1916, Har Folder, Box 7.

36. *The Commoner,* October 1916, 9:3

37. K. P. to Mimosa Pittman, March 12, 1913, Personal Correspondence, Mrs. Key Pittman, 1910–1913 Folder, Box 54

38. K. P. to Bernard M. Baruch, July 1, 1930, B Folder, Box 43

39. K. P. to George B. Thatcher, January 25, 1916, T Folder, Box 10

40. Baker, *op. cit.,* VII, 127

41. *Washington Post,* April 20, 1914

42. *New York Times,* May 15, 1915, 5:3

43. K. P. to John W. Kern, December 4, 1915, Committee on Naval Affairs Folder, Box 89

44. *The* [Cincinnati] *Enquirer,* March 16, 1916

45. K. P. to Mimosa Pittman, March 21, 1916, Personal Correspondence, Mrs. Key Pittman, 1916–1921 Folder, Box 55

46. *The Washington Herald*, March 28, 1916, 2:3

47. K. P. to Prince A. Hawkins, January 18, 1916, Haw Folder, Box 7

48. K. P. to Sam P. Davis, February 17, 1917, D Folder, Box 6

49. *Congressional Record*, 64 Cong. 2 Sess. Vol. 54, Pt. 3 (February 7, 1917), p. 2737

50. K. P. to Woodrow Wilson, March 27, 1917, The White House Folder, Box 68

51. *Congressional Record*, 65 Cong. Special Sess. Vol. 55, Pt. 1 (April 4, 1917), p. 251

52. K. P. to Harley Harmon, October 17, 1918, Har Folder, Box 7

53. *New York Times*, October 27, 1918, 1:1

54. Baker, *op. cit.*, VIII, 562

55. K. P. to Woodrow Wilson, November 15; 27, 1918, The White House Folder, Box 68

56. *Congressional Record*, 65 Cong. 3 Sess. Vol. 57, Pt. 1 (December 2, 1918), pp. 3–5

57. *New York Times*, August 20, 1919, 1:8, 2:3. A complete transcript of the conference can be found in *ibid.*, pp. 8–11. See also: Statement of Key Pittman, *Congressional Record*, 66 Cong. 1 Sess. Vol. 58, Pt. 4 (August 20, 1919), pp. 4048 ff.; Thomas A. Bailey, *Woodrow Wilson and the Great Betrayal* (New York: Macmillan, 1947), p. 86; John A. Garraty, *Henry Cabot Lodge* (New York: Knopf, 1953), pp. 366 ff.

58. *New York Times*, August 16, 1919, 1:1

59. Senate Resolution 168, 66 Cong.

60. *Congressional Record, loc. cit.*, pp. 4048, 4054

61. *New York Times*, August 21, 1:8; August 22, 2:5; August 27, 1919, 1:7

62. K. P. to William Hard, July 7, 1926, H Folder, Box 13

63. K. P. to W. M. Riddle, August 28, 1919, League of Nations Folder, Box 91

64. K. P. to Bernard M. Baruch, July 1, 1930, B Folder, Box 43

65. *New York Times*, February 10, 1:5; February 11, 1920, 1:8

66. As quoted in Bailey, *op. cit.*, p. 254

67. K. P. to Bernard M. Baruch, July 1, 1930, B Folder, Box 43

68. *Loc. cit.* See also K. P. to H. R. Cooke, February 20, 1928, C-General Folder, Box 11

69. K. P. to Mimosa Pittman, December 13, 1915, Personal Correspondence, Mrs. Key Pittman, 1914–1915 Folder, Box 54; K. P. to Mimosa Pittman, February 18; March 20, 1916, Personal Correspondence, Mrs. Key Pittman, 1916–1921 Folder, Box 55

70. K. P. to Mimosa Pittman, February 27, 1913, Personal Correspondence, Mrs. Key Pittman, 1910–1913 Folder, Box 54

71. K. P. to Mimosa Pittman, January 8; February 8; 25; March 22, 1916; Personal Correspondence, Mrs. Key Pittman, 1916–1921 Folder, Box 55

72. K. P. to Mimosa Pittman, November 24, 1915; December 17, 1915; Personal Correspondence, Mrs. Key Pittman, 1914–1915 Folder, Box 54

73. K. P. to Mimosa Pittman, December 29, 1915, *ibid*

74. K. P. to Mimosa Pittman, April 16, 1913, Personal Correspondence, Mrs. Key Pittman, 1910–1913 Folder, Box 54

75. K. P. to Mimosa Pittman, September 19, 1904, Personal Correspondence, Mrs. Key Pittman, 1904–1905 Folder, Box 53

76. See Charlotte Buhler and D. Welty Lefever, *A Rorschach Study of the Psychological Characteristics of Alcoholics* (New Haven: Laboratory of Applied Psychology, 1948), 64 pp.; Donald G. Murphy, "Psychological Correlations of Alcohol Addictions" (unpublished Ph.D. dissertation, Teachers College, 1957), 109 pp.

77. K. P. to Mimosa Pittman, February 17, 1913, Personal Correspondence, Mrs. Key Pittman, 1910–1913 Folder, Box 54

78. Mimosa Pittman to K. P., n.d., Personal Correspondence, Mrs. Key Pittman, 1910–1913 Folder, Box 54. Mrs. Pittman is answering K. P.'s letter of February 17, 1913

79. The Johns Hopkins Hospital Examination Report, June 15, 1923, Personal Correspondence, Mrs. Key Pittman, 1922–1925 Folder, Box 55. See also Ruth Fox, "Treatment of Alcoholism," in Harold E. Himwich (ed.), *Alcoholism: Basic Aspects and Treatment* (Washington: American Association for the Advancement of Science, 1957), pp. 171 ff.

80. Mimosa Pittman to Humboldt Gates, October 26, 1915, Personal Correspondence, Mrs. Key Pittman, 1914–1915 Folder, Box 54

81. K. P. to Mimosa Pittman, December 22, 1935, Personal Correspondence, Mrs. Key Pittman, 1926–1936 Folder, Box 55

82. K. P. to Mimosa Pittman, December 22, 1935, Personal Correspondence, Mrs. Key Pittman, 1926–1936 Folder, Box 55. See also George N. Thompson, "The Psychiatry of Alcoholism," in George N. Thompson (ed.), *Alcoholism* (Springfield: Charles C. Thomas, 1956), pp. 452 ff.

NOTES TO CHAPTER III

1. As quoted in William E. Leuchtenburg, *Perils of Prosperity* (Chicago: University of Chicago, 1958), p. 84

2. K. P. to Mrs. Minnie L. Bray, March 24, 1920, Br Folder, Box 6; K. P. to J. T. Goodin, April 17, 1920, Go Folder, Box 7, Key Pittman Papers, Library of Congress (hereafter cited by Folder and box number); *New York Times*, August 7, 1920, 3:1

3. K. P. to James D. Phelan, October 5, 1920, Campaign of 1920 Folder, Box 147

4. The Reminiscences of James W. Gerard, Oral History Project, Columbia University, p. 70; *Nevada State Journal*, September 15, 1920, 1:1

5. *San Francisco Chronicle*, October 2, 1920, 4:2–3

6. *The Seattle Daily Times*, October 5, 1920

7. K. P. to R. P. Dunlap, July 25, 1921; July 28, 1921; D Folder, Box 12; K. P. to A. L. Scott, July 6, 1922, S Folder, Box 15

8. *Congressional Record*, 67 Cong. 1 Sess. Vol. 61, Pt. 5 (August 3, 1921), p. 4601; (August 4, 1921), pp. 4626–4630

9. Arthur Capper, *The Agricultural Bloc* (New York: Harcourt, Brace, 1922), p. 12

10. K. P. to R. P. Dunlap, July 28, 1921, D Folder, Box 12; K. P. to Boyd Moore, April 21, 1922, Newspapers (1920–1927) Folder, Box 14

11. K. P. to Charles Henderson, May 14, 1921, H Folder, Box 13

12. *Congressional Record*, 67 Cong. 2 Sess. Vol. 62, Pt. 7 (May 12, 1922), p. 6801; K. P. to R. P. Dunlap, April 22, 1921, D Folder, Box 12

13. K. P. to Bernard M. Baruch, February 10, 1923, B Folder, Box 43

14. James Bryce, *The American Commonwealth* (New York: Macmillan, 1911), I, 103

15. *Congressional Record,* 67 Cong. 1 Sess. Vol. 61, Pt. 5 (August 11, 1921), pp. 4855, 4860; (August 16, 1921), pp. 5041–5045, 5055–5056; (August 19, 1921), p. 5270

16. K. P. to Samuel W. Belford, May 10, 1922, B-General Folder, Box 11

17. *Congressional Record,* 67 Cong. 2 Sess. Vol. 62, Pt. 6 (May 3, 1922), pp. 6257–6258; Pt. 7 (May 12, 1922), pp. 6799–6801; Pt. 8 (May 29, 1922), pp. 7852–7858

18. *Nevada State Journal,* November 3, 1922, 4:1

19. Joseph H. Baird, "Key Pittman: Frontier Statesman," *American Mercury,* L (July 1940), 310–312

20. *Congressional Record,* 67 Cong. 2 Sess. Vol. 62, Pt. 5 (March 25, 1922), p. 4541; (March 27, 1922), pp. 4614–4615; (March 24, 1922), p. 4493

21. *Congressional Record, loc. cit.,* Pt. 3 (February 15, 1922), p. 2587; (February 23, 1922), pp. 2940–2942

22. Merlo J. Pusey, *Charles Evans Hughes* (New York: Macmillan, 1951), II, 500; *The Commoner,* March 1922, pp. 1, 13; April 1922, p. 1. See also K. P.'s correspondence with William Jennings Bryan, Treaties Folder, Box 94

23. For Pittman's 1922 campaign, see the William Woodburn File, W. Folder, Box 16

24. *Infra,* pp. 112–116

25. *Nevada State Journal,* November 1, 1922, 2:3

26. K. P. to Mimosa Pittman, August 26, 1922, Personal Correspondence, Mrs. Key Pittman, 1922–1925 Folder, Box 55

27. K. P. to Mimosa Pittman, October 7, 1922; October 29, 1922; Personal Correspondence, Mrs. Key Pittman, 1922–1925 Folder, Box 55

28. Bernard M. Baruch to K. P., May 14, 1923; K. P. to Bernard M. Baruch, May 16, 1923, B-General Folder, Box 11

29. K. P. to Frances Friedhoff, April 29, 1924, F Folder, Box 12; K. P. to D. H. Pettingell, January 14, 1924, Fish Hatchery-Humboldt River Folder, Box 104

30. K. P. to J. G. Scrugham, May 12, 1924, S Folder, Box 15; K. P. to Samuel W. Belford, May 12, 1924, B-General Folder, Box 11

31. K. P. to Samuel Belford, May 12, 1924; June 16, 1924, B-General Folder, Box 11

32. *Official Report of the Proceedings of the 1924 Democratic National Convention,* p. 270

33. K. P. to L. L. Aitken, July 28, 1924, A-General Folder, Box 11

34. *Proceedings,* pp. 273–279. See also *New York Times,* June 30, 1924, 6:8

35. K. P. to John Sharp Williams, July 28, 1924, W Folder, Box 16

36. K. P. to William McKnight, August 29, 1924, Mc Folder, Box 13; K. P. to Clifford P. Morehouse, May 8, 1924, M Folder, Box 13; K. P. to J. G. Scrugham, May 12, 1924, S Folder, Box 15

37. *Proceedings,* pp. 226, 333. See also *New York Times,* June 30, 1924, p. 1

38. K. P. to George B. Thatcher, August 29, 1924, T Folder, Box 16; K. P. to William McKnight, August 29, 1924, Mc Folder, Box 13; *New York American,* August 28, 1924, 7:3–4; *Proceedings,* p. 333

39. K. P. to George B. Thatcher, May 20, 1924, T Folder, Box 16; K. P. to William A. Kelly, June 3, 1924, K Folder, Box 13

40. *Proceedings,* pp. 618; 790; 895

41. K. P. to William McKnight, July 23, 1924, Mc Folder, Box 13

42. K. P. to Samuel W. Belford, July 24, 1924, B-General Folder, Box 11

43. *Proceedings,* pp. 1028, 1038

44. K. P. to W. B. Pittman, August 13, 1924, W. B. Pittman Folder, Box 46

182   *Notes*

45. K. P. to John Sharp Williams, July 28, 1924, W Folder, Box 16
46. K. P. to Norman H. Davis, July 23, 1924, D Folder, Box 12
47. K. P. to Samuel W. Belford, August 26, 1924, B-General Folder, Box 11; K. P. to William McKnight, August 26, 1924; August 29, 1924; Mc Folder, Box 13; *New York Times*, August 25, 1924, 3:1
48. K. P. to Mimosa Pittman, August 19 [1924], Personal Correspondence, Mrs. Key Pittman, 1922–1925 Folder, Box 55
49. K. P. to George B. Thatcher, August 29, 1924, T Folder, Box 16
50. K. P. to William McKnight, September 27, 1924, Mc Folder, Box 13
51. K. P. to Mimosa Pittman, September 5, 1924, Personal Correspondence, Mrs. Key Pittman, 1922–1925 Folder, Box 55
52. K. P. to S. M. Pickett, August 26, 1924, P Folder, Box 14
53. K. P. to William McKnight, October 23, 1924, Mc Folder, Box 13
54. Samuel W. Belford to K. P., October 25, 1924; November 11, 1924; B-General Folder, Box 11
55. Will Rogers, *How We Elect Our Presidents*, edited by Donald Day (Boston: Little, Brown, 1952) , p. 144
56. *Nevada State Journal*, November 2, 1924, 4:5–6
57. K. P. to Samuel W. Belford, November 13, 1924, B-General Folder, Box 11
58. The Reminiscences of John W. Davis, Oral History Project, Columbia University, pp. 149–150
59. K. P. to Mr. and Mrs. George W. Friedhoff, December 1, 1924, F Folder, Box 12; K. P. to Frances Friedhoff, April 29, 1924, F Folder, Box 12; K. P. to Mrs. Frances Parkinson Keyes, December 18, 1925, K Folder, Box 13
60. K. P. to William Woodburn, December 26, 1926, W Folder, Box 16. For Pittman's work on behalf of the interests of his constituents during this period, see Boxes 69, 73–76, 104, 105, 108, 113
61. *Congressional Record*, 68 Cong. 1 Sess. Vol. 65, Pt. 11 (June 7, 1924) , pp. 1198 ff.; 68 Cong. 2 Sess. Vol. 66, Pt. 2 (January 6, 1925) , p. 217; Pt. 5 (March 2, 1925) , p. 5126; Spanish Springs Project Folder, Box 112
62. *Congressional Record*, 69 Cong. 2 Sess. Vol. 68, Pt. 1 (December 22, 1926) , p. 936
63. *Loc. cit.*, 1 Sess. Vol. 67, Pt. 5 (March 4, 1926) , p. 4986
64. *Loc. cit.*, 2 Sess. Vol. 68, Pt. 1 (December 21, 1926) , p. 849
65. *Ibid.* (December 9, 1924) , pp. 301, 305, 306; (December 12, 1924) , p. 516; Pt. 5 (February 25, 1927) , p. 4759; 70 Cong. 1 Sess. Vol. 69, Pt. 4 (March 13, 1928) , p. 4635
66. *Loc. cit.*, 69 Cong. 2 Sess. Vol. 68, Pt. 4 (February 11, 1927) , p. 3518; 70 Cong. 1 Sess. Vol. 69, Pt. 6 (April 12, 1928) , p. 6823; Pt. 9 (May 25, 1928) , pp. 9879–9880
67. K. P. to E. N. Steininger, August 23, 1928, Newspapers (1928) Folder, Box 14
68. K. P. to John E. Robbins, February 23, 1928, R Folder, Box 15. See K. P. to William Woodburn, December 23, 1926, W. Folder, Box 16
69. K. P. to John E. Robbins, April 4, 1928, R Folder, Box 15; K. P. to Henry C. Schmidt, May 4, 1928, S Folder, Box 15
70. K. P. to William Woodburn, May 14, 1928, W Folder, Box 16. See also Democratic National Committee Folder, especially K. P. to Mrs. Henry Moskowitz, Box 12, for details of Smith's preconvention organization
71. K. P. to William Woodburn, June 11, 1928, W Folder, Box 16; K. P. to A. L. Scott, June 11, 1928, S Folder, Box 15

72. The Reminiscences of Claude Bowers, Oral History Project, Columbia University, pp. 77–78

73. K. P. to Mrs. Henry Moskowitz, June 18, 1928, Democratic National Committee Folder, Box 12; K. P. to Joseph Robinson, June 18, 1928, R Folder, Box 15

74. *New York Herald Tribune,* June 27, 1928, 6:4

75. "Proceedings of the Executive Meeting of the Committee on Resolutions and Platform," June 28, 1928, p. 38, Democratic National Convention, 1928 Folder, Box 149

76. K. P. to Oscar W. Underwood, July 6, 1928, U Folder, Box 16; K. P. to Judge Joseph M. Proskauer, July 2, 1928, P Folder, Box 14; *Official Report of the Proceedings of the 1928 Democratic National Convention,* pp. 200–204

77. Emily Smith Warner and Hawthorne Daniel, *The Happy Warrior* (New York: Doubleday, 1956) , p. 201

78. Joseph T. Robinson to K. P., July 2, 1928, R Folder, Box 15. See Frances Parkinson Keyes, "The American Woman and the Democratic Party," *Delineator,* CXIII (November 1928) , 17 ff.; K. P. to Mrs. Izetta Jewel Miller, July 6, 1928, M Folder, Box 13

79. Alfred E. Smith, *Up to Now* (New York: Garden City, 1929) , pp. 383–384; *Nevada State Journal,* November 4, 1:8; November 3, 1928, 1:6; K. P. to James A. Farley, July 11, 1932, Democratic National Convention, 1932 Folder, Box 149

80. *Nevada State Journal,* October 23, 1:4–5; October 27, 3:3; November 1, p. 3; November 3, 1:6; November 4, 1928, 1:8

81. K. P. to Peter G. Gerry, September 13, 1928, Campaign Committees, 1928 Folder, Box 11

82. K. P. to Mrs. Henry Moskowitz, March 9, 1929, Campaign Committees, 1928 Folder, Box 11; K. P. to James J. Hoey, February 7, 1929, H Folder, Box 13

83. *Congressional Record,* 71 Cong. 1 Sess. Vol. 71, Pt. 5 (November 22, 1929) , p. 5967

84. Arthur W. Macmahon, "First Session of the Seventy-first Congress," *American Political Science Review,* XXIV (1930) , 38

85. *Congressional Record, loc. cit.,* Pt. 1 (April 16, 1929) , p. 42. See also Gilbert C. Fite, "The Agricultural Issue in the Presidential Campaign of 1928," *Mississippi Valley Historical Review,* XXXVII (1950–1951) , 653 ff.; Theodore Saloutos and John D. Hicks, *Agricultural Discontent in the Middle West 1900–1939* (Madison: University of Wisconsin, 1951) , pp. 404 ff.

86. *New York Times,* July 31, 1928, 1:6. See E. E. Schattschneider, *Politics, Pressures and the Tariff* (New York: Prentice Hall, 1935) , p. 7; Abraham Berglund, "The Tariff Act of 1930," *American Economic Review,* XX (1930) , 467 ff.

87. *Congressional Record,* 71 Cong. 1 Sess. Vol. 71, Pt. 4 (September 12, 1929) , p. 3542; Pt. 5 (November 5, 1929) , p. 5173

88. *Ibid.,* p. 5175; 71 Cong. 2 Sess. Vol. 72, Pt. 5 (March 7, 1930) , p. 4920; 1 Sess. Vol. 71, Pt. 5 (November 4, 1929) , p. 5141

89. State of Nevada, *Report of the Commissioner of Labor for the Period 1929–1930* (Carson City: State Printing Office, 1931) , p. 13

90. *Annual Report of the Director of the Mint for the Fiscal Year 1931,* pp. 32–33; *Nevada State Journal,* January 7, 1930, 7:5.

91. *Congressional Record,* 72 Cong. 1 Sess. Vol. 75, Pt. 8 (April 28, 1932) , p. 9109. See John N. Webb and Malcolm Brown, *Migrant Families* (Washington: United States Government Printing Office, 1938) , pp. 44–45

92. K. P. to John W. Davis, December 17, 1931, D Folder, Box 12

93. *Ibid.*

94. S 4755, 72 Cong.

95. *Congressional Record,* 72 Cong. 1 Sess. Vol. 75, Pt. 12 (June 21, 1932), p. 13562

96. *Ibid.,* Pt. 8 (April 28, 1932), p. 9110

97. K. P. to William S. Boyle, November 12, 1930, B-General Folder, Box 11

98. K. P. to Charles L. Richards, November 8, 1930, R Folder, Box 15; K. P. to W. G. Greathouse, November 10, 1930, G Folder, Box 12

NOTES TO CHAPTER IV

1. *Annual Report of the Director of the Mint for the Fiscal Year 1944,* pp. 87, 91. For a comprehensive discussion of the congressional silver bloc and silver legislation 1918 to 1946, see: Everett L. Cooley, "Silver Politics in the United States, 1918–1946" (unpublished Ph.D. dissertation, University of California, Berkeley, 1951)

2. U. S., Congress, House, Committee on Banking and Currency, *Hearings, Silver Purchases Under the Pittman Act,* 68 Cong. 2 Sess. 1925, pp. 5–6; U. S., Congress, Senate, Committee on Banking and Currency, *Hearings, Silver Purchased Under the Pittman Act,* 68 Cong. 1 Sess. 1924, pp. 4, 24

3. *Congressional Record,* 67 Cong. 2 Sess. Vol. 62, Pt. 11 (August 26, 1922), p. 11832; article by K. P., Special Nevada Edition of the *San Francisco Bulletin,* June 13, 1921

4. *Congressional Record,* 65 Cong. 2 Sess. Vol. 56, Pt. 6 (April 22, 1918), p. 5435

5. *Congressional Record,* 65 Cong. 2 Sess. Vol. 56, Pt. 5 (April 18, 1918), pp. 5241–5250; U. S., *Statutes at Large,* XL (1918), p. 535

6. *Reno Evening Gazette,* May 6, 1919

7. *Annual Report of the Director of the Mint for the Fiscal Year 1944,* p. 87

8. K. P. to Walter C. Lamb, June 13, 1920, Silver Folder, Box 111, Key Pittman Papers, Library of Congress (hereafter cited by folder and box number)

9. See Neil Carothers, "Silver—A Senate Racket," *Lehigh University Publications,* VI (January 1932), 7

10. U. S., Congress, Senate, Committee on Mines and Mining, *Hearings, Appointment of Silver Commission,* 67 Cong. 4 Sess. 1923

11. See U. S., Congress, Senate, Subcommittee of the Commission of Gold and Silver Inquiry, *Silver Purchased Under the Pittman Act, Hearings,* 64 Cong. 4 Sess. 1923, 268 pp.

12. K. P. to Charles E. Alden, May 16, 1923, Members of Commission Folder, Box 137; U. S., Congress, Senate, Commission of Gold and Silver Inquiry, *Progress Report,* 68 Cong. 1 Sess. 1924, pp. 23 ff.

13. U. S., Congress, Senate, Commission of Gold and Silver Inquiry, *Silver Producer's Convention,* 67 Cong. 4 Sess. 1923, p. 17; K. P. to C. Berkeley Taylor, July 17, 1923, T Folder, Box 138

14. *Congressional Record,* 68 Cong. 1 Sess. Vol. 65, Pt. 4 (March 25, 1924), p. 4914

15. U. S., Congress, Senate, Banking and Currency Committee, *Hearings, Silver Purchases Under the Pittman Act,* 68 Cong. 1 Sess. 1924, pp. 1–21, 33

16. *Congressional Record,* 68 Cong. 1 Sess. Vol. 65, Pt. 10 (May 29, 1924), p. 9857; Andrew W. Mellon to George P. McLean, April 17, 1924, Silver—To Complete Purchases Folder, Box 112

17. K. P. to John G. Kirchen, June 16, 1924, Silver—To Complete Purchases Folder, Box 112

18. *Congressional Record,* 69 Cong. 1 Sess. Vol. 67, Pt. 12, p. 536; 2 Sess. Vol. 68, Pt. 6, p. 236

19. Handy and Harman, *Review of the Silver Market for 1926,* pp. 1–3; Handy and Harman, *Review of the Silver Market for 1928,* pp. 4–5

20. *Congressional Record,* 71 Cong. 1 Sess. Vol. 71, Pt. 2 (May 16, 1929) , p. 1389; Vol. 71, Pt. 3 (June 11, 1929) , pp. 2631–2633; K. P. to Bernard M. Baruch, November 11, 1930, B Folder, Box 140

21. K. P. to Alben W. Barkley, June 13, 1929, Silver Tariff Folder, Box 101

22. *Congressional Record,* 71 Cong. 2 Sess. Vol. 72, Pt. 5 (March 19, 1930) , p. 5615

23. K. P. to W. H. Venable, February 27, 1930, Silver Tariff Folder, Box 101

24. K. P. to J. G. Scrugham, May 13, 1930, Silver Tariff Folder, Box 101

25. K. P. to James V. Keys, June 3, 1930, Silver Tariff Folder, Box 101

26. K. P. to Frank H. Norcross, May 13, 1930, Silver Tariff Folder, Box 101

27. U. S., Congress, Senate, Subcommittee of the Committee on Foreign Relations, *Hearings, Commercial Relations with China,* 1930, p. 12

28. K. P. to Claude Bowers, February 16, 1931, B Folder, Box 140

29. See K. P. to Homer Mooney, December 13, 1930, M Folder, Box 144

30. *Commercial Relations with China, loc. cit.,* pp. 19, 11–36, 123–134

31. K. P. to Norman H. Davis, January 22, 1931, Key Pittman Folder, Box 47, Norman H. Davis Papers, Library of Congress (hereafter cited as Davis Papers)

32. *New York Times,* December 17, 1930, III, 1:7

33. K. P. to Charles S. Thomas, December 18, 1931, T Folder, Box 146

34. K. P. to L. F. Harden, November 4, 1930, H Folder, Box 143

35. *Congressional Record,* 71 Cong. 3 Sess. Vol. 74, Pt. 5 (February 12, 1931) , p. 4701

36. Senate Resolution 442, 71 Cong. 3 Sess.

37. *Congressional Record,* 71 Cong. 3 Sess. Vol. 74, Pt. 6 (February 20, 1931) , pp. 5493–5494

38. Carothers, *op. cit.,* p. 8

39. K. P. to Norman H. Davis, April 23, 1931, Key Pittman Folder, Box 47, Davis Papers

40. *Hong Kong Daily Press,* July 6, 1931

41. K. P. to Bernard M. Baruch, August 19, 1931, China Correspondence Book, Box 197

42. For a discussion of this point, see Allan Seymour Everest, *Morgenthau the New Deal and Silver* (New York: Kings Crown, 1950) , pp. 101–106; Wei-Ying Lin, *China Under Depreciated Silver 1926–1931* (Shanghai: The Commercial Press, 1935) , pp. 79 ff.

43. *New York Times,* February 21, 1931, 8:6; May 8, 1931, 22:4; W. H. (Coin) Harvey, *The Book,* Rogers, Arkansas, 1930

44. K. P. to A. E. Cahlan, May 18, 1932, C-General Folder, Box 11

45. K. P. to A. G. Prichard, December 17, 1931, P Folder, Box 145

46. K. P. to A. T. McCarter, February 9, 1933, Mc Folder, Box 145; K. P. to Mary McNamara, February 27, 1933, Newspaper Folder, Box 145

47. K. P. to Charles S. Thomas, April 6, 1932, T Folder, Box 146

48. "The Lausanne Agreement," *International Conciliation,* CCLXXXII (Septem-

ber 932) , 37. See also Dean E. Traynor, *International and Financial Conferences in the Interwar Period* (Washington: Catholic University, 1949) , pp. 91–92

49. Henry L. Stimson to Herbert Hoover, December 27, 1932, U. S., Congress, House, Committee on Foreign Affairs, *Hearings, International Monetary and Economic Conference, London, England,* 1933, p. 3

50. K. P. to A. G. Makenzie, July 16, 1932, M Folder, Box 144; K. P. to Rene Leon, August 6, 1932, L Folder, Box 144

51. Senate Resolution 67, 73 Cong.; K. P. to Signor M. Guido, May 6, 1933, Italy Folder, Sen. 73A–F10:112, Papers of the United States Senate Committee on Foreign Relations, National Archives

52. *Infra,* pp. 150 ff.

53. H. V. Kaltenborn, *Fifty Fabulous Years 1900–1950* (New York: Putnam, 1950) , pp. 182–183

54. Raymond Moley, *After Seven Years* (New York: Harper, 1939) , p. 218

55. James Cox, *Journey Through My Years* (New York: Simon and Schuster, 1946) , pp. 351–383; Harry Barnard, *Independent Man: The Life of Senator James Couzens* (New York: Scribner, 1958) , pp. 268–274

56. The Reminiscences of James Warburg, Oral History Project, Columbia University, p. 1148. For a summary of the London conference, see: Robert Ferrell, *American Diplomacy in the Great Depression* (New Haven: Yale University, 1957) , pp. 255–277. Professor Ferrell did not have access to the voluminous diary maintained by James Warburg during the conference, which is an invaluable source, especially for the "behind-the-scene" meetings.

57. Cordell Hull, *The Memoirs of Cordell Hull* (New York: Macmillan, 1948) , pp. 254–255

58. *The Times* [London], June 12, 1933

59. Jeannette P. Nichols, "Roosevelt's Monetary Diplomacy in 1933," *American Historical Review,* LVI (1950–1951) , 308

60. *San Francisco Chronicle,* May 10, 1937, p. 9

61. The Reminiscences of James Warburg, *loc. cit.,* pp. 486, 487, 998, 1250

62. K. P. to Francis H. Brownell, August 30, 1933, B Folder, Box 140

63. Department of State, *Executive Agreement Series,* No. 63

64. Hull, *op. cit.,* p. 266

65. K. P. to George W. Snyder, November 8, 1933, S Folder, Box 145

66. K. P. to Henry Morgenthau, Jr., December 11, 1933, Depts.-Govt. Folder, Box 142

67. K. P. to Louis McH. Howe, November 1, 1933, Depts.-Govt. Folder, Box 142; K. P. to Josephus Daniels, November 9, 1933, D Folder, Box 142

68. Everest, *op. cit.,* p. 30

69. *New York Times,* June 25, 1933, 2:4

70. *New York Times,* December 22, 1933, 1:6

71. Edward S. Corwin, *The President: Office and Powers, 1787–1957* (New York: New York University, 1957) , p. 392

72. K. P. to F. D. R., January 9, 1934; Cordell Hull to K. P., May 1, 1934, Depts.-Govt. Folder, Box 142

73. *Salt Lake Telegram,* December 22, 1933, 1:2–3

74. K. P. to *Nevada State Journal,* December 21, 1933, Newspaper Folder, Box 145

NOTES TO CHAPTER V

1. K. P. to R. L. Douglas, June 25, 1932, Democratic National Convention, 1932 Folder, Box 149, Key Pittman Papers, Library of Congress (hereafter cited by folder and box number)

2. *New York Times,* May 29, 1932, IX, 3:7

3. *New York Times,* April 8, 1932, 1:3; April 9, 1932, 1:1

4. K. P. to William S. Boyle, May 2, 1932, B-General Folder, Box 11

5. K. P. to Homer S. Cummings, June 25, 1932, Democratic National Convention, 1932 Folder, Box 149

6. K. P. to R. L. Douglas, June 25, 1932, D Folder, Box 12

7. James A. Farley, *Behind the Ballots* (New York: Harcourt, Brace, 1938), pp. 132 ff.

8. K. P. to Scott Ferris, June 27, 1932; K. P. to Arthur Mullen, June 27, 1932; K. P. and Harry B. Hawes to Tom Connally, June 27, 1932; Democratic National Convention, 1932 Folder, Box 149

9. Farley, *op. cit.,* pp. 134–136; James A. Farley, *Jim Farley's Story* (New York: McGraw-Hill, 1948), p. 19

10. K. P. to Alfred Pittman, July 16, 1932, Key-Pittman Genealogy Folder, Box 1

11. K. P. to F. D. R., July 19, 1932, Democratic National Convention, 1932 Folder, Box 149; F. D. R. to K. P., August 30, 1932, Roosevelt-F. D. R., 1932–1939 Folder, Box 16

12. K. P. to F. D. R., July 19, 1932; August 11, 1932; Roosevelt-F. D. R., 1932–1939 Folder, Box 16

13. K. P. to William McKnight, October 4, 1932, Mc Folder, Box 13

14. K. P. to Louis Howe, August 19, 1932, H Folder, Box 13

15. *New York Times,* September 18, 1932, pp. 1, 32; *Nevada State Journal,* September 20, 1932, 1:8; K. P. to F. D. R., October 4, 1932, Roosevelt-F. D. R., 1932–1939 Folder, Box 16

16. K. P. to Raymond Moley, October 4, 1932; February 15, 1933; M Folder, Box 13

17. K. P. to Mary McNamara, February 7, 1934, Mc Folder, Box 13

18. The Reminiscences of James Warburg, Oral History Project, Columbia University, pp. 495–498

19. *Congressional Record,* 73 Cong. 1 Sess. Vol. 77, Pt. 3 (April 21, 1933), p. 2077

20. *Congressional Record,* 73 Cong. 2 Sess. Vol. 78, Pt. 1 (January 15, 1934), pp. 614–615

21. *Ibid.,* Pt. 2 (January 26, 1934), p. 1459

22. *Ibid.* (January 27, 1934), pp. 1463–1465

23. *Ibid.,* p. 1475; (January 29, 1934), pp. 1492–1493; (January 26, 1934), pp. 1393, 1439

24. K. P. to Henry Morgenthau, Jr., February 16, 1934, Correspondence M Folder, Sen. 73A–F10 (112C), Papers of the United States Senate Foreign Relations Committee, National Archives (hereafter cited as F.R.C.)

25. See Everett L. Cooley, "Silver Politics in the United States, 1918–1946" (unpublished Ph.D. dissertation, University of California, Berkeley, 1951), pp. 138–146 for a discussion of the Dies and Fiesinger bills

26. Confidential Conference with Senators, April 14, 1934, U. S. Senate Folder,

Box 37, President's Secretary's File, Franklin D. Roosevelt Papers, Hyde Park, N. Y. (hereafter cited as F. D. R.)

27. K. P. to F. D. R., April 25, 1935, Depts.-Govt. Folder, Box 142

28. K. P. to Henry Morgenthau, Jr., April 13, 1934, Depts.-Govt. Folder, Box 142; U. S., Congress, Senate Document 173, *Holders of Silver,* 73 Cong. 2 Sess. 1934

29. K. P. to E. C. Mulcahy, April 28, 1934, M Folder, Box 13

30. K. P. to F. D. R., April 25, 1934, Depts.-Govt. Folder, Box 142

31. *New York Times,* May 17, 1934, 1:1; James White to *Nevada State Journal,* May 16, 1934, Newspaper Folder, Box 145

32. *Congressional Record,* 73 Cong. 2 Sess. Vol. 78, Pt. 9 (May 22, 1934), p. 9215

33. Handy and Harman, *Annual Review of the Silver Market for 1934,* pp. 4–5

34. K. P. to Paul Gardner, August 30, 1934, Lovelock, Nevada Folder, Box 20

35. K. P. to F. D. R., April 17, 1934; F. D. R. to K. P., April 24, 1934, President Roosevelt Folder, Box 23

36. Mimosa Pittman to Harry and Eppes Hawes, September 27, 1934, Mrs. Pittman Folder, Box 21

37. *Tonopah Daily Times,* November 3, 1934; Burton K. Wheeler to *Nevada State Journal,* October 11, 1934, Publicity Folder, Box 22

38. K. P. to George L. Swartz, January 30, 1940, S Folder, Box 15

39. The article appeared in *Plain Talk,* X (November 1934)

40. F. D. R. to K. P., September 7, 1934, Box 745, President's Personal Files, Franklin D. Roosevelt Papers, Hyde Park, N. Y. (hereafter cited as P.P.F., F. D. R.)

41. K. P. to Joseph O'Mahoney, November 12, 1934; K. P. to Alben W. Barkley, November 12, 1934; K. P. to M. M. Neely, November 13, 1934, Miscellaneous—Official Folder, Box 21

42. K. P. to F. D. R., February 19, 1935, Box 745, P.P.F., F. D. R.

43. Harold L. Ickes, *The Secret Diary of Harold L. Ickes* (New York: Simon and Schuster, 1954), I, 302; see also K. P. to Harold L. Ickes, February 22, 1935, Box 55, Harold L. Ickes Papers, Library of Congress

44. K. P. to F. D. R., February 19, 1935, Box 745, P.P.F., F. D. R.

45. *Congressional Record,* 74 Cong. 1 Sess. Vol. 79, Pt. 5 (April 11, 1935), p. 5404; *Annual Report of the Director of the Mint for the Fiscal Year 1935,* p. 26. See also F. D. R. to K. P., April 15, 1935, Depts.-Govt. Folder, Box 142

46. Allan Seymour Everest, *Morgenthau the New Deal and Silver* (New York: Kings Crown, 1950), pp. 51 f.; K. P. to F. D. R., April 10, 1935, Depts.-Govt. Folder, Box 142

47. K. P. to F. D. R., April 23, 1935, The White House Folder, Box 81

48. *Congressional Record,* 74 Cong. 1 Sess. Vol. 79, Pt. 12 (August 15, 1935), p. 13242

49. K. P. to Duncan U. Fletcher, June 7, 1935, Committee Members Folder, Box 141

50. See K. P.'s Correspondence with John J. Raskob, Consolidated Virginia Mining Corporation 1935–1938 Folder, Box 159

51. Handy and Harman, *Annual Review of the Silver Market for 1936,* pp. 2–6; Everest, *op. cit.,* pp. 60–61

52. *Congressional Record,* 74 Cong. 2 Sess. Vol. 80, Pt. 7 (May 25, 1936), pp. 7874–7877; *New York Times,* May 25, 1936, p. 29

53. K. P. to Marvin H. McIntyre, September 21, 1937, The White House Folder, Box 81

54. K. P. to Ed W. Clark, August 2, 1937, C-General Folder, Box 11

55. *Congressional Record,* 75 Cong. 2 Sess. Vol. 82, Pt. 1 (November 22, 1937), p. 219; Pt. 3 (December 10, 1937), pp. 418–419

56. *New York Times,* September 29, 1938, 43:1; October 2, 1938, III, 1:5; October 8, 1938, 23:6

57. F. D. R. to K. P., July 13, 1938, The White House Folder, Box 81

58. *Congressional Record,* 76 Cong. 1 Sess. Vol. 84, Pt. 1 (January 16, 1939), p. 357; John G. Townsend, Jr. to John L. Dynan, January 6, 1939, Pt. 2, pp. 1281–1282

59. U. S., Congress, Senate, *Special Committee on the Investigation of Silver,* 76 Cong. 1 Sess. 1939, p. 407

60. Handy and Harman, *Annual Review of the Silver Market for 1938,* pp. 22–23

61. See Everest, *op. cit.,* pp. 70–75; *infra,* pp. 253–255

62. K. P. to *Nevada State Journal,* July 6, 1939, Newspaper Folder, Box 145

63. F. D. R. to Marvin H. McIntyre, September 12, 1936, Nevada Folder, Box 300, Office File, F. D. R.

64. C. D. Baker to K. P., December 19, 1932, B Folder, Box 11

65. K. P. to Bill Kennett, March 14, 1933, K Folder, Box 13

66. K. P. to James A. Farley, May 28, 1933, 73 Congress, Committee Correspondence Folder, Sen 73A–F10 (112B), F. R. C.

67. K. P. to Louis M. Howe, May 27, 1933, The White House Folder, Box 81

68. K. P. to William McKnight, August 17, 1933, Mc Folder, Box 13

69. K. P. to F. D. R., August 25, 1933; September 28, 1933; F. D. R. to K. P., August 29, 1933; The White House Folder, Box 81

70. K. P. to Harold L. Ickes, September 27, 1933; Harold L. Ickes to K. P., October 11, 1933; Box 116, Harold L. Ickes Papers, Library of Congress (hereafter cited as Ickes Papers); Ickes, *op. cit.,* I, 101–102, 105

71. K. P. to Harold L. Ickes, October 20, 1933; October 30, 1933; Box 116, Ickes Papers

72. See Burlew Folder, Box 35, Ickes Papers; Ickes, *op. cit.,* I, 440; II, 292–293; III, 219

73. *New York Times,* December 21, 1937, 8:3

74. K. P. to F. D. R., December 19, 1937, The White House Folder, Box 81; K. P. to William S. Boyle, January 15, 1938, B-General Folder, Box 11

75. Ickes, *op. cit.,* II, 305; Harold L. Ickes to F. D. R., February 8, 1938, Burlew Folder, Box 35, Ickes Papers

76. U. S., Congress, Senate, Committee on Public Lands and Surveys, *Hearings, Nomination of Ebert K. Burlew,* 75 Cong. 1938

77. See Nevada Folder, Box 300, Office File, F. D. R.

78. K. P. to James A. Farley, October 27, 1937, Farley Folder, Box 19

79. K. P. to George W. Friedhoff, January 13, 1940, F Folder, Box 12

80. K. P. to Sam Rayburn, July 22, 1936, Democratic National Committee Folder, Box 12

81. K. P. to Breckinridge Long, April 24, 1934, L Folder, Box 13

82. See for example K. P. to Homer S. Cummings, April 29, 1935; K. P. to F. D. R., April 29, 1935, Correspondence B Folder, Sen. 74A–F9 (123B), F.R.C.; K. P. to R. L. Douglas, May 9, 1940, Trade Agreements—Important Correspondence Folder, Box 157

83. See William S. Boyle to James A. Farley, April 10, 1935; December 20, 1938; Nevada Folder, Box 300, Office File, F. D. R.

84. K. P. to Harold L. Ickes, November 28, 1938, Ickes vs. Pittman—Las Vegas Wash, 1939 Folder, Box 74

85. K. P. to Claude Mackey, November 30, 1938; December 2, 20, 1938; Ickes vs. Pittman—Las Vegas Wash, 1939 Folder, Box 74

86. Harold L. Ickes to Alva B. Adams, March 6, 1939; Harold L. Ickes to K. P., March 10, 1939; *ibid.*

87. *The Washington Sunday Star,* August 13, 1939. See also K. P. to E. P. Carville, March 17, 1939, Ickes vs. Pittman—Las Vegas Wash, 1939 Folder, Box 74

88. Breckinridge Long Diary, January 2, 1940, Library of Congress (hereafter cited as Long Diary)

89. *Reno Evening Gazette,* March 6, March 7, 1939

90. K. P. to James G. Scrugham, June 20, 1939; July 22, 1939, Ickes vs. Pittman—Las Vegas Wash, 1939 Folder, Box 74

91. K. P. to Oliver Goerman, August 9, 1939, *ibid.*

92. Ickes, *op. cit.,* II, 588, 693

93. K. P. to F. D. R., August 12, 1939, Ickes vs. Pittman—Las Vegas Wash, 1939 Folder, Box 74

94. K. P. to Claude Mackey, November 9, 1939; February 19, 1940; F. D. R. to K. P., December 9, 1939, *ibid.* With the Senator's death in November, 1940, the Las Vegas Wash project was dropped.

95. Breckinridge Long Diary, January 2, 1940

96. K. P. to Harry MacSheery, January 29, 1940, M Folder, Box 13; K. P. to George W. Friedhoff, January 13, 1940, F Folder, Box 12

97. *Congressional Record,* 76 Cong. 3 Sess. Vol. 86, Pt. 1 (January 3, 1940), pp. 8–9; Pt. 3 (March 25, 1940), pp. 3321 ff.

98. Breckinridge Long Diary, November 28, 1939. See also entries for January 2, 1940; March 4, 1940; March 29, 1940

99. K. P. to John E. Robbins, April 8, 1940; K. P. to Lee Ellsworth, April 7, 1940; Reciprocal Trade Agreements, 1940 Folder, Box 158

100. Breckinridge Long Diary, January 2, 1940

NOTES TO CHAPTER VI

1. Henry Adams, *The Education of Henry Adams* (New York: Random House, 1931), p. 274; George H. Haynes, *Charles Sumner* (Philadelphia: Jacobs, 1909), p. 331

2. *Today,* January 20, 1934, p. 5

3. K. P. to Charles S. Thomas, February 2, 1932, T Folder, Box 146

4. As quoted in George N. Thompson, "The Psychiatry of Alcoholism," in George N. Thompson (ed.), *Alcoholism* (Springfield: Charles C. Thomas, 1956), p. 460

5. *New York Times,* March 15, 1933, 1:4; January 12, 1933, 1:5

6. Cordell Hull to Senate Committee on Foreign Relations, May 17, 1933, *Papers Relating to the Foreign Relations of the United States, 1933,* Department of State Publication 3839 (Washington: Government Printing Office, 1950), I, 365

7. See *Congressional Record,* 73 Cong. 1 Sess. Vol. 77, Pt. 2 (April 13, 1933), pp. 1683–1702; (April 14, 1933), pp. 1746–1778

8. Tom Connally, *My Name Is Tom Connally* (New York: Crowell, 1954), p. 206

9. K. P. to Cordell Hull, May 10, 1933, Correspondence D Folder, Sen. 73A–F10 (112B) , Papers of the United States Senate Foreign Relations Committee, National Archives (hereafter cited as F.R.C.)

10. *Congressional Record, loc. cit.,* Vol. 77, Pt. 5 (May 30, 1933) , pp. 4577–4578

11. Cordell Hull, *The Memoirs of Cordell Hull* (New York: Macmillan, 1948) , I, 228–229; Cordell Hull to Sam D. McReynolds, April 5, 1933 and William Phillips to Hugh Wilson, June 1, 1933, *Papers . . . 1933, loc. cit.,* I, 365, 378. See also Robert A. Divine, "Franklin D. Roosevelt and Collective Security, 1933," *Mississippi Valley Historical Review,* XLVIII (June 1961) , 48–57

12. Hull, *op. cit.,* p. 387

13. K. P. to Carrie Chapman Catt, February 26, 1934, Sen. 73A–F10 (112B) , F.R.C.

14. Memorandum by John S. Dickey, Assistant to the Assistant Secretary of State, January 3, 1935, *Papers Relating to the Foreign Relations of the United States, 1935* (Washington: Government Printing Office, 1953) , I, 383–385

15. K. P. to F. D. R., January 4, 9, 11, 1935, Box 202, President's Personal Files, Franklin D. Roosevelt Papers, Hyde Park, N. Y. (hereafter cited as P.P.F., F. D. R.)

16. Francis B. Sayre to F. D. R., January 9, 1935, *Papers . . . 1935, loc. cit.,* pp. 385–386

17. *Congressional Record,* 74 Cong. 1 Sess. Vol. 79, Pt. 1 (January 16, 1935) , p. 480

18. William E. Borah to William Randolph Hearst, February 4, 1935, World Court Folder, Box 391, William E. Borah Papers, Library of Congress

19. See Peter B. Morris, "Father Coughlin and the New Deal" (unpublished Master's thesis, Columbia University, 1958) , pp. 70–73

20. *Congressional Record, loc. cit.* (January 29, 1935) , p. 1143

21. The Reminiscences of Henry L. Stimson, Oral History Project, Columbia University, pp. 5 f.

22. F. D. R. to Joseph T. Robinson, January 30, 1935; F. D. R. to Elihu Root, February 9, 1935; in Elliott Roosevelt (ed.) , *F. D. R. His Personal Letters, 1928–1945* (New York: Duell, Sloan and Pearce, 1950) , I, 448, 451

23. K. P. to F. D. R., February 19, 1935, Box 745, P.P.F., F. D. R.

24. *The Washington Herald,* April 7, 1935, 3:1–3

25. *New York Times,* March 24, 1935, IV, 8:7

26. Memorandum by Walter C. Lamb to K. P., April 11, 1935, Correspondence M Folder, Sen. 74A–F9 (123C) , F.R.C.; memorandum by Joseph C. Green of the Division of Western European Affairs, *Papers . . . 1935, loc. cit.,* I, 329–330

27. K. P. to Wallace S. Murray, April 11, 1935, Correspondence M Folder, Sen. 74A–F9 (123C) , F.R.C.

28. Memorandum by the Secretary of State to President Roosevelt, April 11, 1935, *Papers . . . 1935, loc. cit.,* I, 331–332

29. *Congressional Record,* 74 Cong. 1 Sess. Vol. 79, Pt. 10 (July 1, 1935) , p. 10463; Hull, *op. cit.,* p. 410

30. Connally, *op. cit.,* p. 219

31. K. P. to Cordell Hull, July 17, 1935, Secretary of State Folder, Sen. 74A–F9 (123C) , F.R.C.

32. *Congressional Record, loc. cit.,* Vol. 79, Pt. 13 (August 23, 1935) , p. 14283; Connally, *op. cit.,* p. 219

33. Hull, *op. cit.,* p. 411

34. F. D. R. to K. P., August 19, 1935, Box 745, P.P.F., F. D. R.

35. Memorandum to the President from K. P., August 19, 1935, Box 745, P.P.F., F. D. R.

36. Telephone conversation between K. P. and Steve Early, August 19, 1935, Box 745, P.P.F., F. D. R. Record was kept by Steve Early

37. *Congressional Record, loc. cit.* (August 20, 1935), pp. 13775 ff.

38. See Joseph Green to Jay Pierrepont Moffat, October 12, 1935, Papers of Jay Pierrepont Moffat, Houghton Library, Harvard University (hereafter cited as Moffat Papers)

39. Philip C. Jessup, *Neutrality: Its History, Economics and Law* (New York: Columbia University, 1936), IV, 124

40. Charles A. Beard, *American Foreign Policy in the Making, 1932–1940* (New Haven: Yale University, 1946), pp. 165–166; Basil Rauch, *Roosevelt from Munich to Pearl Harbor* (New York: Creative Age, 1950), pp. 27–28

41. F. D. R. to William E. Dodd, December 2, 1935, in Roosevelt (Elliott), *op. cit.*, I, 530–531

42. See John D. Armstrong, "The Search for the Alcoholic Personality," in Selden D. Bacon (ed.), *Understanding Alcoholism, The Annals of the American Academy of Political and Social Science*, CCCXV (January 1958), 40 ff.

43. *New York Times,* December 21, 1935, 8:6; December 22, 1935, 24:2

44. Harold L. Ickes, *The Secret Diary of Harold L. Ickes* (New York: Simon and Schuster, 1954), I, 490

45. Joseph Green to Jay Pierrepont Moffat, November 25, 1935, Moffat Papers

46. Hull, *op. cit.,* pp. 460–461

47. *Congressional Record,* 74 Cong. 2 Sess. Vol. 80, Pt. 3 (February 27, 1936), pp. 2901–2902; H. J. Res. 422, 74 Cong.

48. K. P. to Pat Harrison, January 4, 1936, Correspondence P Folder, Sen. 74A–F9 (123C), F.R.C.

49. K. P. to Cordell Hull, January 8, 1936, Secretary of State Folder, Sen. 74A–F9 (123C), F.R.C.

50. Hiram Johnson to K. P., January 9, 1936, Correspondence J Folder, Sen. 74A–F9 (123B), F.R.C.

51. As quoted in *The Literary Digest,* February 29, 1936, p. 5

52. Joseph Green to Jay Pierrepont Moffat, April 22, 1936, Moffat Papers

53. R. Walton Moore to F. D. R., n.d., Office File 1561, F. D. R.; Memorandum of Conversation between R. Walton Moore and Key Pittman, February 3, 1936, Neutrality-1936 Folder, Box 14, Papers of R. Walton Moore, Hyde Park, New York (hereafter cited as Moore Papers)

54. F. D. R. to K. P., January 29, 1936, Office File 1561, F. D. R.

55. See U. S., Congress, Senate Committee on Foreign Relations, *Hearings, Neutrality Legislation,* 74 Cong. 2 Sess. 1936; John C. Donovan, "Congress, and the Making of Neutrality Legislation, 1935–1939" (unpublished doctoral dissertation, Harvard University, 1949) pp. 88 ff.

56. R. Walton Moore to F. D. R., January 23, 1936, F. D. R., 1936 Folder, Box 17, Moore Papers

57. *Congressional Record,* 74 Cong. 2 Sess. Vol. 80, Pt. 2 (February 17, 1936), p. 2176; (February 18, 1936), pp. 2287, 2292, 2298

58. *Congressional Record, loc. cit.,* Pt. 4 (March 23, 1936), p. 4372

59. R. Walton Moore to F. D. R., January 5, 1937, R. Walton Moore Folder, Office File, F. D. R.

60. *Congressional Record,* 75 Cong. 1 Sess. Vol. 81, Pt. 1 (January 6, 1937), p. 74

61. Telephone message of James A. White to the White House, January 6, 1937, Office File 1561, F. D. R.

62. Claude G. Bowers to K. P., June 26, 1937, Spanish Civil War Folder, Sen. 75A–F9–1 (105E), F.R.C.

63. Hull, *op. cit.,* p. 509

64. Breckinridge Long Diary, January 24, 1937, Library of Congress (hereafter cited as Long Diary)

65. *New York Times,* January 23, 1937, 1:4; January 30, 1937, 6:6; memorandum by K. P. to F. D. R., December 29, 1936, F. D. R. 1937 Folder, Box 17, Moore Papers

66. *New York Times,* February 2, 1937, 22:5; February 21, 1937, 1:3.

67. R. Walton Moore to F. D. R., January 30, 1937, Office File 1561, F. D. R.

68. U. S., Congress, Senate Committee on Foreign Relations, *Hearings Relative to Proposed Legislation on Neutrality,* 75 Cong. 1 Sess. 1937, pp. 8, 16–17

69. R. Walton Moore to F. D. R., February 15, 1937; March 4, 1937, Neutrality 1937 Folder, Box 14, Moore Papers

70. *Congressional Record,* 75 Cong. 1 Sess. Vol. 81, Pt. 2 (February 3, 1937), p. 1490; (March 1, 1937), p. 1666. See also K. P. to Joseph Barber, Jr., February 20, 1937, Correspondence B Folder, Sen. 75A–F9–1, F.R.C.

71. K. P. to Herbert Wright, May 22, 1937, Correspondence C Folder, Sen. 75A–F9–1 (105F), F.R.C.

72. *Congressional Record, loc. cit.,* Pt. 4 (April 29, 1937), pp. 3937 ff.

73. K. P. to Walter C. Clark, June 12, 1937, C-General Folder, Box 11; *New York Times,* February 21, 1937, 1:3

NOTES TO CHAPTER VII

1. K. P. to Joseph P. Kennedy, May 2, 1938, European Affairs Folder, Sen. 75A–F9–1 (105C), Papers of the United States Senate Foreign Relations Committee, National Archives (hereafter cited as F.R.C.)

2. Joseph P. Kennedy to K. P., April 14, 1938, European Affairs Folder, Sen. 75A–F9–1 (105C); Joseph E. Davies to K. P., December 23, 1938, Joseph E. Davies Folder, Sen. 76A–F9–1 (122L), F.R.C.

3. K. P. to Joseph P. Kennedy, May 2, 1938, European Affairs Folder, Sen. 75A–F9–1 (105C), F.R.C.

4. *Congressional Record,* 75 Cong. 3 Sess. Vol. 83, Pt. 6 (May 2, 1938), pp. 6017, 6030

5. F. Jay Taylor, *The United States and the Spanish Civil War* (New York: Bookman Associates, 1956), pp. 90–92

6. Cordell Hull to K. P., May 12, 1938, as quoted in Taylor, *op. cit.,* p. 175

7. Harold L. Ickes, *The Secret Diary of Harold L. Ickes* (New York, Simon and Schuster, 1954), II, 388

8. Claude G. Bowers, *My Mission to Spain* (New York: Simon and Schuster, 1954), p. 419

9. Jay Pierrepont Moffat Diary, January 19, 1939, Houghton Library, Harvard University (hereafter cited as Moffat Diary)

10. *New York Times,* December 23, 1938, 1:8; December 24, 1938, 6:3; December 25, 1938, 1:2

11. Samuel I. Rosenman (ed.) , *The Public Papers and Addresses of Franklin D. Roosevelt,* 1939 volume (New York: Random House, 1941) , pp. 1 ff.

12. K. P. to R. Walton Moore, October 13, 1938, Neutrality-1938 Folder, Box 15, Papers of R. Walton Moore, Franklin D. Roosevelt Library, Hyde Park, N. Y. (hereafter cited as Moore Papers)

13. Breckinridge Long Diary, February 3, 1939, Library of Congress (hereafter cited as Long Diary)

14. Cordell Hull, *The Memoirs of Cordell Hull* (New York: Macmillan, 1948) , pp. 613, 641; Moffat Diary, January 23, 1939

15. Confidential memorandum from K. P. to F. D. R., January 11, 1939, Box 745, President's Personal Files, Franklin D. Roosevelt Papers, Hyde Park, N. Y.) hereafter cited as P.P.F., F. D. R.)

16. Moffat Diary, March 15, 1939

17. F. D. R. to Cordell Hull, March 28, 1939, Box 52, Secretary's File, F. D. R.; William L. Langer and S. Everett Gleason, *The Challenge to Isolation, 1937–1940* (New York: Harper, 1952) , pp. 79–80

18. Carlton Savage to R. Walton Moore, February 24, 1939, Neutrality-1939 Folder, Box 15, Moore Papers

19. Moffat Diary, April 6, 8, 10, 1939

20. Hull, *op. cit.,* p. 641; F. D. R. to Cordell Hull, March 28, 1939, Box 52, Secretary's File, F. D. R.

21. *New York Times,* March 19, 1939, 1:4; 35:3; R. Walton Moore to F. D. R., March 18, 1939, Neutrality-1939 Folder, Box 15, Moore Papers

22. *Washington Post,* March 20, 1939, 1:1

23. *New York Times,* March 30, 1939, 8:2; R. Walton Moore to F. D. R., March 18, 1939, Neutrality-1939 Folder, Box 15, Moore Papers

24. K. P. to Henry L. Stimson, April 30, 1939, Neutrality Hearings Folder, Sen. 76A–F9 (122H) , F.R.C.

25. Moffat Diary, April 7, 1939

26. K. P. to Cordell Hull, May 16, 1939, Cordell Hull Folder, Sen. 76A–F9 (122M) , F.R.C.

27. K. P. to Bernard M. Baruch, April 26, 1939, Neutrality Hearings Folder, Sen. 76A–F9 (122H) , F.R.C.

28. Moffat Diary, May 3, 1939

29. *New York Times,* March 26, 1939, 29:2–3

30. R. Walton Moore to F. D. R., May 12, 1939, Neutrality-1939 Folder, Box 15, Moore Papers. See also Moffat Diary, May 16, 1939

31. Memo by Carlton Savage, May 19, 1939, as quoted in Langer and Gleason, *op. cit.,* pp. 138–139

32. K. P. to Cordell Hull, May 16, 1939, Cordell Hull Folder, Sen. 76A–F9 (122M) , F.R.C.; F. D. R. to R. Walton Moore, Neutrality-1939 Folder, Box 15, Moore Papers

33. Cordell Hull to K. P., May 27, 1939, Cordell Hull Folder, Sen. 76A–F9 (122M) , F.R.C.

34. *New York Times,* May 30, 1939, 6:1

35. Hull, *op. cit.,* pp. 643–644

36. Press Conference No. 560, Box 213, F. D. R.; Langer and Gleason, *op. cit.,* p. 143

37. F. D. R. to Pat Harrison, July 6, 1939, in Elliott Roosevelt (ed.) , *F. D. R. His Personal Letters, 1928–1945* (New York: Duell, Sloan and Pearce, 1950) , II, 902

38. K. P. to Marguerite M. Wells, July 20, 1939, Neutrality-General Folder, Sen. 76A–F9 (122H) , F.R.C.

39. Joseph Alsop and Robert Kinter, *American White Paper* (New York: Simon and Schuster, 1940) , pp. 44–46; Hull, *op. cit.*, pp. 649–651

40. K. P. to Toyohiko Kagawa, August 12, 1939, China-Japan Folder, Sen. 76A–F9 (122B) , F.R.C.

41. F. D. R. to K. P., May 24, 1939, in Roosevelt (Elliott) , *op. cit.*, II, 887

42. *Congressional Record*, 76 Cong. 1 Sess. Vol. 84, Pt. 7 (June 23, 1939) , pp. 7777 ff.

43. F. D. R. to K. P., June 27, 1939, in Roosevelt (Elliott) , *op. cit.*, II, 898

44. Morgenthau Diary, June 23, 1939, as quoted in Allan Seymour Everest, *Morgenthau the New Deal and Silver* (New York: Kings Crown, 1950) , p. 72

45. Henry Morgenthau, Jr., "The Morgenthau Diaries," *Collier's*, CXX (October 11, 1947) , 79; see also Long Diary, July 6, 1939; *Congressional Record, loc. cit.*, Pt. 8 (July 5, 1939) , p. 8559

46. *New York Times*, May 21, 1939, VIII, p. 12

47. Tom Connally, *My Name Is Tom Connally* (New York: Crowell, 1954) , p. 228

48. Rosenman, *op. cit.*, pp. 512 ff.; Moffat Diary, September 21, 1939

49. Hull, *op. cit.*, p. 693

50. *New York Times*, September 23, 1939, 1:1

51. *Congressional Record*, 76 Cong., 2 Sess. Vol. 85, Pt. 2 (October 1, 1939) , pp. 243, 247

52. Moffat Diary, October 20, 1939

53. Cordell Hull to K. P., November 3, 1939, Commendatory Letters Folder, Box 44, Key Pittman Papers, Library of Congress (hereafter cited by folder and box number)

54. K. P. to William H. Metson, April 4, 1940, Mexican Lands Folder, Sen. 76A–F9 (122F) , F.R.C.; K. P. to John P. Reynolds, July 5, 1940, John Reynolds Folder, Box 78

55. Long Diary, March 12, 1940

56. *New York Times*, February 19, 1940, 8:5; February 16, 1940, 1:5

57. Sumner Welles, *The Time for Decision* (New York: Harper, 1941) , pp. 74, 91, 103

58. *Congressional Record*, 76 Cong. 3 Sess. Vol. 86, Pt. 3 (March 11, 1940) , p. 2654

59. Long Diary, March 12, 1940

60. *Congressional Record, loc. cit.*, Pt. 15 (June 3, 1940) , p. 3469

61. *New York Times*, June 26, 1940, 6:2–3; June 27, 1940, 12:2

62. Ickes, *op. cit.*, III, 219

63. K. P. to John E. Robbins, June 8, 1940, R Folder, Box 15

64. Long Diary, January 2, 1940

Bibliography

1. *Manuscript Collections*

Key Pittman Papers, 201 boxes, Library of Congress
Papers of the United States Senate Committee on Foreign Relations, National Archives

---

Records of the Office of the Secretary of Agriculture, National Archives
William E. Borah Papers, Library of Congress
Reminiscences of Claude Bowers, Oral History Project, Columbia University
Reminiscences of John W. Davis, Oral History Project, Columbia University
Norman H. Davis Papers, Library of Congress
Reminiscences of James W. Gerard, Oral History Project, Columbia University
Harold L. Ickes Papers, Library of Congress
Breckinridge Long Papers, Library of Congress
Jay Pierrepont Moffat Papers, Harvard University
R. Walton Moore Papers, Hyde Park, New York
Reminiscences of William Phillips, Oral History Project, Columbia University
Franklin D. Roosevelt Papers, Hyde Park, New York
Reminiscences of James Warburg, Oral History Project, Columbia University

2. *Newspapers and Magazines*

In addition to those in clipping scrapbooks

The Literary Digest
Nevada State Journal [Reno]
New York Herald Tribune
New York Times

196

Nome [Alaska] *Daily Chronicle*
Nome [Alaska] *Weekly News*
Outlook and Independent
Reno Evening Gazette
Salt Lake Telegram
San Francisco Examiner
Time
Tonopah [Nevada] *Miner*
Washington Post

3. *State and Federal Documents*

Annual Reports of the Director of the Mint, 1913–1944
Congressional Record, 1913–1940
STATE OF MISSISSIPPI, *Mississippi Reports*, Vol. LV
STATE OF NEVADA, *Report of the Commissioner of Labor for the Period 1929–1930*. Carson City: State Printing Office, 1931
TERRITORY OF ALASKA, *Alaska Report*, Vol. I
U. S., Congress, House, Committee on Banking and Currency, *Hearings, Silver Purchases Under the Pittman Act*, 1925
———, Committee on Foreign Affairs, *Hearings, International Monetary and Economic Conference, London, England*, 1933
———, Senate, Commission of Gold and Silver Inquiry, *Progress Report*, 1924
———, Commission of Gold and Silver Inquiry, *Silver Producer's Convention*, 1923
———, Committee on Banking and Currency, *Hearings, Silver Purchased Under the Pittman Act*, 1924
———, Committee on Foreign Relations, *Hearings, Neutrality Legislation*, 1936
———, Committee on Foreign Relations, *Hearings, Relative to Proposed Legislation on Neutrality*, 1937
———, Committee on Mines and Mining, *Hearings, Appointment of Silver Commission*, 1923
———, Committee on Public Lands and Surveys, *Hearings, Nomination of Ebert K. Burlew*, 1938
———, *Special Committee on the Investigation of Silver*, 1939
———, Subcommittee of the Commission of Gold and Silver Inquiry, *Silver Purchased Under the Pittman Act, Hearings*, 1924
———, Subcommittee of the Committee on Banking and Currency, *Hearings, Purchase of Silver Produced in the United States with Silver Certificates*, 1932

U. S., Congress, House, Subcommittee of the Committee on Foreign Relations, *Hearings, Commercial Relations with China,* 1930

——, Subcommittee of the Committee on Public Lands and Survey, *Hearings, Public Park and Recreational Site for the State of Nevada,* 1939

——, Congress, Senate Document 173, *Holders of Silver,* 1934

——, Department of State, *Executive Agreement Series,* 1933 volume

——, *Press Releases,* 1933–1940

——, *Papers Relating to the Foreign Relations of the United States,* 1933–1940

The War of the Rebellion: Official Records of the Union and Confederate Armies, Series I, Volume XXIV

4. Miscellaneous Documents

Annual Catalogue of the Southwestern Presbyterian University, 1890–1891

LEAGUE OF NATIONS, *Journal of the Monetary and Economic Conference, London,* 1933

Official Report of the Proceedings of the 1924 Democratic National Convention

Official Report of the Proceedings of the 1928 Democratic National Convention

5a. *Unpublished Doctoral Dissertations*

CARLSON, EARLAND IRVING, "Franklin D. Roosevelt's Fight for the Presidential Nomination." University of Illinois, 1955

COOLEY, EVERETT L., "Silver Politics in the United States, 1918–1946." University of California, Berkeley, 1951

DONOVAN, JOHN C., "Congress, and the Making of Neutrality Legislation, 1935–1939." Harvard University, 1949

ELLIOTT, RUSSELL RICHARD, "The Tonopah, Goldfield, Bullfrog Mining Districts, 1900–1915." University of California, Berkeley, 1946

MURPHY, DONALD G., "Psychological Correlations of Alcohol Addictions." Teachers College, Columbia University, 1957

5b. *Unpublished Master's Essay*

MORRIS, PETER B., "Father Coughlin and the New Deal." Columbia University, 1958

6. *Articles*

"The Lausanne Agreement." *International Conciliation,* CCLXXXII (September 1932) , 37 ff.

"Nevada's Nabob." *Plain Talk,* X (November 1939)

ARMSTRONG, JOHN D., "The Search for the Alcoholic Personality." In Selden D. Baker (ed.) , *Understanding Alcoholism, The Annals of the American Academy of Political and Social Science,* CCCXV (January 1958) , 40 ff.

BAIRD, JOSEPH H., "Key Pittman: Frontier Statesman." *American Mercury,* L (July 1940) , 306–313

BERGLUND, ABRAHAM, "The Tariff Act of 1930." *American Economic Review,* XX (1930) , 467 ff.

BORCHARD, EDWIN M., "The Arms Embargo and Neutrality." *American Journal of International Law,* XXX (1933) , 293–298

BRATTER, HERBERT M., "The Silver Episode II." *The Journal of Political Economy,* XLVI (1938) , 802–837

CAROTHERS, NEIL, "Silver—A Senate Racket." *Lehigh University Publications,* VI (January 1932) , 1 ff.

COLE, WAYNE C., "Senator Key Pittman and American Neutrality Policies, 1933–1940." *Mississippi Valley Historical Review,* XLVI (1959–1960) , 644–662

COUCH, BERTRAND F., and JAY A. CARPENTER, "Nevada's Metal and Mineral Production (1859–1940, Inclusive) ." *University of Nevada Bulletin,* XXXVII (November 1943) , 152 ff.

DIVINE, ROBERT A., "Franklin D. Roosevelt and Collective Security, 1933." *Mississippi Valley Historical Review,* XLVIII (1961–1962) , 42–59

FITE, GILBERT C., "The Agricultural Issue in the Presidential Campaign of 1928." *Mississippi Valley Historical Review,* XXXVII (1950–1951) , 653–672

FOX, RUTH, "Treatment of Alcoholism." In Harold E. Himwich (ed.) , *Alcoholism: Basic Aspects and Treatment,* Washington: American Association for the Advancement of Science, 1957, 171 ff.

ICKES, HAROLD L., "My Twelve Years with F. D. R.," *Saturday Evening Post,* June 26, 1948, 30 ff.

KEYES, FRANCES PARKINSON, "The American Woman and the Democratic Party," *Delineator,* CXIII (November 1928) , 17 ff.

MACMAHON, ARTHUR W., "First Session of the Seventy-first Congress." *American Political Science Review,* XXIV (1930) , 38 ff.

———, "Second Session of the Seventy-first Congress," *American Political Science Review,* XXIV (1930) , 920 ff.

MCNEILY, J. S., "Climax and Collapse of Reconstruction in Mississippi,

1874–76." *Publications of the Mississippi Historical Society,* XII (1912), 320 ff.

MERRIT, DIXON, "History Is Made at Houston." *Outlook,* CIL (July 11, 1928), 416 ff.

MORGENTHAU, JR., HENRY, "The Morgenthau Diaries." *Collier's,* CXX (October 11, 1947), 16 ff.

MORROW, WILLIAM W., "The Spoilers." *California Law Review,* IV (January 1916), 89–113

NICHOLS, JEANNETTE P., "Roosevelt's Monetary Diplomacy in 1933." *American Historical Review,* LVI (1950–1951), 295–317

———, "Silver Inflation and the Senate in 1933." *Social Studies,* XXV (January 1934), 12–18

RIDGEWAY, GORDON R., "Populism in Washington." *The Pacific Northwest Quarterly,* XXIX (October 1948), 284–311

SPRINGMEYER, GEORGE, "History of the Progressive Party in Nevada." In Sam P. Davis (ed.), *The History of Nevada,* Reno: Elms (ed.), 1913, 453–457

THOMPSON, GEORGE N., "The Psychiatry of Alcoholism." In George N. Thompson (ed.), *Alcoholism,* Springfield: Charles C. Thomas Publisher, 1956, 452 ff.

WIER, JEANNE ELIZABETH, "The Mystery of Nevada." In Thomas C. Donnelly (ed.), *Rocky Mountain Politics,* Albuquerque: University of New Mexico, 1940, 88–114

7. *Autobiographies, Biographies, Collected Letters, and Monographs Cited in Text*

In and About Vicksburg, Vicksburg: Gibraltar Publishing Company, 1890

ADNEY, TAPPAN, *The Klondike Stampede.* New York: Harper, 1900

ALSOP, JOSEPH and ROBERT KINTER, *American White Paper.* New York: Simon and Schuster, 1940

ATWATER, ELTON, *American Regulation of Arms Exports.* Washington: Carnegie Endowment for International Peace, 1941

BAILEY, THOMAS A., *Woodrow Wilson and the Great Betrayal.* New York: Macmillan, 1947

BAKER, RAY STANNARD, *Woodrow Wilson, Life and Letters,* Volume IV. New York: Doubleday, 1931

BANKSON, RUSSELL A., *The Klondike Nugget.* Caldwell, Idaho: Caxton, 1935

BARNARD, HARRY, *Independent Man: The Life of Senator James Couzens.* New York: Scribner, 1958

BEARD, CHARLES A., *American Foreign Policy in the Making, 1932–1940*. New Haven: Yale University, 1946

BEATTY, BESSIE, *Who's Who in Nevada*. Los Angeles: Home Printing, 1907

BECKER, ETHEL ANDERSON, *Klondike '98*. Portland: Binfords and Mort, 1949

BERTON, PIERRE, *Klondike Fever*. New York: Knopf, 1958

BLUM, JOHN MORTON, *From the Morgenthau Diaries: Years of Crisis 1928–1938*. Boston: Houghton Mifflin, 1959

BOWERS, CLAUDE G., *My Mission to Spain*. New York: Simon and Schuster, 1954

BRYCE, JAMES, *The American Commonwealth*. New York: Macmillan, 1911

BUHLER, CHARLOTTE, and D. WELTY LEFEVER, *A Rorschach Study of the Psychological Characteristics of Alcoholics*. New Haven: Laboratory of Applied Psychology, 1948

BURNS, JAMES M., *Congress on Trial*. New York: Harper, 1949

CANTRIL, HADLEY (ed.), *Public Opinion, 1935–1946*. Princeton: Princeton University, 1951

CAPPER, ARTHUR, *The Agricultural Bloc*. New York: Harcourt, Brace, 1922

CONNALLY, TOM, *My Name Is Tom Connally*. New York: Crowell, 1954

COOPER, WALLER RAYMOND, *Southwestern at Memphis, 1848–1948*. Richmond: John Knox, 1949

CORWIN, EDWARD S., *The President: Office and Powers, 1787–1957*. New York: New York University, 1957

COX, JAMES, *Journey Through My Years*. New York: Simon and Schuster, 1946

CRAWFORD, ARTHUR WHIPPLE, *Monetary Management Under the New Deal*. Washington: American Council on Public Affairs, 1940

DAVIS, SAM P. (ed.), *The History of Nevada*. Reno: Elms, 1913

DIVINE, ROBERT A., *The Illusion of Neutrality*. Chicago: University of Chicago, 1962

EVEREST, ALLAN SEYMOUR, *Morgenthau the New Deal and Silver*. New York: Kings Crown, 1950

FARLEY, JAMES A., *Behind the Ballots*. New York: Harcourt, Brace, 1938

——, *Jim Farley's Story*. New York: McGraw-Hill, 1948

FERRELL, ROBERT, *American Diplomacy in the Great Depression*. New Haven: Yale University, 1957

HANDY and HARMAN, *Annual Review of the Silver Market, 1920–1940*

HARVEY, W. H. (COIN), *The Book*. Rogers, Arkansas, 1930

HOOKER, NANCY HARVISON (ed.), *The Moffat Papers: Selections from the Diplomatic Journals of Jay Pierrepont Moffat, 1919–1943*. Cambridge: Harvard University, 1956

The Memoirs of Cordell Hull. New York: Macmillan, 1948

The Secret Diary of Harold L. Ickes. New York: Simon and Schuster, 1954

JESSUP, PHILIP C., *Neutrality: Its History, Economics and Law,* Volume IV. New York: Columbia University, 1936

LANGER, WILLIAM L., and S. EVERETT GLEASON, *The Challenge to Isolation, 1937–1940.* New York: Harper, 1952

LILLARD, RICHARD G., *Desert Challenge: An Interpretation of Nevada.* New York: Knopf, 1949

LIN, WEI-YING, *China Under Depreciated Silver 1926–1931.* Shanghai: The Commercial Press, 1935

LINK, ARTHUR S., *Wilson: The New Freedom.* Princeton: Princeton University, 1956

MOLEY, RAYMOND, *After Seven Years.* New York: Harper, 1939

NEVADA CHAMBER OF COMMERCE, *Greater Nevada.* Reno, 1915

NEVINS, ALLAN, *Hamilton Fish.* New York: Dodd, Mead, 1937

O'CONNOR, RICHARD, *High Jinks on the Klondike.* New York: Bobbs-Merrill, 1954

O'SHAUGHNESSY, M. M., *Hetch-Hetchy: Its Origins and History.* San Francisco, 1934

PASVOLSKY, LEO, *Current Monetary Issues.* Washington: The Brookings Institution, 1933

PORTER, KIRK H., and DONALD BRUCE JOHNSON, compilers, *National Party Platforms 1840–1956.* Urbana: University of Illinois, 1956

PUSEY, MERLO J., *Charles Evans Hughes.* New York: Macmillan, 1951

RAUCH, BASIL, *Roosevelt from Munich to Pearl Harbor.* New York: Creative Age, 1950

ROGERS, WILL, *How We Elect Our Presidents,* edited by Donald Day. Boston: Little, Brown, 1952

ROOSEVELT, ELLIOTT (ed.), *F. D. R. His Personal Letters, 1928–1945.* New York: Duell, Sloan and Pearce, 1950

ROSENMAN, SAMUEL I. (ed.), *The Public Papers and Addresses of Franklin D. Roosevelt,* 1939 volume. New York: Random House, 1941

SALOUTOS, THEODORE, and JOHN D. HICKS, *Agricultural Discontent in the Middle West 1900–1939.* Madison: University of Wisconsin, 1951

SCHATTSCHNEIDER, E. E., *Politics, Pressures and the Tariff.* New York: Prentice Hall, 1935

SCHLESINGER, JR., ARTHUR M., *The Coming of the New Deal.* Boston: Houghton Mifflin, 1959

SCRUGHAM, JAMES G. (ed.), *Nevada.* New York: The American Historical Society, 1935

SMITH, ALFRED E. *Up to Now.* New York: Garden City, 1929

SULLIVAN, EDWARD, *The Fabulous Wilson Mizner.* New York: Henkle, 1935

TAYLOR, F. JAY, *The United States and the Spanish Civil War*. New York: Bookman Associates, 1956

TRAYNOR, DEAN E., *International and Financial Conferences in the Interwar Period*. Washington: Catholic University, 1949

VINSON, JOHN CHALMERS, *The Parchment Peace: The United States Senate and the Washington Conference*. Athens: University of Georgia, 1955

WEBB, JOHN N., and MALCOLM BROWN, *Migrant Families*. Washington: United States Government Printing Office, 1938

WELLES, SUMNER, *The Time for Decision*. New York: Harper, 1941

WICKERSHAM, JAMES, *Old Yukon: Tales, Trails, and Trials*. Washington: Washington Law Book, 1938

WILSON, WOODROW, *The New Democracy: Presidential Messages, Addresses, and Other Papers (1913–1917)*, edited by Ray Stannard Baker and William E. Dodd. New York: Harper, 1926

WREN, THOMAS (ed.), *A History of the State of Nevada*. New York: Lewis, 1904

Index

Adams, Alva, 117
Agricultural Bloc (Senate), 46, 61, 68
Arms Embargo (1933), 132–134
Austin, Warren R., 165n.

Baker, Newton: Democratic National Convention (1924), 52–53; mentioned, 64, 99
Baker, Raymond T., 31, 76
Bankhead, John H., 163
Barkley, Alben, 82, 111, 165n.
Baruch, Bernard: contributes to Pittman campaign (1922), 50n.; mentioned, 40, 50, 158, 162
Beach, Rex, 15
Beard, Charles, 143, 144, 144n.
Belford, Sam, 47–48, 52, 58
Blease, Cole L., 64
Bloom, Sol, 163, 164
Bone, Homer T., 138n., 141, 142, 148, 153, 165n.
Borah, William E.: World Court (1934–1935), 136, 136n.; neutrality, 139, 142, 146, 147, 148, 153, 163, 169; mentioned, 38, 46, 83, 131
Borchard, Edwin, 147
Bowers, Claude: neutrality, 150; mentioned, 63, 84, 157
Boyle, William, 97, 124
Bratter, Herbert M., 90–91
Bruce, Edward, 90
Bruce, William, 60
Bryan, Charles W., 56–57
Bryan, William Jennings: bimetallism (1904), 19; supports Pittman (1916), 34; Pittman criticizes, 35–36; criticizes Pittman, 49; Democratic National Convention (1924), 54; mentioned, 20, 26, 57, 58, 67, 75
Bryan, William Jennings, Jr., 87
Bryce, James: opinion of U.S. Senate, 47
Buckley, Robert J., 72

Bukner family, 6
Bullitt, William, 101n., 160
Burlew, Ebert: promotion, 124–125; mentioned, 123
Butler, Jim: discovers Tonopah, 16–17
Byrnes, James, 101n., 112, 169

Capper, Arthur, 46
Caraway, T. H., 64
Catt, Carrie Chapman, 135
Chandler, Charles S., 49–50
Clark, Bennett C., 138n., 139, 142, 143n., 153, 154, 162, 168, 169
Commission of Gold and Silver Inquiry (1923), 79, 80, 81
Connally, Tom, 98, 133, 139, 167, 168
Coolidge, Calvin, 44, 58, 59, 60, 99
Copeland, Royal, 112n.
Corning, Parker, 62
Corwin, Edward S., 94
Coughlin, Charles E.: World Court (1934–1935), 136, 136n.
Couzens, James, 89, 90
Cox, James: presidential election (1920), 44, 45; World Monetary and Economic [London] Conference (1933), 89, 90, 91, 92n.; mentioned, 67
Cummings, Homer, 52, 97
Cummins, Albert, 38

Daniels, Josephus, 64
Davies, Joseph E., 155
Davis, John W.: Democratic National Convention (1924), 56; presidential election (1924), 57, 58; mentioned, 67, 72, 99
Davis, Norman, 56, 86, 141
Dawson, Canada: description (1897), 12
Democratic National Conventions: (1924), 51–57; (1928), 61–66; (1932), 96–98

205